Achieving Strategic Goals Through Executive Development

Achieving Strategic Goals Through Executive Development

William P. Nilsson

Addison-Wesley Publishing Company, Inc.
Reading, Massachusetts • Menlo Park, California
Don Mills, Ontario • Wokingham, England • Amsterdam • Bonn
Sydney • Singapore • Tokyo • Madrid • Bogotá
Santiago • San Juan

Library of Congress Cataloging-in-Publication Data

Nilsson, William P.
  Achieving strategic goals through executive development.

  Bibliography: p.
  Includes index.
  1. Executives—Training of. 2. Strategic planning.
I. Title.
HD38.2.N54 1987   658.4'012   86-32201
ISBN 0-201-12751-2

Copyright © 1987 by Addison-Wesley Publishing Company, Inc.

All rights reserved. No part of this publication may be reproduced, stored in a retrieval system, or transmitted, in any form or by any means, electronic, mechanical, photocopying, recording, or otherwise, without the prior written permission of the publisher. Printed in the United States of America.

Published simultaneously in Canada.

Cover design by Hannus Design Associates
Text design by Robert Moschetto and Allan Johnson.
Set in 10 point Aster by Compset, Inc., Beverly, MA.

ISBN 0-201-12751-2

ABCDEFGHIJ-AL-8987
First printing, May 1987

For Sheila and Laurie

CONTENTS

Preface   xiii

1. INTRODUCTION: LINKING EXECUTIVE DEVELOPMENT TO BUSINESS STRATEGY   1

   Competing in a Complex International Marketplace   1

   Current Executive Development Practices and Their Limitations   3

   Why Business Strategy Must Drive Executive Development   4

   Linkages between Strategy, Operations, and Executive Development   7

   An Unconventional Approach to Executive Development   9

   An Overview of the Book   11

   References   13

PART I   A STRATEGIC FRAMEWORK   15

2. STRATEGY   17

   Some Basic Definitions   17

   Strategy as a Real-Time Management Process   19

   Relating Strategy to Organizational Factors   21

   Strategic Position   22

   Strategy as a Repositioning Process   24

   Basic Considerations in Business Strategy Formulation   25

Functional Strategies as Components of Business Strategy   29

Importance of Executive Development to Strategy Formulation   31

References   31

3. STRATEGIC ISSUES   33

Strategic Issues: Impediments to Strategy Execution   34

Identifying Strategic Issues   35

Using Strategic Issues as a Management Tool   40

Strategic Issues for XYZ Products, Inc.: An Example   42

Synchronizing Executive Development Goals to Strategic Issues   45

References   47

4. STRATEGY IMPLEMENTATION THROUGH TACTICAL PLANNING   49

Goal Congruency and Sharing the Vision   49

The Tactical Planning Process   50

Guidelines for Tactical Plans   55

Evaluating a Tactical Plan   58

Linking Management and Executive Development to Tactical Planning   59

Summary of Part I   60

References   61

PART II OPERATIONS   63

5. STRATEGY EXECUTION: A FUNCTIONAL MODEL   65

Management as a Series of Linked Processes   66

The Importance of Interfunctional Teamwork   74

Some Processes for Developing Interfunctional Teamwork   75

The Need for Concurrent Executive Development 77
Measures of Performance 77
References 78

6. TOTAL QUALITY CONTROL: A TOOL FOR IMPROVING THE QUALITY OF MANAGEMENT 79

TQC Basics 80
The Deming Prize and the Deming Cycle 82
Process Analysis 85
Measuring Process Performance 90
Cause and Effect Analysis 92
Corrective Action 95
Application of TQC to the Process of Management 96
References 97

7. PROCESS IMPROVEMENT AND EXECUTIVE DEVELOPMENT 99

The General and Functional Management Processes 101
Evaluating the Effectiveness of Executive Processes 106
Cause and Effect Analysis 110
Process Performance Measurement Compared to Performance Appraisal 111
Alternatives for Executive Process Improvement 112
Summary of Part II 113
References 114

PART III EXECUTIVE DEVELOPMENT 115

8. EXECUTIVE DEVELOPMENT STRATEGY FORMULATION 117

Basic Responsibilities 117
Determining Overall Needs 123
Developing the Strategy 128

Gaining Strategy Approval   132
Acquiring Resources   133
Involving Executives in the Development Process   134
Program Ownership and the "Best Practices" Model   135
Executive Development as a Worldwide Activity   137
Planning for Strategy Implementation   138
References   141

9. EXECUTIVE DEVELOPMENT PROGRAM DESIGN   143

Needs Analysis and Program Investigation   144
Establishing Specific Training Objectives   148
Confirming Objectives with Top Management and Discussing Program Alternatives   149
Designing the Program Structure   150
Developing Specific Methods for Meeting Module Objectives   154
Defining Module Content and Identifying Content Experts   158
Finalizing the Executive Program Agenda   160
Program Packaging   160
A Strategy Example: A Management Seminar for Senior Executives   164
References   166

10. PROGRAM DEVELOPMENT AND PRODUCTION   169

Overall Project Management   169
Staffing Assignments   171
The Project Schedule, Checkpoints, and Project Reviews   172
The Project Budget   175
Use of Module Task Forces   177
Selection of Materials and Media   178
Content Development   179

Development of Leaders' Materials   184
Content Testing and Pilot Runs   185
Program Production Considerations   186
Quality Assurance   191
References   192

11. MARKETING EXECUTIVE DEVELOPMENT   193

Appraising Where You Stand and Setting Marketing Objectives   193

Essential Elements of Marketing for Training and Development Directors   196

Applying Marketing Techniques to Executive Development   198

Marketing an Executive Development Program   200

References   207

12. PROGRAM IMPLEMENTATION AND EVALUATION   209

Program Management   209

Participant Selection   212

Instructor Training, Coaching, and Evaluation   213

Program Logistics   215

Classroom Operations   219

Program Evaluation and Followup   221

Program Support   223

Strategy for Program Updating and Ultimate Obsolescence   224

Summary of Part III   225

APPENDIXES

A. A MODEL FOR MANAGEMENT DEVELOPMENT   227

B. TEN STRATEGIC ISSUES FOR TRAINING AND DEVELOPMENT   233

C. TELEVISION, COMPUTERS, AND SIMULATIONS AS EXECUTIVE
   DEVELOPMENT RESOURCES   241

Bibliography   257

Index   259

PREFACE

In February 1985, my wife, Sheila, and I spent two weeks in northern Italy visiting our daughter, Laurie, who was studying at Stanford's campus in Florence. At the time, I was also making some final decisions on what I wanted to do after completing twenty-five years with Hewlett-Packard in June. Somewhere between the hours of viewing Michelangelo and Botticelli and sampling the wine and pasta, I reached the conclusion to leave HP to strike out on my own. I had three objectives in mind: to spend some time further refining and documenting my experiences and ideas on the general subject of the linkages between business strategy and executive development, to volunteer some time to the California State Department of Education to pursue how the management effectiveness of our schools could be increased, and to do some private consulting. My strategy for meeting the first of these objectives included writing this book. The second objective was expanded to occupy about 30 percent of my time as a result of HP's offer to financially support my work with the state. The project was completed in November of 1986. The consulting objective is just getting underway.

While managing Hewlett-Packard's executive development program, I became intrigued with the power of executive development as a tool for business strategy implementation. During this period, I also had many opportunities to discuss the linkages between strategy execution and development activity with colleagues in other corporations in the United States and abroad. As my interest grew, I became determined to further develop some methods for integrating these linkages into executive development strategy formulation.

My purpose in writing this book is to argue that executive development *must* be driven by business strategy. There is no other way to achieve an adequate return on executive development investment. The relationships between an organization's strategy and its management and executive training efforts need to be identified and managed by both the top management team and the training and development people. For this reason, the book is written for both executives and training and development professionals. It is hoped that training and development people will find some different approaches for more closely aligning their efforts with the needs of the firm. Executives may discover that executive development can be their "secret weapon" to build competitive advantage. Both groups may rediscover the importance of their working closely together to enhance their organization's overall effectiveness.

There is no way I could adequately recognize the many contributions made by others to this work. The people at Hewlett-Packard have had the major influence on my ideas, for I spent a quarter of a century in the HP environment. The philosophies and examples of Bill Hewlett and Dave Packard have been etched indelibly into my thinking. John Young taught me the value of "one-page" strategies and strategic issues. The opportunity to join HP was provided by Bob Grimm and Ed Morgan, my first boss. Bob Boniface and Al Oliverio taught me much of what I know about selling and marketing, and they encouraged and coached my early development in sales and marketing management. John Doyle helped me to better understand how successful management practices can be articulated and perpetuated. They all emphasized the importance of an organization's values and philosophies and were strong role models.

My colleagues on the Conference Board Council on Education, Training, and Development helped me learn about management and executive practices in other companies and confirmed many of the ideas in this book. Ruth Shaeffer of the Conference Board provided advice and encouragement during my years on the Council.

I am particularly indebted to several members of the faculty at the Stanford Graduate School of Business, who were not only outstanding instructors for HP executive development programs but also excellent coaches for me. The late

Alex Robichek taught me the mechanics of an effective executive development seminar and things to consider when selecting instructors. Hal Leavitt and Gene Webb had major influence on my recognition of the importance of process as well as task and, when communicating, feelings as well as facts. Chuck Horngren's emphasis on goal congruency has been carried over into my approach to strategic management. Jim Howell demonstrated the impact that an outstanding teacher can have on a program as well as making the "dismal" science of economics exciting to executives.

Tom Peters shared his early research on excellent companies in a number of HP seminars and was willing to spend many hours with me discussing the relevance of his research to the training of executives. "Getting the basics right first" has its roots in these early discussions. Bill Ouchi introduced me to the importance of organizational culture and, through his research, confirmed the importance of philosophy and values in a training and development curriculum.

During the last half of 1985 and for most of 1986, I had the opportunity to work closely with Bill Honig, California's Superintendent of Public Instruction, and his executive team in Sacramento. This was a chance to try many of my ideas in the public sector environment. I found that there are many more similarities than differences.

I found that writing a book is a lot like training for your first marathon—it's easy to underestimate the magnitude of the effort required. I could not have completed the task without the encouragement of my wife and her willingness to spend long hours reading, commenting on, and rereading the many drafts of each chapter. Scott Shershow at Addison-Wesley provided much needed support and assistance during the preparation and editing of the manuscript.

Los Altos Hills, California
January 1987

Achieving Strategic Goals Through Executive Development

CHAPTER 1

INTRODUCTION: LINKING EXECUTIVE DEVELOPMENT TO BUSINESS STRATEGY

COMPETING IN A COMPLEX INTERNATIONAL MARKETPLACE

"Oil shock waves roll through the North Sea." "Computers that come awfully close to thinking." "America's computer heavyweights slug it out in Europe." "Imports keep clobbering machine tool makers." "The U.S. trade deficit with Japan: A new record." "High tech to the rescue." These quotations were titles for news items recently appearing in one month's issues of *Business Week*.[1] Fierce competition, exchange rate fluctuations, technological obsolescence, and economic uncertainty are major concerns for all executives in every industry and country. Executives are faced with the realities of navigating through a maze of complexities to better position their firms relative to competitors.

This concern about the changing business environment, particularly increased competition, is a common theme in shareholder reports. In its 1985 annual report, General Electric stated:

> During the past five years, we've shared with you our assessment of the increasingly more competitive 1980s — and our strategy for winning in this era of greatly intensified worldwide competition. In an environment of accelerated technological and market change and slower worldwide growth, a company — and its businesses — must change faster than the world around it. That's why General Electric embarked five years ago on a long term strategy to become the most compet-

itive enterprise in the world — not only in the 1980s, but, in the 1990s and beyond.[2]

Along with the constant turmoil in the industrial environment itself, a revolution is happening in world markets, and this revolution focuses on quality and productivity. Customers expect high-quality products at low cost, and companies, notably those around the Pacific rim, are finding new ways to meet these customer expectations. The companies that are winning in the marketplace have developed methods to achieve superior product quality at the same time that they have been increasing the productivity of physical and human resources. Higher quality has come from doing a better job of making the product in the first place. Moreover, this has resulted in a productivity increase because manufacturing costs are lower when there is less scrap and rework. New manufacturing technologies have contributed significantly to productivity increases. Further gains in output have come from cooperative efforts among employees and their participation in the management of operations.[3]

To compete in these more complex markets, executives are creating innovative strategies to optimize their firm's performance, but in more highly competitive markets the margins for error in *strategy implementation* are substantially reduced. Many markets are growing at much slower rates than in the past, and implementation mistakes will not be masked by more than enough business for all. Executive teams must execute properly the first time.

Executing right the first time requires that employees, at all levels, have the necessary skills to function successfully, including the skill to use their minds to think about better ways to do their jobs. Japanese companies have demonstrated dramatically the wisdom of harnessing the minds of their workers, but thinking workers need to keep up to date with rapidly changing workplace technologies. This updating is effected through continual programs of training and education for all employees.[4] To effectively lead these employees managers need to stay up to date also. Consequently, management and executive development must be a continuous

Introduction: Linking Executive Development to Business Strategy

process that is carefully aligned to the changes taking place in the firm, its industry, and its markets.

The objective of this book is to outline a strategy for enhancing a firm's overall effectiveness, particularly the organization's ability to compete in a complex and changing environment, by linking executive development to business strategy. I believe that executive training should be focused on those processes that are critical to the implementation of the firm's business strategy. Furthermore, the achievement of this linkage between training and strategy requires the close attention of the chief executive officer and the other members of the top management team.[5]

CURRENT EXECUTIVE DEVELOPMENT PRACTICES AND THEIR LIMITATIONS

Conventional management and executive development approaches suffer several limitations that make linkages with corporate strategy difficult. First, these approaches are typically generic — that is, all managers are treated as if they have the same problems. This approach is usually most effective for building basic managerial skills. Second, most management development programs are designed and implemented by practitioners who have had little experience with the actual operating problems of a specific company. This makes it difficult to build realism into the training. Third, management development is often treated as something that other people "do" to managers, and therefore the executives of the organization seldom feel ownership of the process. Fourth, many executive development programs are conducted by an outside organization entirely away from the firm's environment. When they return to the company, executives typically find that their associates have difficulty relating to the new methods and techniques acquired from the program. This makes transfer of learning back to the job extremely difficult, if not impossible. Fifth, traditional executive development efforts focus an extraordinary amount of time on executive succession planning. Large data bases of existing and potential executive talent are maintained, and the development effort is directed at "holes" in a manager's education and experience. This activity deserves some attention, but time spent on executive succession planning is time not spent on building executive implementation skills.

It is important to consider these limitations when thinking about the development of your organization's executives. Your organization may not be of sufficient size to warrant extensive training activities designed and conducted within the firm. In that case don't abandon executive development because you are unable to find the "right" program. Choose the programs and activities that come closest to meeting your specific needs. You will do a much better job of implementing your business strategy when you link executive development to your strategy. If you can design and conduct your own programs, this linkage can be optimized. If not, all is not lost. When you must rely exclusively on outside programs, spend the time necessary to get as close a linkage to your strategy as possible. The discussion on formulating an executive development strategy in Chapter 8 will include things to look for in selecting outside executive training programs.

WHY BUSINESS STRATEGY MUST DRIVE EXECUTIVE DEVELOPMENT

The ultimate goal for a business is to provide products and services to its customers at a competitive advantage over those other firms attempting to provide similar products and services. Every activity of the business should be concentrated on achieving this objective. Businesses develop strategies to guide these activities, and these strategies are implemented through a series of interrelated functional activities including product development, marketing, and manufacturing. To perform these activities in an optimal manner, and thereby maximize the chances for successful implementation of the strategy, this book argues that executive development needs to be closely linked to the strategy. Primary emphasis

Introduction: Linking Executive Development to Business Strategy

for executive development should be on the continual development and fine tuning of those functional and general management skills necessary for operationalizing the firm's strategy.

Strategies are poorly executed when goals are unclear to those charged with implementation. For this reason, an increasing number of chief executive officers have recognized that a formal executive development program is also an effective vehicle for communicating goals throughout the organization. Benefits provided by this communication include

- A deeper understanding of the basic values and principles that guide the organization;
- A greater understanding of the environment in which the business competes and ways for the firm to optimize performance in this environment;
- Gaining commitment to those key, essential actions that dictate the success or failure of the business.

An executive development program used in this manner can have great impact on changing the behavior of the organization. In 1969 Dave Packard, cofounder with Bill Hewlett of Hewlett-Packard Company, took a leave of absence to become Deputy Secretary of Defense. After three years in Washington, he returned to his company to find that short-term debt had increased significantly and that top management was about to convert this debt to long term — despite HP's strong tradition of financing the business from internally generated funds. Long-term debt was considered necessary only when firms were unable to manage their operations to generate sufficient cash for continuing to meet expenses and finance growth.

Packard concluded that in his absence some of the executives and managers had failed to pay attention to the underlying principles that guided the company's management. Some behavior modification was in order. He called for the development of a management training program for all executives that would stress the basic business management principles that he wished to have followed.

I became involved in this story after being asked to set up a corporate department to design and implement a seminar along with an overall strategy for management and executive development at Hewlett-Packard. The first task was to develop a program to meet the needs seen by Dave Packard. A comprehensive executive seminar was launched in the spring of 1975, and sessions were held until nearly all general and functional managers had attended. The sessions on finance, accounting, economics, general management, and other topics contributed greatly to providing executives with the background knowledge they needed to do their jobs. However, there is no question in my mind that the enduring benefit of the seminar was the message that Dave communicated on how he wanted the company managed and the behavior change that ensued.

Another example of how executive development is used to change behavior was the response of AT&T to the challenge presented by divestiture in January 1984. Until then the telephone business in the United States had been strongly regulated by the government and dominated by AT&T. Divestiture meant that AT&T would have to compete with a number of aggressive firms in a nonregulated environment. This would require a significant change in operating style. Brooke Tunstall of AT&T cited six actions that would be necessary to change the firm's culture for competing in this new competitive environment, including "Gear training to support cultural values." The Bell Advanced Management Program was developed for senior managers, and its curriculum included business strategy formulation and implementation, finance, marketing, and the management of change.[6]

Executive development programs are frequently used to reinforce and perpetuate a firm's culture and distinctive skills. 3M is consistently used as an example of a firm that excels in product innovations. At a Conference Board Council meeting a couple of years ago, Bob Backlund, executive director of Staffing, Development, and Services at 3M, told me that his company had recently implemented an executive development program on maintaining innovation.

Whether the goal is senior management education, communication of top management expectations, or implementing change in an organization, executive development is an extremely effective tool provided that it is driven by the strategy and goals of the organization.

LINKAGES BETWEEN STRATEGY, OPERATIONS, AND EXECUTIVE DEVELOPMENT

Figure 1–1 is a model showing the primary linkages between executive development and business strategy. The four major elements of the model are top management, strategy, operations, and development.

Top Management

The top management team, particularly the CEO, has the overall responsibility for guiding the activities of the organization toward the successful implementation of strategy. A basic responsibility is strategy formulation — the course of action to meet the organization's strategic goals. Top management leadership is required to translate strategic goals into specific action steps.

Strategic Framework

This element of the model defines the goals that the organization is striving to achieve and the actions to reach these goals. It includes a statement of strategic goals and a description of the organization's strategy. A key component of the strategy is a list of strategic issues — that is, those forces that tend to impede the successful implementation of the strategy. Strategic issues are particularly useful for providing a focus for specific executive development activities. Additional inputs to the strategy element are the actions of customers and competitors as well as the economic and political forces affecting the business climate. As will be discussed in Chapter 4, strategies are implemented through discrete actions, or tactics, that need to be congruent throughout the organization. Tactics are developed and managed through goal-congruent tactical plans.

Operations

This element includes the functional activities of the business, such as product development, marketing, manufacturing, quality assurance, finance, and personnel. Closely associated with these functional activities are the activities provided by outside organizations, including the firm's suppliers, banks, and independent distributors.

Figure 1-1 Linking Executive Development to Business Strategy

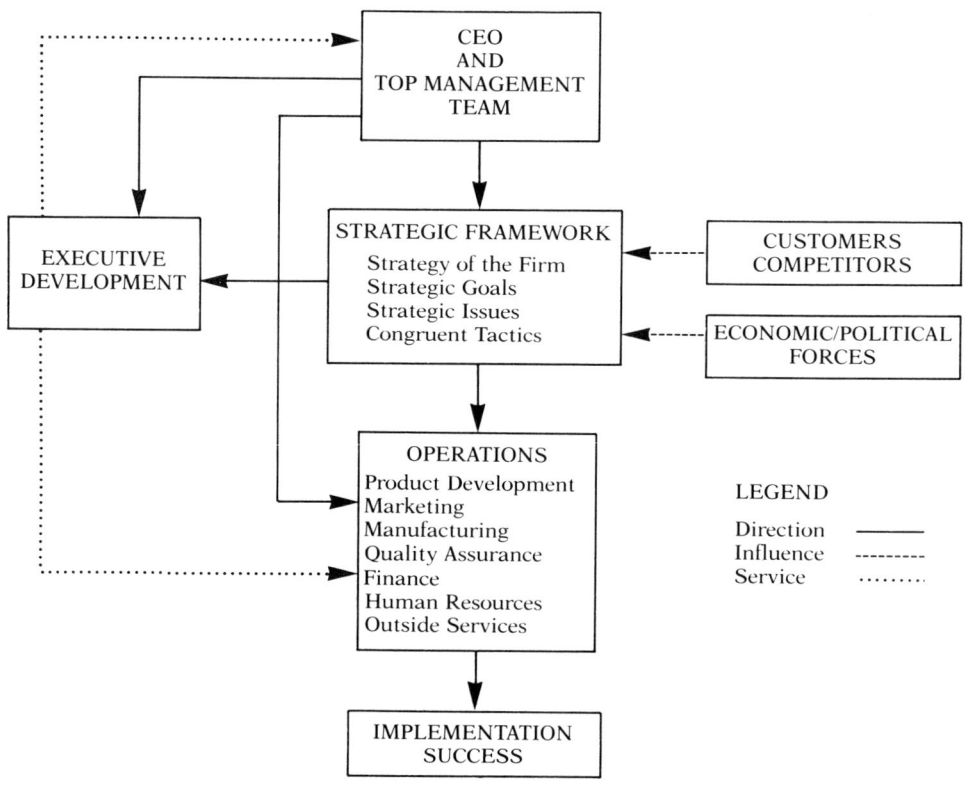

Executive Development

Although normally a component of the personnel or human resources function, executive development is shown separately to emphasize critical linkages. This element includes all of the activities that are designed to make sure that executives have the necessary knowledge and skills to operationalize the firm's strategy. Major activities in executive development are needs assessment, program design, program development, and the implementation of the programs that contribute to the developmental needs of the executive team.

AN UNCONVENTIONAL APPROACH TO EXECUTIVE DEVELOPMENT

In 1975, when I was asked to put together an overall strategy for developing managers and executives at Hewlett-Packard, particular emphasis needed to be placed on the development of the large number of new general and functional managers who would be needed during the late 1970s and 1980s. Although I had been with Hewlett-Packard since 1960, my educational background was in engineering and my HP experience was in marketing, including various assignments in field sales, marketing, and general management. My qualifications for this new job were nontraditional. I had no choice but to take an unconventional approach to my new responsibilities by relying on the applications of marketing principles to management and executive training.

The transition to developing HP managers turned out to be smoother than anticipated because much of what I had learned in marketing was directly applicable to training managers. Needs analysis sounded a lot like market research; program pilot runs corresponded to test marketing. Designing a program to meet executive needs was a process similar to designing a product to meet customer needs. Moreover, I was particularly helped by having already "walked in the shoes" of the managers for whom our strategy was intended. I knew how difficult the transitions to functional and general manager were.

My first step was to design an overall model for management and executive development. We needed something tangible to guide our development program efforts so that we would have an overall strategy with one program building on another. A model would also serve me well in selling the strategy to the HP top management team.[7] Although the model dealt with all levels of management, my personal interest and focus were on those programs aimed at senior managers. I borrowed from my marketing background and realized that executive development programs would be successful only to the extent that executives "owned" their programs. For this ownership to occur, the design and development of the program had to involve the executive team, and the programs had to provide immediate help to the executives in the day-to-day activities of their jobs. If we could very closely couple curriculum to the implementation of strategy, program ownership would be assured. Our strategy for executive development would then be successful.

The major departures from more traditional strategies for executive development were the close linkages between the development function and the top management team, the day-to-day operations of the entities, and the strategy for the company. As illustrated in Figure 1–1, executive development was one of the key processes requiring top management direction. The resources provided for executive development were focused on activities that *directly* supported the strategic goals of the company. Moreover, executive development was seen by top management as a tool for implementing strategy.

The top management team — in considering the needs of customers, the actions of competitors, and environmental factors affecting the firm's business operations — has the primary responsibility for shaping business strategy. Strategy is implemented by functional operations under the leadership of the top management team. The link advocated in this book is the general direction provided by the CEO to executive development activities. Following the model, the CEO should routinely call on the resources of executive development to optimize the performance of functional operations. As will be discussed in Chapter 3, there are many things that get in the way of strategic goal achievement. Through the process of

Introduction: Linking Executive Development to Business Strategy

identifying these implementation impediments, a list of "strategic issues" that require general attention can be developed. A significant number of these issues can be resolved by providing executives with additional skills and knowledge. Specific strategies for the training of executives need to be shaped by these strategic issues.

How successful was the approach taken at Hewlett-Packard? During the period 1975 to 1985, HP's annual revenues grew from less than $1 billion to over $6 billion. The number of operating entities (divisions and sales regions worldwide) grew from about thirty to over 100, including many divisions that consist of two or three relatively autonomous operations. Each HP entity has a general manager and several functional managers, so this rapid growth in entities is a measure of the need to develop executive talent. All HP senior managers have been developed internally with one or two exceptions.[8] In *Fortune* magazine's survey for ranking corporate reputations Hewlett-Packard was listed in the top five for "most admired company" for the years 1983, 1984, and 1985. During these same years, HP was ranked number one in "ability to attract, develop, and keep talented people."[9] There are many contributing factors to this performance in addition to executive development activity. Nevertheless, executive development made a significant contribution to this performance.

AN OVERVIEW OF THE BOOK

This book has been written for general managers who would like to gain some additional insight into how executive development can contribute significantly to successful strategy implementation, and for human resources managers and professionals who have the responsibility for developing and implementing strategies for executive and management development. Part I presents an overall strategic framework that defines specific connecting links to executive training. Chapter 2 reviews the principles of strategic management, recognizing that line managers have the ultimate responsibility for both strategy formulation and execution. The concepts of strategic position and functional strategies are introduced, and strategy is further defined as a real-time repositioning process. Chapter 3 discusses strategic issues and presents a model for discovering topics that should be included in an executive development strategy. Chapter 4 outlines a process for strategy implementation through goal-congruent tactical planning that integrates the operations of functional departments into the firm's business strategy.

Part II deals with strategy implementation, beginning with a model for interfunctional relationships in Chapter 5. Chapter 6 outlines the basic principles of total quality control and presents a case for looking at management as a series of interrelated processes that need to be continuously improved. Chapter 7 establishes the relationship between the need for continual process improvement and the activities of executive development.

Part III completes the strategy, operations and development model by covering techniques for developing executive training programs that relate specifically to strategic issues and operational needs. Chapter 8 describes a process for executive development strategy formulation and outlines specific roles for the top management team and the training department. A strategy for gaining program ownership by the targeted participants is described. Chapters 9 and 10 show a process for designing, developing, and producing an executive development program, and a seminar developed for senior managers at Hewlett-Packard is used to illustrate the steps. Included in the process are techniques for needs analysis, selecting instructors, sharing the development work through module task forces, overall project management, and methods for testing the design prior to program implementation. In Chapter 11 the importance of marketing an executive development program is discussed, and the key steps for a marketing program are outlined. Finally, Chapter 12 covers program implementation and evaluation. Included in this discussion are seminar management practices and a strategy for gaining management commitment to program evaluation and followup.

The appendixes include detailed treatments of several topics introduced in the book. These include a model for management development and a discussion of ten strategic issues for the training and development function. Television, computers, and simulations have become powerful media for executive training, and Appendix C summarizes the author's experience in these areas. A detailed bibliography concludes the book.

REFERENCES

1. *Business Week,* May 19, 1986, pp. 30 and 64; May 26, 1986, p. 122; June 2, 1986, p. 92; June 9, 1986, p. 26; and June 16, 1986, p. 100.
2. From General Electric Company, *Annual Report 1985,* p. 2.
3. For a detailed treatment of the challenges facing U.S. Industry, see *Global Competition — The New Reality,* Report of the President's Commission on Industrial Competitiveness, U.S. Government Printing Office, Washington, D.C., 1985.
4. For a discusssion on the Japanese approach to employee training, see Shigeko M. Asher and Ken Inoue, "Industrial Manpower Development in Japan," *Finance & Development,* September 1985, p. 23, and G. F. Brown and A. R. Read, "Personnel and Training Policies — Some Lessons for Western Companies," *Long Range Planning,* April 1984, pp. 48–57.
5. This book defines *executives* as senior managers at or above the level of the functional manager. *Top management* and *the top management team* are defined as the chief executive officer and those executives reporting directly to the CEO. The other executives in the organization are referred to as the *executive team.*
6. W. Brooke Tunstall, "Cultural Transition at AT&T," *Sloan Management Review,* Fall 1983, pp. 15–26.
7. See Appendix A for a detailed description of this management development model.
8. See the 1975 and 1985 Hewlett-Packard Company Annual Reports.
9. See "Ranking Corporate Reputations," *Fortune,* January 10, 1983, pp. 34–44, and "America's Most Admired Corporations," *Fortune,* January 9, 1984, pp. 50–62, and January 7, 1985, pp. 18–30.

PART I
A STRATEGIC FRAMEWORK

CHAPTER 2
STRATEGY

Strategies drive business actions. Executives are paid to formulate and implement successful strategies. When strategic goals are met, executives earn their salaries; when goals are consistently missed, those responsible are replaced. Executive development must provide the knowledge and skills for effective strategy formulation, and this topic occupies a central position in most executive development curricula. Managers who are responsible for executive development need to thoroughly understand the principles of strategy development and implementation and why these principles must form the basis for all executive training activity.

This chapter outlines a general framework for strategy development derived primarily from my experiences at Hewlett-Packard, first as a line executive and subsequently as an architect of the company's executive training strategy. The framework that will be presented is particularly useful for developing linkages between business strategy and the executive development process. A detailed treatment of strategy is beyond the scope of this book. Readers are referred to the many excellent books on strategy. Michael Porter's *Competitive Strategy* and *Competitive Advantage* and Kenichi Ohmae's *The Mind of the Strategist* provide in-depth treatment of many of the concepts introduced in the following sections.[1]

SOME BASIC DEFINITIONS

There is frequently confusion, if not strong differences of opinion, over the definitions of the basic terms used in the discussion of strategy. The following definitions are consistent with current usage in most organizations and academic circles.

The important thing is to establish a consistent set of definitions for your own organization.

Mission

The broadly stated purpose of the business organization is its mission — the reason that the organization exists. For example, Genentech, a major firm in the biotechnology field, states its mission as follows: "Genentech was founded to apply genetic engineering techniques to the production of important health care products."[2]

Goals and Objectives

It is generally agreed that goals and objectives are the same things, and no distinction between them is made in this book. For business organizations, goals or objectives are established for specific markets, for development or acquisition of technologies that will be used in products to serve these markets, for sales volume, and for profitability. Additional goals may be established for market share, for specific capabilities in manufacturing, for the people in the organization, and for contributions to society in general. These types of goals will be referred to as the organization's *strategic goals* or *strategic objectives*. A major strategic goal for General Electric is to be number one or two in market share in the businesses in which they have chosen to compete.[3]

Strategy

Strategies are specific plans for achieving the organization's strategic goals or strategic objectives. The term *strategy* is often confused with the terms *goals* and *objectives*. A strategy is the means for achieving goals or objectives. It consists of specific, current actions — not just good intentions. Hayes and Wheelwright characterize strategy as a "pattern of decisions" made by a firm to reach desired goals.[4] Strategies do not necessarily have to be explicit, but implicit strategies, like implicit navigation, can lead to foundering.

Tactics

Tactics are the specific actions that the company takes during a convenient planning period, usually corresponding to the fiscal year, to implement strategy. A common misunderstanding is that strategies are always long-term actions and tactics short-term. Time horizons are inconsistent with our previous definition of *strategy*. For example, the plan that a person makes to drive to the mountains for skiing is a strategy to reach the mountains. The actions that the person takes to get there are tactics. This book will refer to *tactics* as components of strategy implementation. Tactics are *driven* by strategy. As will be discussed in more detail in Chapter 4, tactics will be used to refer to specific tasks to be completed during the organization's yearly planning cycle.

Figure 2-1 shows the hierarchical relationship between mission, goals, strategy, and tactics. It is not necessary to dwell on semantics. Just remember that strategies are the means for achieving goals and tactics are merely a convenient subdivision for the strategic actions necessary to achieve them.

STRATEGY AS A REAL-TIME MANAGEMENT PROCESS

In the past many business firms had strategic planning units in their organizations, and these units were responsible for developing master strategic plans for the enterprise. In recent years executives have recognized that the managers who are responsible for implementing strategy should play the major role in strategy development.[5] This process of strategic management has begun to replace classical strategic planning in the business school classroom and in U.S. business firms. A pioneer of this concept is Dan Thomas, who taught the strategic management process at the Harvard and Stanford Business Schools and now consults for major international firms.

The major premise of the strategic management approach is that large central planning staffs are not close

A Strategic Framework

enough to the dynamics of a business to either develop realistic strategies or be able to fine tune strategies on a real-time basis in response to a rapidly changing marketplace. Changes in the business environment — particularly new developments in technology, shifting government policy, and actions of aggressive competitors — take place faster than conventional strategic planning cycles can accommodate. Today's management responsibilities include the duty to manage strategy on a real-time basis. Moreover, strategies should be designed to take advantage of any opportunities that develop during implementation.

The central player in the real-time process of strategic management is the chief executive officer or the general manager of a strategic business unit or SBU. For this reason ex-

Figure 2-1   Basic Definitions

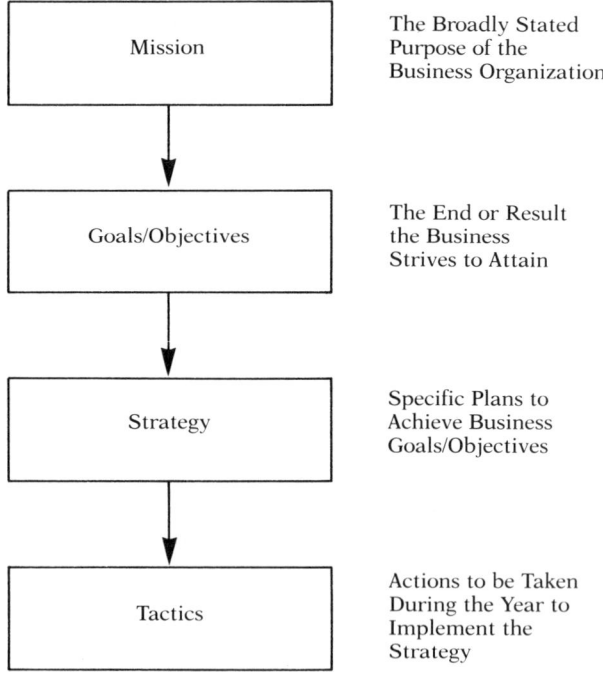

ecutive development efforts aimed at the general management levels should include heavy doses of strategic management principles and skills. These same skills and principles need also to be included in programs aimed at the functional levels. Strategies are necessarily formulated at the top of the organization, but implementation is carried out at successively lower levels. A significant responsibility of CEOs and SBU managers is to make sure that a set of interlocking strategies is developed for each functional unit of the business, and this task is easier when functional executives have been through similar training.

RELATING STRATEGY TO ORGANIZATIONAL FACTORS

Effective strategies cannot be developed without considering a number of factors that affect the organization. Executives need to ask a number of questions during the planning process. Are you organized in a way that will make it possible to achieve your strategic goals? Do you have the skills within the organization to implement the strategy? Are the political and economic environments supportive? Several years ago a very helpful model that relates strategy to other organizational elements was developed at McKinsey & Company. Commonly called the *McKinsey 7S Framework*, it clearly describes the relationships between strategy, structure, skills, staff, style, systems, and superordinate goals (more recently renamed *shared values*).[6] This model serves as an excellent guide during strategy formulation and is particularly helpful in developing a management and executive training strategy.

To survive as a viable business, every organization has some distinctive skills. These skills give it an edge over competitors. To achieve strategic goals, an organization's strategy should be congruent with these distinctive skills. To gain a further competitive advantage the organization should direct its employee and management development efforts toward building a stronger base of distinctive skills. For example, Motorola has enjoyed several decades of strong growth as an innovative high technology business concentrating in communications and semiconductors. During the last several years increased competition from companies in the Far East has been a major impediment to Motorola's continued high-growth performance. Motorola has taken several steps to strengthen its own competitive position. A major executive development program was launched to provide key managers with a better understanding of their Far Eastern competitors and methods for more effectively competing with these organizations. Compared to its domestic competitors, Motorola has developed some distinctive skills in response to competitive threats from across the Pacific.[7]

STRATEGIC POSITION

A summary statement of an organization's strategic goals can be used to define a strategic position to which the organization aspires. The distance between this strategic position and the firm's present position represents the gap that the strategy needs to address. Strategic positions are illustrated in Figure 2–2. Point A in the figure represents the organization's current strategic position, and it corresponds to some relative measure of success along the Y axis. Past strategies have placed the firm in this position. Strategies yet to be implemented are designed to carry the organization to a higher level of success, indicated by strategic position B.

The current strategic position is defined by answering the question, "Where are we today?" The answer needs to be phrased in terms of the firm's product offerings (particularly quality as perceived by the customer), markets and marketing capabilities, technology strengths (and weaknesses), manufacturing capabilities, financial resources, and organizational capabilities including employee and management knowledge and skills.

Another item that affects a firm's strategic position is the way that people throughout the organization treat customers. I recently experienced two extremes of customer satisfaction on a trip to Los Angeles to make a presentation at La Verne University. The airline I had chosen put forth little

Strategy

effort to make the trip enjoyable for its passengers. I didn't hear one *please* or *thank you* from any of the crew on either leg of the flight. In sharp contrast to the airline, the staff at the Clarion Hotel in Ontario went out of their way to make a brief visit a delightful experience. The waiters and waitresses were helpful, friendly, and polite. Every member of the staff I encountered made an effort to show his or her appreciation for my patronage. The hotel must have included customer satisfaction as an important component of its view of strategic position.

The strategic position concept is most meaningful when used as a tool to compare a company's current position rela-

Figure 2-2   Strategic Positions

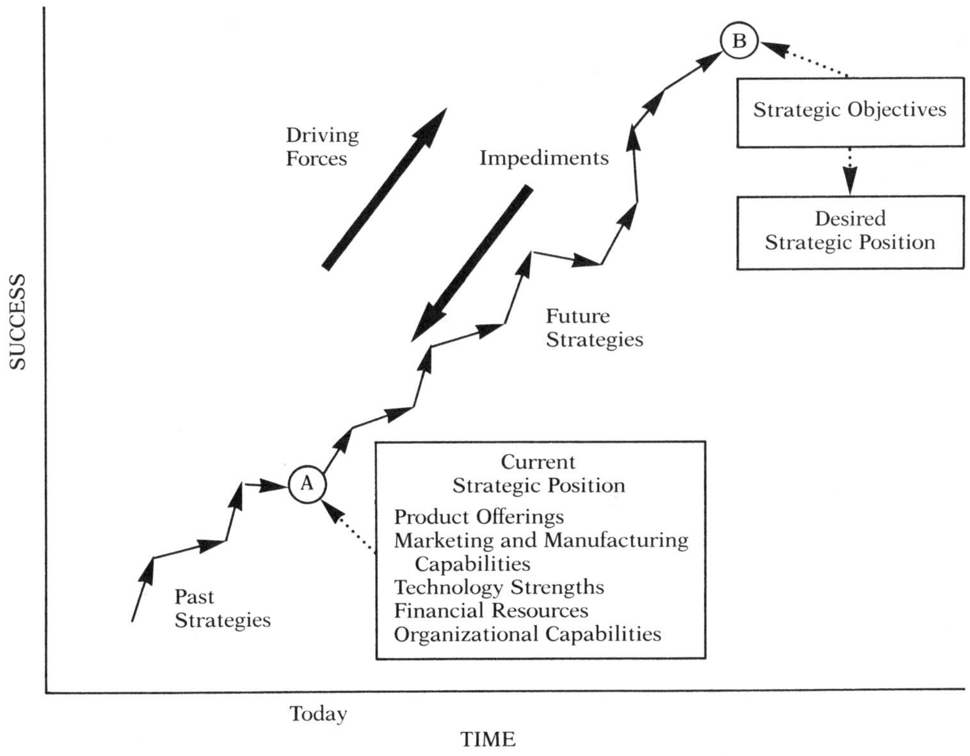

Y-axis: SUCCESS; X-axis: TIME (Today)

- Past Strategies → A (Current Strategic Position: Product Offerings, Marketing and Manufacturing Capabilities, Technology Strengths, Financial Resources, Organizational Capabilities)
- Driving Forces
- Impediments
- Future Strategies → B
- Strategic Objectives → Desired Strategic Position

tive to that of competitors and to the position to which the firm aspires in the future. Achieving strategic objectives results in a new strategic position, and the goal of strategy is to arrive at a strategic position of significant strength compared to competitors.

"Where there is no competitive differential," as Kenichi Ohmae puts it, "the giant will always win."[8] Ohmae, Porter, and others who have contributed greatly to the literature on strategy forcibly argue that a strategy that disregards the capabilities and actions of competitors will be ineffective.[9] Success comes from doing things better than your competitors. Ohmae's comment goes a long way to explain why so many businesses today develop strategies based on finding a market niche to meet customer needs that larger, established firms have ignored.

STRATEGY AS A REPOSITIONING PROCESS

A useful way to view strategy is as a repositioning process. This process is illustrated in Figure 2–2 by the future strategies designed to reposition the firm to position *B*. These strategies consist of a series of congruent tactical actions that move a firm's strategic position closer to the desired objective.

Take as an example the strategic position of the U.S. automobile industry compared to those of the Japanese and Germans. Steadily declining market share has been due primarily to product quality. Ask your friends why they purchased a Japanese or German car, and nine times out of ten they will respond by saying "better quality for the money." U.S. manufacturers will not be able to regain market share until prospective buyers perceive that domestic quality is comparable to or better than that of the imports at a competitive price. Chrysler, Ford, and General Motors have identified future strategic positions that include quality as a major component. Ford stresses quality in every advertisement I have recently seen.

Ford Motor Company's Taurus and Sable project is evidence of their repositioning effort. A report in *Business Week* called the Taurus and Sable "four-star successes." It went on to say,

> Customers are snapping them up faster than the company can turn them out. . . . How did Ford pull it off? . . . It studied customer wants and needs like never before, made quality the top priority, and streamlined its operations and organization. Top management is so pleased with the outcome that the Taurus approach will be the blueprint for all future development programs."[10]

A number of forces, both positive and negative, affect this repositioning effort. These include forces that are economic, social, environmental, technical, political, and cultural. Successful strategy implementation requires that top management teams thoroughly understand the actions of these forces on their chosen strategy and, when necessary, modify the strategy accordingly. The unexpected changes in these forces are the principal reasons that strategy must be managed on a real-time basis. Executive development activities need to address the forces that act on strategic repositioning efforts. Executives need to develop the necessary knowledge and skills to be able to identify and deal with the forces that may influence strategy implementation.

BASIC CONSIDERATIONS IN BUSINESS STRATEGY FORMULATION

Figure 2–3 outlines the key steps in developing a strategy for repositioning a firm to a desired strategic position. The starting point for strategy development is an accurate assessment of your organization's current strategic position. What are the actual strengths and weaknesses of your products and services, marketing program, available technologies, financial position, manufacturing capabilities, and organizational strengths? How are you perceived by your customers? Are you easy to do business with? Do your products and services offer exceptional quality? Important factors are the distinctive strengths or competencies of your organization and its

A Strategic Framework

Figure 2-3   Key Steps in Strategy Development

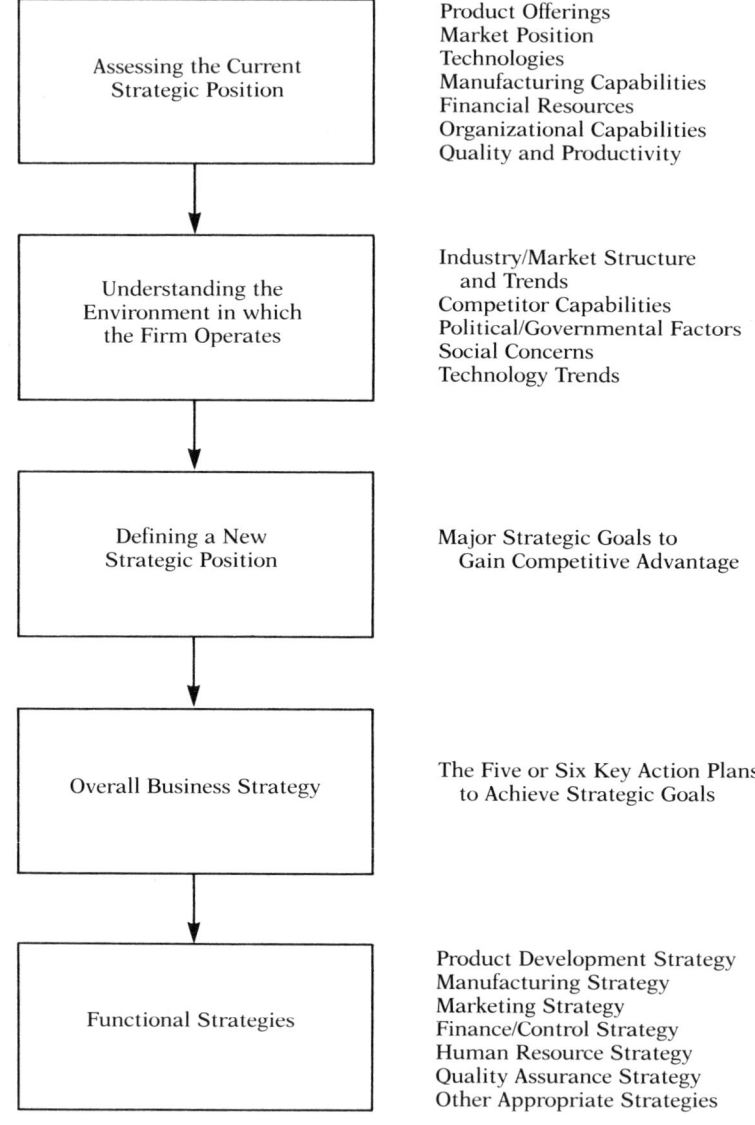

people. Successful strategies are usually built on these strengths. For example, the marketing competency of IBM has become legendary as have the innovation skills of 3M. How well is your firm linking your distinctive skills to your strategy? Anyone doubting the importance of this linkage only has to look at how IBM took advantage of its marketing skills in creating the overwhelming success of the IBM PC.

The second basic step in strategy formulation is to understand the environment in which your firm does business. A thorough understanding of the environment will include traditional factors such as economic, political, and social issues. What trends are apparent? How do governmental actions like deregulation of industries or emphasis on product safety affect your business? Critical forces in the environment are your competitors. How well do you understand their organizations, strategies, strengths and weaknesses, products, and marketing emphasis? What trends for change do you see in your industry? How well can your firm cope with industry trends and actions of competitors? Most important are trends in your marketplace. What are your current customer expectations and how are they likely to change?

The next step in strategy formulation is to define a future strategic position for your organization that is consistent with your company's current and conservatively projected capabilities. This definition must also recognize the capabilities of your competitors and where they are heading. It must be consistent with future customer expectations. The process of defining a strategic position is an attempt at defining the future. Although there is no way of knowing the future, most companies attempt forecasts of conditions that would influence their operations. "What if" exercises can be helpful to evaluate ideas for future strategic goals. Many businesses construct several likely scenarios against which they can test proposed strategies.

The next step is to develop an overall strategy for reaching the desired strategic position. The top management team's challenge is to figure out some specific ways for the firm to gain and hold a competitive advantage over competitors. Michael Porter makes the argument that competitive advantage is possible only by achieving a lower price, by offering a differentiated product relative to the offerings of competitors, or by focusing on a particular market segment to achieve lower cost or differentiation. In *Competitive Advantage*, he describes some specific approaches.[11] Whatever approach is taken to develop the actual strategy, it should be simple and easily understood by the people in the organization who must implement it. Current trends favor short strategic plans; John Young, CEO of Hewlett-Packard, challenges managers to be able to put a strategy on one sheet of paper. The important thing about a business strategy is to define those few key actions that all parts of the organization must implement to achieve strategic goals. These few actions can then form the foundation for strategies to guide each function within the firm.

An excellent example of strategic repositioning in the face of strong competitive threats is provided by reviewing reported activities at Black & Decker Corporation over the past several years.

Black & Decker is a manufacturer of small power tools, appliances, and rechargeable household devices with 1985 sales of about $1.7 billion. The company enjoys a strong market position in portable electric power tools. It has over twenty-five plants in nine countries and traditionally localized the design of its power tools for individual country needs. A few years ago a Japanese company, Makita Electric Works, Ltd., entered the world market for power tools with a global strategy — that is, it designed, manufactured, and marketed a standardized product on a worldwide basis. One of the principal advantages of this strategy is a manufacturing cost that is lower than the cost for products customized for each country.

Black & Decker began to see an erosion in its market share, due primarily to the new competition from Makita. To meet this aggressive competition Black & Decker had to evaluate its strategic position. It responded with a global strategy of its own, based on standardizing the design for small home power tools. As reported in *Fortune*, an advanced design electric motor, 25 percent smaller while at the same time 25 percent more powerful than existing motors, became the heart of a new line of portable electric tools that are to be manufactured and marketed on a global basis.[12] One can speculate that an important strategic goal for Black & Decker was the ability to compete on equal cost and quality terms with Makita. A significant element of strategy was the design and manufacture of the new motor. The 1985 annual report described a plan to restructure costs: "The restructuring plan announced on November 12, 1985 is designed to position Black & Decker to compete more effectively in global markets, particularly in the United States where imports are an increasing challenge. Manufacturing and overhead expenses must be reduced to achieve our earnings objectives."[13]

FUNCTIONAL STRATEGIES AS COMPONENTS OF BUSINESS STRATEGY

An effective strategy will provide a firm with a sustainable competitive advantage over others in its industry. This advantage may come from many sources — for example, product features not available from competitors, lower manufacturing costs leading to lower pricing at good margins, or superior marketing and distribution skills. The major Japanese car manufacturers enjoy a lower manufacturing cost per car than U.S. manufacturers, and this differential results in a price advantage of nearly $2000 per car.[14] Japanese goals of providing cars of exceptional quality, packed with user features, at competitive prices have been met largely by paying careful attention to a manufacturing strategy featuring high levels of automation, very low materials inventories, and highly trained worker teams. The overall strategies are dependent on specific strategies in each function that provide some competitive edge.

In developing business strategies, executives need to decide what unique contributions can be made by each function in the firm. The strategies for these functions must address these contributions. In addition, the functional strategies need to be congruent with the overall business strategy, and they must interrelate effectively with one another. Figure 2–4 lists some of the primary components of functional strategies for a manufacturing enterprise.

There are several things to look for in reviewing a strategy. Is the strategy clear to the people who will contribute to its implementation? Are adequate resources available? Does

Figure 2-4   **Some Components of Functional Strategies**

    Marketing Strategy
       Pricing
       Distribution
       Market Segmentation
       Promotion
       Market Research
       After Sales Support
    Manufacturing Strategy
       Capacity
       Shipments
       Manufacturing Methods
       Quality
       Inventory
       Vendors/Subcontractors
    Product Development Strategy
       New Products
       Market Needs Assessment
       Quality of Design
       Manufacturability
       Technology Exploitation
    Financial Strategy
       Capital Acquisition and Management
       Business Basics and Controls
       Cash Flow
       Accounting and Reporting
       Investment
    Human Resources Strategy
       Staffing
       Compensation and Benefits
       Employee Relations
       Training and Development
       Affirmative Action
       Workforce Reshaping
    Quality Assurance Strategy
       Quality Basics
       Quality Development and Promotion
       Total Quality Control

it fit the character of the organization? Is the strategy consistent with the desired goals? Are there sufficient measures of progress? Does it take advantage of key strengths as well as weaknesses? Can it be adapted to significant changes in the competitive situation or to major environmental and political changes?

IMPORTANCE OF EXECUTIVE DEVELOPMENT TO STRATEGY FORMULATION

Because strategy development is a major responsibility of line executives, they need to acquire the knowledge and skills to think and manage strategically. This is not a skill that can be adequately developed by one or two sessions in a traditional executive development program. Most firms would be well advised to retain the services of a skilled consultant to assist them in implementing a more detailed seminar in strategic management. At Hewlett-Packard we found that strategic management skills are developed over a period of time and that the coaching provided by a strategic management consultant is a key component to acquiring these skills. The effectiveness of a strategy, and hence the effectiveness of the training and development effort, can be evaluated only over a considerable period of time.

During the process of strategy development, the top management team of the company will inevitably discover knowledge and skill deficiencies that will inhibit implementation. The discovery of these deficiencies is a key part of knowing where to concentrate executive development efforts.

REFERENCES

1. Michael E Porter, *Competitive Strategy*, New York, The Free Press, 1980; Michael E. Porter, *Competitive Advantage*, New York, The Free Press, 1985; Kenichi Ohmae, *The Mind of the Strategist*, New York, McGraw-Hill, 1982.
2. From Genentech, Inc., *Annual Report 1985*, p. 5.
3. "Central to our strategy is being number one or two in market

share in 15 critical businesses which we've grouped into three circles: core manufacturing, technology, and services." General Electric Company, *Annual Report 1985*, p. 2.
4. Robert H. Hayes and Steven C. Wheelwright, *Restoring Our Competitive Edge — Competing Through Manufacturing*, New York, John Wiley & Sons, 1984, p. 30.
5. For a summary of the shift from strategic planning to strategic management, see, "The New Breed of Strategic Planner," *Business Week*, September 17, 1984.
6. For a description of this model, see Robert H. Waterman, Jr., Thomas J. Peters, and Julien R. Phillips, "Structure Is Not Organization," *Business Horizons*, June 1980, pp. 12-26.
7. "Looking to the future, businesses throughout Motorola studied their organizational effectiveness and devised structures that would enable them to better serve growing customer needs. Each Motorola officer spent a week of concentrated study on 'Asia: Past, Present, and Future,' and how it relates to the company's businesses." Motorola Inc., *Annual Report 1984*, p. 18.
8. Ohmae, *The Mind of the Strategist*, p. 214.
9. Porter, *Competitive Advantage*.
10. "How Ford Hit the Bull's-Eye with Taurus," *Business Week*, June 30, 1986, p. 69.
11. See Porter, *Competitive Advantage*, chs. 3 and 4.
12. Bill Saporito, "Black and Decker's Gamble on 'Globalization,'" *Fortune*, May 14, 1984.
13. Black & Decker, *1985 Annual Report*, p. 2.
14. "38th Annual Report on American Industry," *Forbes*, January 13, 1986, p. 68.

CHAPTER 3
STRATEGIC ISSUES

Winston Churchill, Mao Tse-tung, and Lee Iacocca have at least one thing in common. Each succeeded in meeting extremely ambitious goals in the face of huge odds. The odds against England's survival in 1940 were astronomical. In the 1930s Mao and his followers were forced to retreat north. Chrysler faced bankruptcy in the late 1970s. Yet Churchill could see an allied victory. Mao was designing the framework for a new China. Iacocca was convinced that Chrysler would survive and prosper.

Like all successful leaders, Churchill, Mao, and Iacocca looked beyond their current difficulties and developed a strategy for success. Each had a strong vision of where he was heading and the ability to get his people to not only share this vision but also commit to its fulfillment. Each took precisely the right action to make the vision come true.

Much of the recent research and literature on effective leadership points to the same basic themes. Warren Bennis and Burt Nanus, in their study of ninety successful leaders, found that the ability to develop a "vision" and get everyone in the organization to share it was a fundamental component of successful leadership.[1] Hal Leavitt uses the term *pathfinding* to describe the processes of establishing a vision and finding the right problems to address.[2] In his study of general managers, John Kotter concludes that the first task of a general manager is "agenda setting."[3] Strategy development is the way that businesses articulate visions and set agendas to reach the goals that are defined within the visions.

STRATEGIC ISSUES: IMPEDIMENTS TO STRATEGY EXECUTION

Most strategies outline in detail the steps that an organization must take to achieve strategic goals. But what about all the things that might get in the way of your well laid out plans? In my experience few organizations devote enough attention to identifying these impediments and for this reason are likely to miss reaching many of their goals.

In the preceding chapter the concept of strategic position was used to describe the effectiveness of a company relative to its own past performance and to that of its competitors. A new strategic position, one that improves the position of the company, is defined by specific strategic goals. Strategies are developed to reposition the firm toward these strategic goals.

Many forces act on this repositioning effort, and the effects of these forces are shown in Figure 3–1. They are divided into two categories, *driving forces* and *restraining forces*. Driving forces consist of all those positive things that might assist the firm in reaching its goals. Some examples are distinctive skills possessed by the employees and managers of the firm, proprietary manufacturing methods, advanced technologies, and financial resources.

Restraining forces make strategy implementation more difficult, and these impediments to strategy execution are strategic issues. Examples in this category include an inexperienced management team, actions by competitors, quality problems with suppliers, and lack of financial resources.

Some forces acting on strategic repositioning efforts can be either driving *or* restraining. The economy is the major example here. When economic growth is robust, it is much easier to reach strategic goals. The two decades of rapid economic growth beginning in the 1950s made it difficult not to succeed. Conversely, the economy became a restraining force for most firms in the early 1980s. Governmental policy is another force that can either aid or impede strategy implementation. Also, luck should be recognized as a rather elusive bidirectional force.

Although management teams welcome forces that aid strategy implementation, our main concern in this book is with impediments to reaching strategic goals. This is where the link between strategy and executive development occurs. Executive development activity must be aimed at the restraining forces to strategy execution.

IDENTIFYING STRATEGIC ISSUES

Hal Leavitt, in his book *Corporate Pathfinders*, suggests that management education in the past has stressed problem solving and solution implementation, not the important manage-

Figure 3-1   Strategic Issues

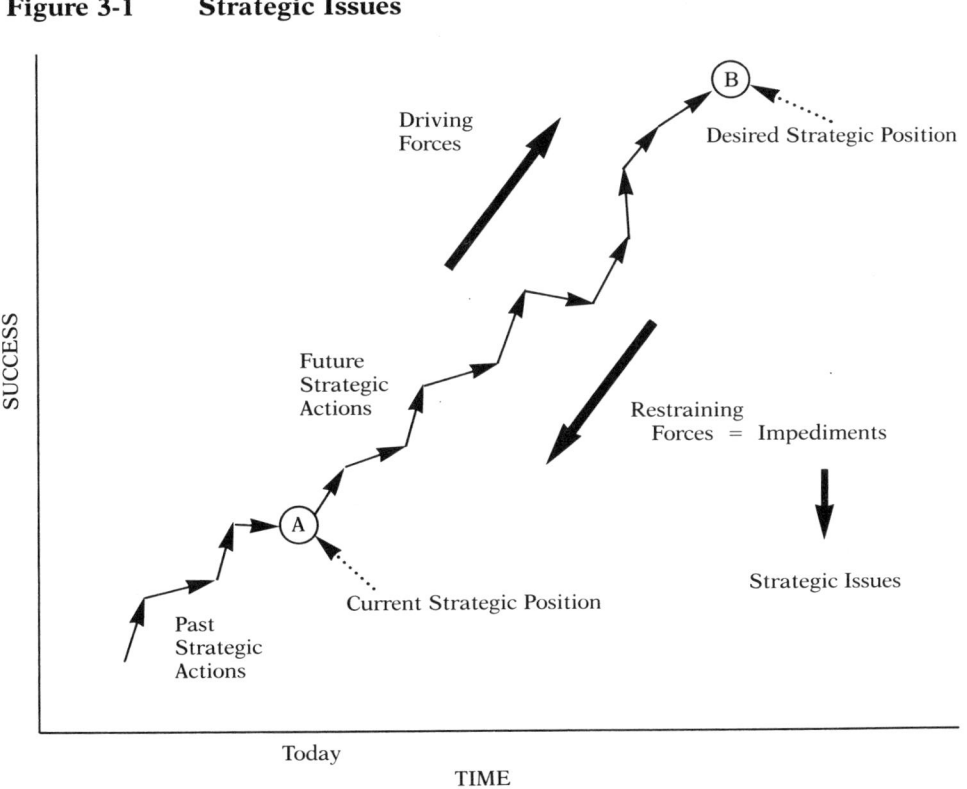

ment task of finding the right problem to address in the first place.[4] Identifying the restraining forces to strategy implementation and developing a list of strategic issues are parts of the pathfinding process that Hal describes. The issues are *the* relevant problems that the business needs to address.

How does one identify the restraining forces to strategy execution? What are the common things that prevent an organization from reaching strategic goals? There are three major reasons for strategy failure:

- The strategy itself;
- Implementation effectiveness and other factors internal to the firm;
- Factors in the environment external to the firm.

Let's look at some examples and do some problem finding in order to identify some strategic issues.

The Effectiveness of the Strategy Itself

This is a difficult assessment because good strategies can fail due to poor implementation or insurmountable economic or other environmental problems. Also, you never really know whether the strategy is good until it has either succeeded or failed. Strategic management must be a dynamic process, and executives must be able to adjust strategic actions as the overall strategy is being carried out. When a firm doubts its strategic management ability, this becomes a major strategic issue for the organization.

Implementation Effectiveness and Factors Internal to the Firm

The people in the organization may not have the knowledge and skills to implement the strategy or, for some reason, the motivation and determination that are necessary. There also may be too many internal obstacles in the way. Common problems in the firm's internal environment are defects in the organizational structure and ineffective communication.

Productivity, quality, customer satisfaction, leadership, and teamwork all influence the ability of a firm to execute its strategy. Problems in any of these areas can be a reason for ineffective implementation. Consider the following themes.

Productivity. Competitive advantage is directly related to a firm's productivity compared to competing companies. Much of the success of Asian companies comes directly from higher productivity compared to their U.S. and European competitors. Manufacturing productivity is but one small part of the problem. The major cost components of many products lie in overhead, administration, research and development, and marketing. Poor productivity in any of these areas results in ineffective strategy execution. Productivity can be a significant strategic issue for most organizations.

Product and service quality. Quality is no longer a frill or a luxury; it is expected. Excellent quality comes from people doing their jobs right the first time, including the job of management. Major gaps in employee and management skills and knowledge are important strategic issues.

Customer satisfaction. Product features do not dictate most purchasing decisions. Customers expect a solution to their specific problem, not some lowest common denominator solution that results from much of today's product development effort. Customers expect to have their needs satisfied. How many strategies take specific actions to guarantee customer satisfaction?

Leadership and teamwork. Strategies are implemented by people in "turned on" work teams at every level in the organization. Leaders of these teams must be able to not only articulate the vision for where the teams are heading but also engender the commitment and enthusiasm necessary for achieving team and company goals.

Lack of vision, commitment, or enthusiasm are significant strategic issues for any organization.

The External Environment

The firm may be affected by actions outside its control. Competitors can upset your market strategy by product innovations and price cutting. There may be a shift in market needs. The economy may turn sour, or government actions might go against the firm's strategy. The following two trends might well create strategic issues for your firm.

Global competition. The winners in hotly contested world markets will be those aggressive competitors who can move easily across national boundaries. Products that are designed and manufactured to meet the common needs of all markets of interest can be produced at lower cost than products customized for each individual market. Failure to think "globally" can easily put a firm at a great disadvantage.[5]

Impact of new technologies. Advances in technology are making a profound impact on methods for engineering, manufacturing, marketing, and administration. Unless executives take steps to acquire these new technologies and methods and apply them to their firm, they will fall behind competitors. Significant changes in job methods have created, for some firms, serious mismatches between available skills and the skills required to adopt more competitive methods. Reshaping the skills of the workforce is a strategic issue for these firms.

Although the firm does not directly influence most of these external factors, executives do have the responsibility to develop strategies that will optimize the firm's performance in the environment that exists. A first step is to recognize changes that will affect the company.

Figure 3–2 is a general listing of the types of impediments that might get in the way of strategy execution. The list is not intended to be all inclusive but suggests the kinds of things that you might consider in developing your own list of strategic issues. As an aid to future strategic issue development it may be worthwhile to modify this list so that it deals directly with your industry and its operating environment.

To develop a list of strategic issues, start by systematically thinking about and listing all those things that need to be done to implement your strategy. Think about the knowledge and skills that your management and employee teams will need. What skills must you develop? What resources will you require? Think about and list all of the things that might impede your implementation efforts. Where are you vulnerable? What competitive and environmental forces pose a po-

Figure 3-2   Identifying Strategic Issues

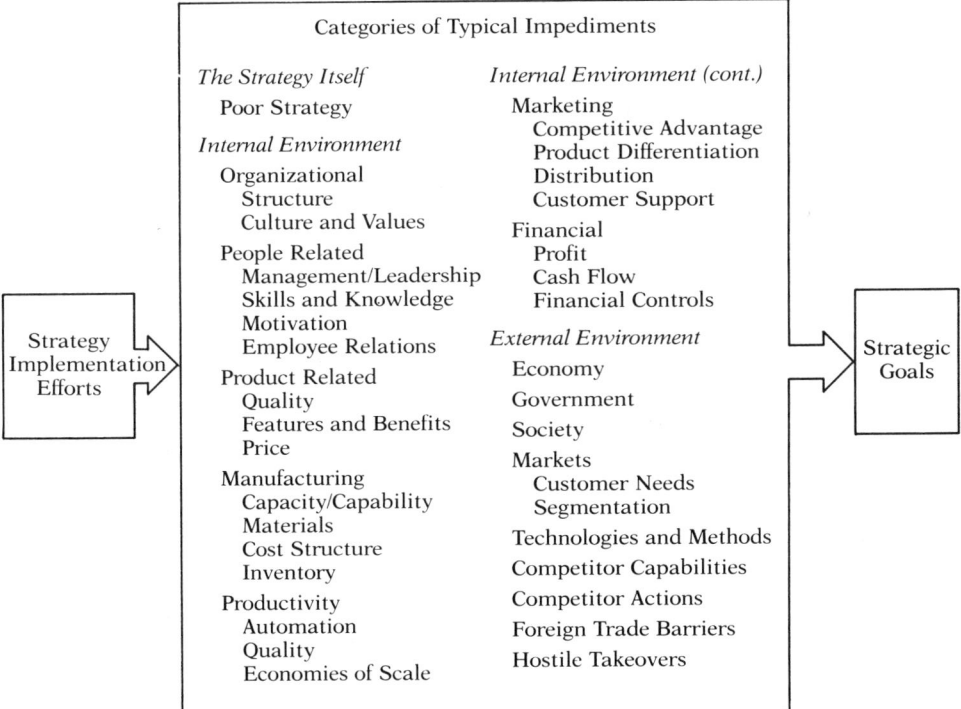

tential threat? Break down your list by categories and subcategories and continue the process until you are sure that you have included every conceivable impediment.

From the list of impediments that you generate, develop a final list of strategic issues. Keep the list to about ten issues because the idea of the exercise is to identify a strategic agenda for the organization. The amount of effort that will be focused on each issue is inversely proportional to the length of the list. The final list does not have to include every item identified in your analysis, only those items that are absolutely critical to your firm's success.

USING STRATEGIC ISSUES AS A MANAGEMENT TOOL

I first saw the application of a list of strategic issues at a Hewlett-Packard general management meeting in 1977. This was the first meeting that John Young led as HP's new president. John used the general management meeting as a forum for setting and communicating expectations. He presented a list of about ten problems that would have to be dealt with in order for the company to optimize its performance and achieve overall business objectives. The list was labeled *strategic issues,* and everyone present at the meeting was expected to direct the efforts of entities and departments to these strategic issues. The presentation of strategic issues became a regular agenda item at future general management meetings.

Each strategic issue was a brief statement — a word or two but never more than one or two lines. The list contained ten issues that easily fit on one page. Each year several issues drop off the list, and several new ones are added. Most issues stay on the list for the two or three years that are required to successfully deal with them.

Shortly after each general management meeting, the list of strategic issues was communicated down through management ranks. Operating entities and departments began to shape their own plans for playing their role in dealing with the issues. For example, in the corporate training organization we reviewed our strategies to ensure that our programs were designed to address these issues. The executive development strategy was specifically adjusted to correspond with the current strategic issues.

To ensure even wider dissemination throughout the company, the issues were presented in a feature article written by Young for the employee magazine, *Measure*. In many ways, the strategic issues became the marching orders for the entire company and formed the basis for achieving goal congruency among operating units worldwide.

How is a list of strategic issues used to increase the effectiveness of a business organization? The biggest problem with implementing a strategy is getting everyone to believe in it and own it. This is a very difficult task and is probably the reason that goals and strategies defined by thick strategic plans frequently fail. A list of strategic issues can be used to focus everyone's attention on the most critical tasks that need to be addressed to meet strategic goals. It gets people to pay attention to doing the right things. The first step in this process is the clear communication of the issues to the management team.

The strategic leader needs to be an evangelist — selling executives, managers, and employees on a few key actions. Of all the tools that a CEO has available, a list of strategic issues may be the most potent. The benefit provided by the strategic issue idea is that it imposes some order on the myriad of things that command a chief executive officer's attention. Once developed, the strategic issues provide a focus for the organization's efforts and resources. Strategic issues, on one page of paper, that are well publicized within the company are a clear communication of top management expectations. Everyone can easily identify with the issues, and individual business unit strategies can address them. It is a marvelous tool for the sharing of the CEO's vision and for gaining goal congruency throughout the organization. You can hold the list of issues in your hand and say, "These are the things we will focus on," and those in the next level of management can take these issues and say to their people, "These are the things we will focus on," and so it goes. The list is a rallying point and a symbol of focused effort.

STRATEGIC ISSUES FOR XYZ PRODUCTS, INC.: AN EXAMPLE

The following example will illustrate the process for using a list of strategic issues to address some common impediments to strategy implementation. Figure 3–3 is a list of strategic issues for XYZ Products, Inc., a hypothetical company in the computer disc memory business. These issues were presented by the CEO at a recent two-day management retreat that was attended by the fifty most senior managers in the firm. After the CEO's presentation, the managers were assigned to groups of ten to analyze each issue and discuss possible actions for dealing with them. Each group shared its ideas at a

Figure 3-3   XYZ Products, Inc. — Strategic Issues

1. Focus Increased Attention to Real-Time Strategic Management to More Closely Match Company Operations with Customer Needs and Expectations.
2. Regain Technology Edge for Products and Manufacturing Processes, Particularly for Compact Disc ROMs.
3. Strengthen International Marketing Implementation Through Expansion of Distribution Channels for Export Markets.
4. Recognize That We Compete in Global Markets Where Success is Often Based on Alliances with Foreign Entities.
5. Refocus Companywide Attention to Customer Expectations for Higher Quality.
6. Expand Total Quality Control Efforts to All Processes and Build Commitment to Continuous Process Improvement at All Levels.
7. Adapt to an Environment of Slower Industry Growth.
8. Establish Financial Control Systems That Closely Link Expenses and Inventory Levels to Incoming Orders.
9. Employee Rewards Based on Sustained Contribution.
10. Productivity of All Assets, Including People and Their Actions.

final retreat session. This is the first step in addressing the issues — get your senior people to understand the rationale behind the issues and to accept responsibility for doing something about them.

The issues echo several predominant themes, including more closely linking company operations to customer expectations, paying attention to advances in technology, global marketing, quality, belt tightening in a business slowdown, and productivity. What are some actions that XYZ's executives might take to get their functions to address the issues that most directly affect them?

Issue 1 will require the attention of all executives, particularly the CEO and the functional managers. The issue suggests that prior strategies were not successful because changing customer expectations were not recognized or strategies were not adjusted to cope with these changes. The CEO will have to decide if the executive team has the necessary strategic management skills and, if it does not, take action to build these skills into the organization. Functional executives need to make the same assessment of their management teams.

XYZ operates in a highly competitive segment of the computer industry where gaining a technology edge is one way to achieve an advantage over competitors. Issue 2 calls attention to the need to keep up to date with technology developments and how they can be applied to new products and manufacturing methods. This is not a short-term issue and may require recruiting people with the required knowledge and experience. More effective continuing education for engineers and scientists may also be necessary.

Issues 3 and 4 describe the need for XYZ to recognize the importance of export markets. Marketing channels with skills in export selling are vital requirements, and the firm must abandon any reluctance to form alliances with foreign companies when this is necessary for entry into a market with high potential. In addition to the CEO, the firm's marketing executives will need to develop strategies for dealing with these two issues. These strategies should become integral elements in XYZ's marketing plan.

Issues 5 and 6 indicate that the firm has fallen behind in product quality and that more effort is needed. An existing program in total quality control has not been implemented throughout the firm, and this needs to be done. The product assurance manager is not the only executive who should be responsible for these issues. All executives need to develop strategies for ensuring that all XYZ operations do each job right the first time. The product assurance manager should lobby hard to make quality a line item in each function's strategy. Moreover, the CEO must provide the overall leadership for a companywide quality effort.

Issues 7 and 8 have probably resulted from a slowing of industry growth, perhaps aggravated by a sluggish economy. Whatever the cause, stricter financial controls are necessary to preserve profit margins. Issue 10 may also be a direct outgrowth of economic problems. However, higher productivity should be a goal in the best of times. Common methods for dealing with economic decline are to look for ways to decrease manufacturing costs and operating expenses, while at the same time increasing orders. This may require the CEO to change investment allocations between functions.

Note that one way to increase customer interest, and therefore orders, is through higher quality and better customer service. Many of these issues interrelate, so that strategies designed to address one issue should be congruent with strategies for the others.

Issue 9 and the people productivity part of issue 10 present an opportunity for human resource executives at XYZ to review the current performance evaluation, compensation, and promotion philosophies. Productivity is intimately tied to the environment in which people work, so attention to leadership skills is an important component for dealing with issue 10.

Implementing the actions suggested above is the final step in addressing strategic issues. Each work group must be asked to think of ways that their activities can help address these issues. Each functional executive and the management teams in each function are responsible for gaining general commitment throughout the company for the actions that will resolve these issues. These actions should be included in the overall strategies for the firm as a whole and for each function. The tactics for carrying out the strategies must also be consistent with the strategic issues.

SYNCHRONIZING EXECUTIVE DEVELOPMENT GOALS TO STRATEGIC ISSUES

Strategic issues are the primary linkage between the business strategy of an organization and effective executive development efforts. Let's again look at the list of strategic issues for XYZ Products to see where some potential linkages exist.

Issue 1. An executive seminar on the process of strategic management would be an effective way to begin to deal with this issue. Best results would be obtained from a seminar designed for the executives with primary responsibility for strategy development and execution. To enhance the immediate transfer of learning back to the job, the seminar should deal with actual situations at XYZ.

Issue 2. There are at least two possible options for the technology issue. The first is to implement a comprehensive continuing education program for the firm's engineering and science professionals, including some awareness seminars for all executives. Another option is for XYZ executives to visit their counterparts in other companies, particularly those companies that excel in technology application to their products and manufacturing processes. Finding out what others are doing is an important first step in formulating a longer-term strategy to regain a technology edge.

Issues 3 and 4. An executive seminar in international business management would be a logical action for addressing these issues, particularly if executives lack an international perspective. Travel by key members of the executive team to high potential markets is another approach. Talking with customers and potential distribution partners is necessary before XYZ can develop a suitable global marketing program.

Issues 5 and 6. It is likely that XYZ executives and managers need to be more strongly convinced of the merits of total quality control, and additional training is one action that can be taken to address these issues. Perhaps the executive team needs simply to focus more attention on continuous process improvement. Apart from providing knowledge and skills, executive seminars are also excellent means for setting top management expectations on a particular topic like quality.

Issues 7 and 8. High growth rates can easily hide many flaws in strategy implementation. When growth slows, executives must identify these flaws and take steps to eliminate them. A training program to provide executives and managers with some financial tools for more effective asset management and expense control is an excellent way to focus more attention on "belt tightening." Asset productivity should be addressed concurrently with the actions for improving asset and expense management.

Issues 9 and 10. To address the issues of employee rewards and productivity, executives should review their current practices for merit pay increases and promotions. If appropriate, training should be conducted to make sure that all members of the management team understand XYZ's practices. Action is also necessary to make sure that all employees understand the pay and promotion philosophy.

Training in executive leadership will help address people productivity. Executives should look for ways to get employees more actively involved in productivity improvement programs. Small group problem-solving activities (such as quality circles) should be used whenever possible.

In Chapter 8 we will return to the strategic issue — executive development linkage — in the discussion on executive development strategy formulation.

REFERENCES

1. Warren Bennis and Burt Nanus, *Leaders*, New York, Harper & Row, 1985.
2. Harold J. Leavitt, *Corporate Pathfinders*, Homewood, Ill., Dow Jones-Irwin, 1986.
3. John P. Kotter, *The General Managers*, New York, The Free Press, 1982.
4. Leavitt, *Corporate Pathfinders*, p. 2.
5. For a discussion of global marketing, see the following: Theodore Levitt, *The Marketing Imagination*, New York, The Free Press, 1983; Kenichi Ohmae, *Triad Power*, New York, The Free Press, 1985; Thomas Hout, Michael Porter, and Eileen Rudden, "How Global Companies Win Out," *Harvard Business Review*, September/October 1982; Theodore Levitt, "The Globalization of Markets," *Harvard Business Review*, May/June 1983.

CHAPTER 4

STRATEGY IMPLEMENTATION THROUGH TACTICAL PLANNING

The key elements to effective strategy implementation are operational plans that reflect the firm's strategy, address strategic issues, and focus efforts throughout the organization on overall strategic goals. This chapter describes a process for developing goal-congruent action plans for the departments and operations within a business entity.

GOAL CONGRUENCY AND SHARING THE VISION

In his book, *The Mind of the Strategist,* Kenichi Ohmae writes, "If we analyze the characteristics of excellent companies . . . strategy . . . and organization are in harmony. Everything is geared to execution. That is how these companies achieve excellent results."[1] On a similar theme, John Young of Hewlett-Packard commented once to a group of senior executives in an advanced management training program that getting your strategy right is the easy part; the real challenge is to get everyone behind you sharing your vision of where you want to go.

Pick up any book about leadership or review the current research data. In every case the principal tasks are (1) articulating and communicating a vision for the organization and (2) translating this vision into tactical actions at all levels.

THE TACTICAL PLANNING PROCESS

Strategies are implemented by the efforts of everyone in the organization. Success comes when all parts of the organization play their proper roles in the strategic plan. Of particular importance is goal congruency at all levels. HP uses the tactical planning process as a tool for building goal congruency between operating entities and the individual functions within an entity. The specific tactical plans that are developed are roadmaps for achieving strategic goals.

Strategies and tactics form an activity hierarchy that begins with the overall business strategy of the organization and ends with the tactical plan that guides an individual work group's contribution to strategy implementation. A question of semantics often enters into a discussion of strategy and tactics: When moving down in the organization, at what point do strategies become tactics? For our discussion on linking management and executive development with business strategy, precise semantics are not critical. *Strategy* is defined as the plan for an organization to meet its strategic goals, and the more detailed action plans for implementing the strategy are defined as *tactics*.

Figure 4-1 is an abbreviated block diagram for a typical organizational structure for a multipurpose enterprise. The basic strategic unit is the division, often referred to as the *strategic business unit* or *SBU*. Divisions that design, manufacture, and market products belonging to the same general family are typically gathered together organizationally into product groups. In very large companies product groups that focus on similar markets may be organized into business sectors as shown in the figure.

The development of tactical plans should begin several months before the start of a new fiscal year. The process starts with the development of specific business sector plans for implementing the firm's business strategy. Product groups in each business sector develop strategies that outline specific goals to be achieved during the next fiscal year that are critical to the implementation of the sector's strategy. During the development of product group plans, sector managers pay

Strategy Implementation Through Tactical Planning

close attention to the goal congruency of group plans within their sectors.

Each division within a product group develops a strategy that articulates the division's targeted contribution to product group strategy implementation. Once the strategies at the business sector, product group, and division levels are aligned, each functional department within a division develops a tactical plan to outline the actions that they will take to implement the division's strategy. The process continues downward through the organization to sections and work

Figure 4-1   Typical Multibusiness Organization

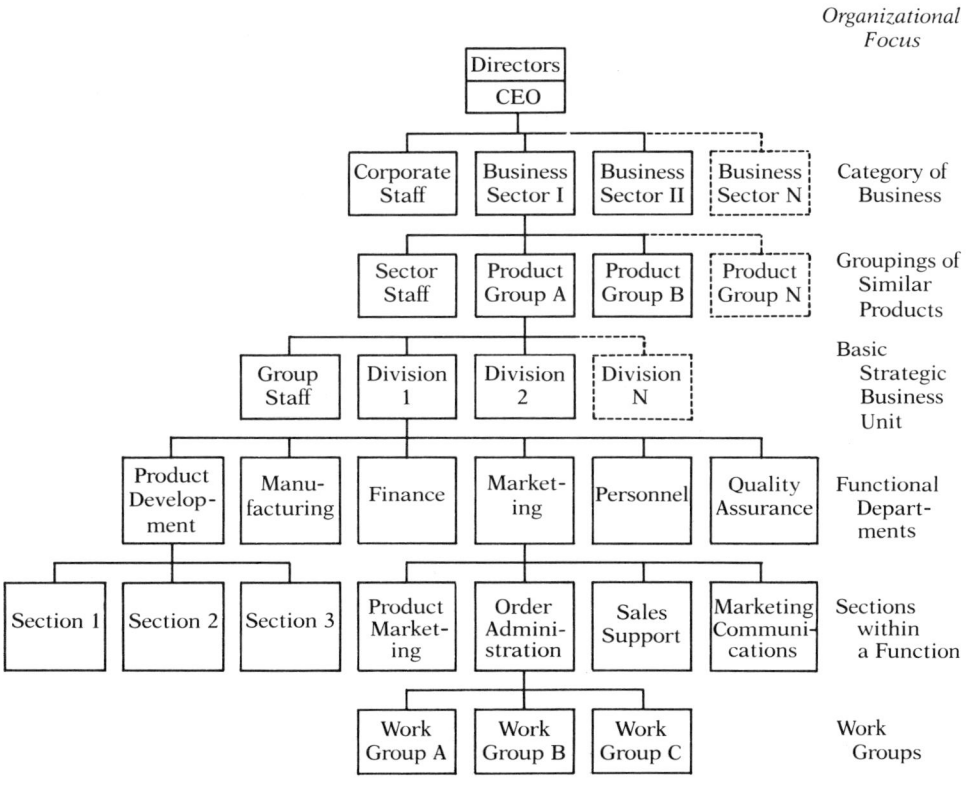

A Strategic Framework

Figure 4-2   Interlocking Tactical Plans

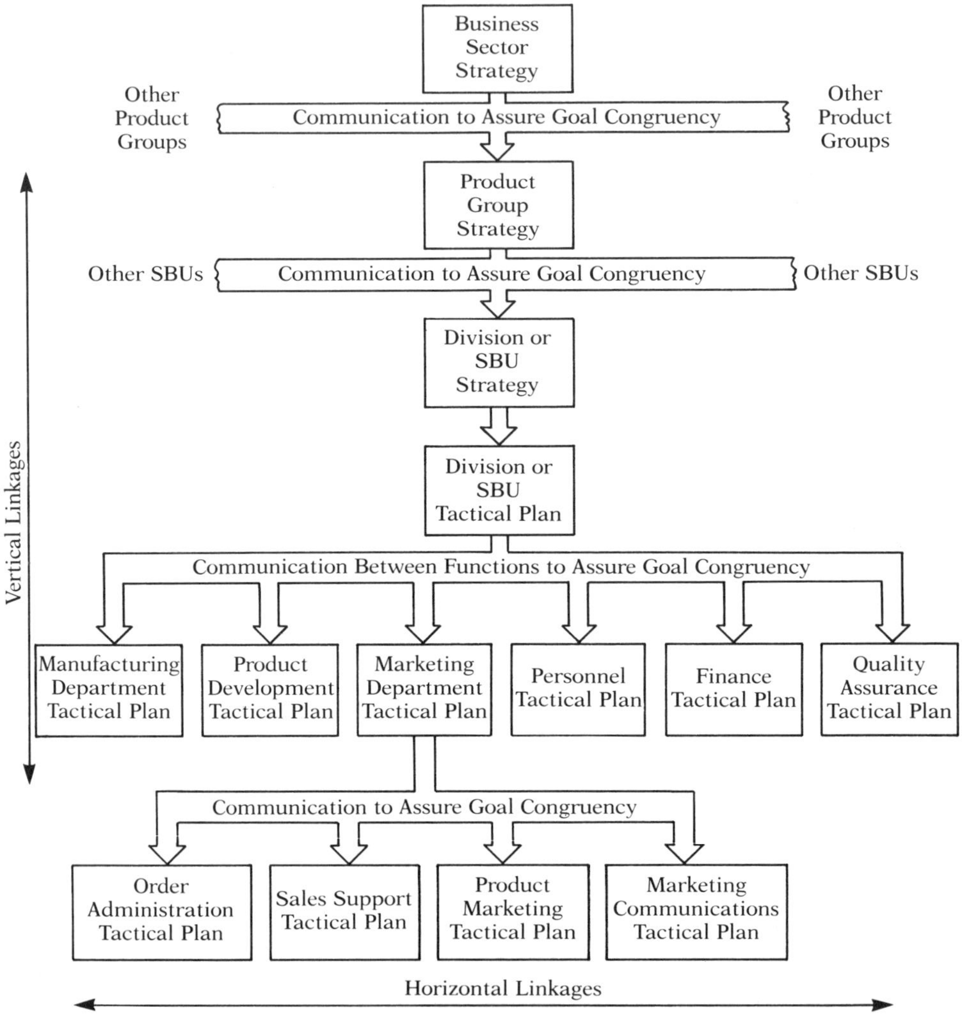

Strategy Implementation Through Tactical Planning

groups, and in some cases tactical plans are developed by individuals. By paying close attention to goal congruency as tactical plans are developed at each level in the organization, the plans of each entity, when viewed together, represent a powerful, focused effort for strategy implementation.

To be most effective, each unit's tactical plan must interlock both vertically and horizontally with the plans of the units surrounding it. Figure 4–2 shows how these tactical plans within a business sector should relate to each other.

To illustrate how tactical plans should interrelate, as well as typical formats for the plans, Figures 4–3, 4–4, and 4–5 show example tactical plans for XYZ Products, Inc., the hypothetical company of Chapter 3. XYZ manufactures memory devices for personal computers. To gain a better position in the marketplace, a major new product, code named BUCKEYE, is under development. When completed, BUCKEYE will contribute a 25 percent increase in sales during the first full year after introduction. For competitive reasons, an intro-

---

Figure 4-3 **XYZ Products, Inc. — FY 1987 Tactical Plan**

1. Launch Buckeye by 9-30-87. Complete Product Design by 3-31-87, Complete Manufacturing Pilot Run by 6-30-87, and have 2000 Units in Inventory by 9-30-87.
2. Develop Comprehensive Marketing Plan for Buckeye by 6-30-87 and a Global Marketing Strategy for All XYZ Products by 9-30-87.
3. Reduce Product Failure Rate of Pinetree, in First Thirty Days Following Shipment, to 10 PPM by 12-30-87.
4. Continue to Concentrate Attention on Employee Communication and Teamwork.
5. Beginning in March 1987, Hold Monthly Employee Communication Meetings Hosted by General Manager. Every Other Month Beginning in April 1987, Expand Meeting to Feature the Mission, Goals, and Operation of the Functional Departments. Product Development in June Followed by Manufacturing, Marketing, Personnel, Finance, and Product Assurance.
6. Manage All Departmental Expenses for the First Half of Fiscal Year 1987 (1-1-87 to 6-30-87) to 95 Percent of Approved Budget Levels.
7. Schedule Customer Visits by Each Member of the Top Management Team. Marketing to Coordinate the Scheduling of Two Visits Per Executive Per Month Throughout Fiscal Year 1987.

duction prior to product availability from stock would dampen customer enthusiasm. Sales for an existing product, PINETREE, which was introduced last year, have been somewhat soft due to a high first-year failure rate. Figure 4–3 is the tactical plan for this company.

The tactical plan lists seven key goals. Goals 1 and 2 are related to BUCKEYE and the need for a global marketing strategy for all XYZ products. A specific failure rate improvement goal for PINETREE is included as item 3 on the tactical plan. The next three items deal with people management and financial goals deemed important by XYZ's management, and specific targets are established in the tactical plan. Although the people management items are difficult to quantify, the management team wanted to focus companywide attention on the need for better employee communication and teamwork. The final goal, item 7, sets specific objectives for getting the management team out to talk directly to the firm's customers.

Figure 4–4 shows a tactical plan developed by the XYZ marketing department to guide its efforts in implementing the overall company plan. The marketing plan establishes specific goals for BUCKEYE that are carried to the next level of detail. The sales promotion group within marketing would carry specific BUCKEYE goals to the next level of detail, and so on.

Figure 4–5 is a sample tactical plan for the personnel department. The first item on this plan addresses the communication and teamwork issue listed on XYZ's overall tactical plan. Personnel has established some specific goals for dealing with this issue. Note that goals are stated simply, responsibilities are assigned, and specific target dates for completion are specified.

GUIDELINES FOR TACTICAL PLANS

I have found the following guidelines helpful in developing tactical plans.

Strategy Implementation Through Tactical Planning

Figure 4-4 **XYZ Products, Inc. — 1987 Marketing Tactical Plan**

1. Develop a Global Marketing Strategy for Increased International Sales. Complete by 9-30-87.
2. Develop a Comprehensive Marketing Plan for Buckeye Including:
    Product Introduction Plan by 3-31-87
    Marketing Communications Plan by 4-30-87
    Product Training Plan by 4-30-87
    Service Plan by 6-30-87
3. Beginning January 1987, Sales Support Section to Schedule Two Customer Visits Per Month by General Manager and Each Functional Manager.
4. Improve Service Response Time by Year End to Four Hours for All Accounts Within 100 Miles of Sales Offices. Provide a Weekend and Holiday On-Call Option for Maintenance Contracts by 6-30-87.
5. Implement a Basic Selling Skills Program for New Sales Representatives by 6-30-87.
6. Implement a Major Account Sales Program by 9-30-87.
7. Maintain Marketing Expenses at 95 Percent of Approved Budget During First Half of Fiscal Year 1987.
8. Set an Example for Leadership and Teamwork for the Rest of the Company.

Figure 4-5 **XYZ Products, Inc. — 1987 Personnel Tactical Plan**

1. Take an Active Role in Assisting the Management Team to Develop Better Communication within the Company Through Scheduling Monthly Communications Meetings Beginning in March 1987. Measure the Overall Effectiveness of This Effort and Provide Quarterly Feedback to the Management Team.
2. Develop a New Employee Orientation Program, and Conduct First Session by 6-30-87. Schedule Quarterly Sessions Thereafter.
3. Initiate by 6-30-87 a Performance Evaluation Overdue Report with a Monthly Summary for Each Manager and Their Immediate Supervisor.
4. Conduct Appropriate Salary Surveys by 9-30-87 to Ensure Competitive Pay.
5. Expand College Recruiting Activity for the 1987 Season to Twenty-Five Campuses. Establish a Measurement System for Recruiting Effectiveness at Each Campus.
6. Update Management Development Training Program for New Managers by 12-31-87 and Produce Instructors' Materials That Will Facilitate the Use of Line Managers as Instructors.

Simplicity

A tactical plan should list those five or six high-priority action items that a manager expects to accomplish over the next twelve months or fiscal year planning cycle. These action items should be the ones that will really make a difference in strategy implementation. They should be listed in brief goal statements. If it were possible for you to stencil the main goals for your organization on the inside of your forehead, select the goals that you might put there.

Goal Definition

Each item or task in the tactical plan should be expressed as a specific goal statement with clear assignment of responsibility and a target completion date. Goals should be realistic and achievable, yet challenge the people in the organization. Statements of tasks requiring lengthy continuous effort should be accompanied by appropriate completion checkpoint dates.

Goal Congruency

Because gaining goal congruency throughout an organization is a major benefit of tactical planning, care should be taken to review tactical plans at each organizational level to ensure that they mesh both vertically and horizontally within the organization. This is particularly important for managers with general or functional management responsibility. In the early stages of plan development, each unit should be encouraged to share its draft tactical plans with other units to facilitate the meshing of the final plans into a goal congruent set.

Relationship to Management by Objectives (MBO)

MBO works only when clear objectives are established and effectively communicated to the individuals who will manage and operate in accordance with these objectives. A division manager at Hewlett-Packard commented a number of years ago that tactical planning is MBO in action. A well-developed tactical plan is an excellent way to state and communicate the objectives for an organization.

Tactical Planning and Participative Management

The wise manager will involve his or her management team or work group in the development of the tactical plan. In this way the work team accepts ownership for the plan. As the management team works together during the course of the year, the construction of a new tactical plan is simply an extension of the team's activities projected into the future.

The Tactical Plan as a Leadership Tool

The manager should use the tactical plan as a working document to lead the work group. It can be used to clearly express a vision of where the work team is heading during the next fiscal period. Although participation of the work team in developing the plan is important, it should be remembered that business goals ultimately flow from the top. Managers cannot abdicate their responsibility for the content of the tactical plan. One of the best bits of advice that I received as a young naval officer was that to lead, you have to be out in front. The tactical planning process is a way of providing this "out in front" leadership, and the document itself serves as an effective chart.

The Tactical Plan as an Operational Tool

To be effective a tactical plan should be used, not buried in a desk drawer or filing cabinet in your office. Organizations should formally review the progress made toward achievement of tactical goals on a regular basis, at least once per quarter. The most effective managers refer to their tactical plans more frequently, and the document becomes dog-eared from frequent use. Changes should be made to the plan to reflect new information or realities.

Tactical Plan Visibility and Ownership

To be of value the tactical plan needs to be owned by the employees of the organization. This means that it must be visible and that progress reports should be made on a frequent and regular basis to all who contribute to its implementation. I found it essential to review the tactical plan with my management team on a monthly basis and with the entire department each quarter at a coffee break meeting. It is important to get people involved to successfully implement the tactical plan.

EVALUATING A TACTICAL PLAN

How can you judge whether a tactical plan is likely to lead to operational success? The following checklist may be helpful in reviewing your tactical plans or the plans of groups that report to you.

- Does the plan fit the business strategy?
- Is it consistent with the basic values of the organization and its basic business objectives?
- Are the goals achievable?
- Will you know when each goal is achieved as well as how much progress has been made toward achievement?
- Are the goals congruent with each other?
- Are the goals congruent with the overall goals of the organization and with the goals of other departments?
- Does the tactical plan form a solid basis for the plans of subordinate departments and work groups?

- Does the plan take into consideration economic and other business realities?
- Is the plan flexible enough to be adaptable to significant changes in the environment or in business conditions?

LINKING MANAGEMENT AND EXECUTIVE DEVELOPMENT TO TACTICAL PLANNING

The tactical plans of the business entity in total and of the functional departments, when taken together, express the major operational focus of the company for the next fiscal period. Take care to ensure that the management and executive development activities are consistent with the requirements of these tactical plans. I can't overemphasize the importance of the involvement of the management team and executive development manager in the entire tactical planning process. This involvement should begin long before the formulation of the actual tactical plans. By staying close to the activities of the functional departments, the training and development manager will be aware of functional and general management strategies as well as operational problems, and the tactical plans will not come as a surprise. This means that the management and executive development plan will most likely match the needs of the management team.

The person responsible for executive development should receive copies of departmental tactical plans in draft form and spend time understanding the issues and expectations behind each action item. Recurring themes that suggest training programs or other developmental activity should be noted. Also, look for items that require or assume adequate communication between departments and that require an understanding of departmental functions by managers and executives in other functions. Often these items suggest the need for additional training in the other functions or training in interfunctional relationships. While reviewing tactical plan drafts, determine how well the existing training plan aligns with the plans for executive training. For example, in the tactical plan example shown in Figure 4–3, the BUCKEYE project is of major importance to the success of XYZ. Successful implementation of the strategy for BUCKEYE will require close coordination and cooperation between engineering, manufacturing, and marketing. From the perspective of a training manager, is this likely to occur? Do the drafts of the functional department tactical plans exhibit goal congruency?

SUMMARY OF PART I

The first part of this book has presented a strategic framework for management and executive development activity. That framework assumes that senior managers today do more than strategic planning: They do strategic management. Strategic management is the continuous attention paid by executives to guiding the activities of the firm toward strategic goals. The same managers who plan also implement, and they must live with the results of their planning and implementation actions.

The concepts of strategic position and strategic issues were introduced to illustrate how executive development can be linked to a firm's business strategy. In repositioning the company toward a future strategic position, many obstacles — defined as strategic issues — may impede progress. Recognizing that the sole purpose of management and executive development activity is to help the management team do a better job implementing the firm's strategy, programs for this development activity must be closely linked to strategic issues.

An effective tool for strategy implementation is the tactical plan. Through active involvement in the tactical planning process, training and development managers can ensure that their management and executive development activities are congruent with the business goals, strategies, and tactical issues facing the company.

REFERENCES

1. Kenichi Ohmae, *The Mind of the Strategist*, New York, McGraw-Hill, 1982. This quotation taken from the Penguin Books edition, p. 207.

PART 2
OPERATIONS

CHAPTER 5

STRATEGY EXECUTION: A FUNCTIONAL MODEL

In his landmark work, *Management*, Peter Drucker distinguishes between effectiveness and efficiency by defining *effectiveness* as "doing the right things" and *efficiency* as "doing things right."[1] The first part of this book, A Strategic Framework, dealt with doing the right things. The second part, Operations, will focus on doing things right.

How do you get the people in an organization to line up behind an overall strategy and do the things required to achieve strategic goals? A first step is to make sure that each function in the organization has an effective strategy for its part of the organization's overall plan. A list of strategic issues can be used to guide this activity. Functional strategies are implemented through specific action plans at each operating level, and goal-congruent tactical plans are an excellent tool to ensure functional strategy execution.

There is, however, another dimension to successful strategy execution, and that is the degree to which the heavily interdependent functions work closely together. This chapter will outline the basic responsibilities of the functional departments, define some critical linkages between functions, and explain why the management of these linkages is essential to strategy implementation success.

Finally, two equally important questions need to be answered. How do you know when a strategy is being implemented successfully? What can be done to improve implementation skills? Chapters 6 and 7 will address these questions through the application of total quality control to the general and functional management processes.

For the executive development practitioner, an understanding of strategy execution is important to management and executive development strategy formulation. The goal of all development efforts should be to generate more effective skills for business strategy execution. A knowledge of strategy execution processes — that is, the functional operations of an organization — is necessary in order to identify those critical knowledge and skill areas that may need attention.

MANAGEMENT AS A SERIES OF LINKED PROCESSES

The complexity of business operations has created an increasing interdependence among the functional elements of business entities. The increased importance of international trade and foreign competition has contributed to this complexity. Advances in technologies for transportation, manufacturing, communication, and new product development make running a business today a challenging task. The sheer number of entities in major multinational corporations makes effective communication and coordination essential for successful strategy implementation. In most large organizations there is no way that any one entity or department within an entity can "check up" on all of the others on whom it depends.

Hewlett-Packard has become a complex organization with over fifty manufacturing divisions and another fifty sales entities throughout the world. None of these entities can succeed without the cooperative effort of many others. I am convinced that much of HP's success is based on the close linkages that have been developed over the years between entities and the functions within these entities. Equally important is the basic trust that exists among managers. No matter what the circumstances, one manager can depend on another to deliver as promised.

Building interentity teamwork within a corporation is difficult enough, but consider also the need for close working relationships between companies and their suppliers and distributors. How can just-in-time inventory management work without careful coordination between vendors and manufacturers? The way that many companies run could never be shown on an organization chart. Companies depend on a complex network of customer types, operational functions, support groups, industry and professional organizations, and public and governmental agencies. Indeed, some businesses function almost totally through networks with few or no manufacturing employees and minimal administrative staff.[2]

To understand strategy implementation requires an understanding of how the components of an organization and its network work together to achieve overall goals. Several models have been developed to assist this understanding. Michael Porter in his book, *Competitive Advantage*, develops the concept of the value chain to describe the contribution that the various elements of a business make to strategy implementation and the interdependences that support this contribution.[3] A recent article by Porter in the *California Management Review* applies his value chain model to the complexities of international competition.[4]

A model based on my experiences at Hewlett-Packard is shown in Figure 5–1. It is useful in analyzing the key linkages between the various elements of a typical business organization. Although the model was developed for a manufacturing entity, it can be readily adapted to meet the needs of service and not-for-profit organizations. It consists of three main organizational elements:

- General management;
- The three line operating functions of product development, marketing, and manufacturing;
- Administrative support, including accounting and finance, personnel, and quality assurance.

The model defines five primary linkages between organizational units, which become more obvious by reviewing the principal objectives of each element.

The primary role of general management is to

- Establish overall objectives for the organization (creating the vision);

Operations

- Develop a strategy to reach objectives;
- Guide strategy implementation efforts;
- Evaluate overall organizational performance;
- Adjust strategic actions in response to major changes in customer expectations or the operating environment.

Figure 5-1   A Functional Model

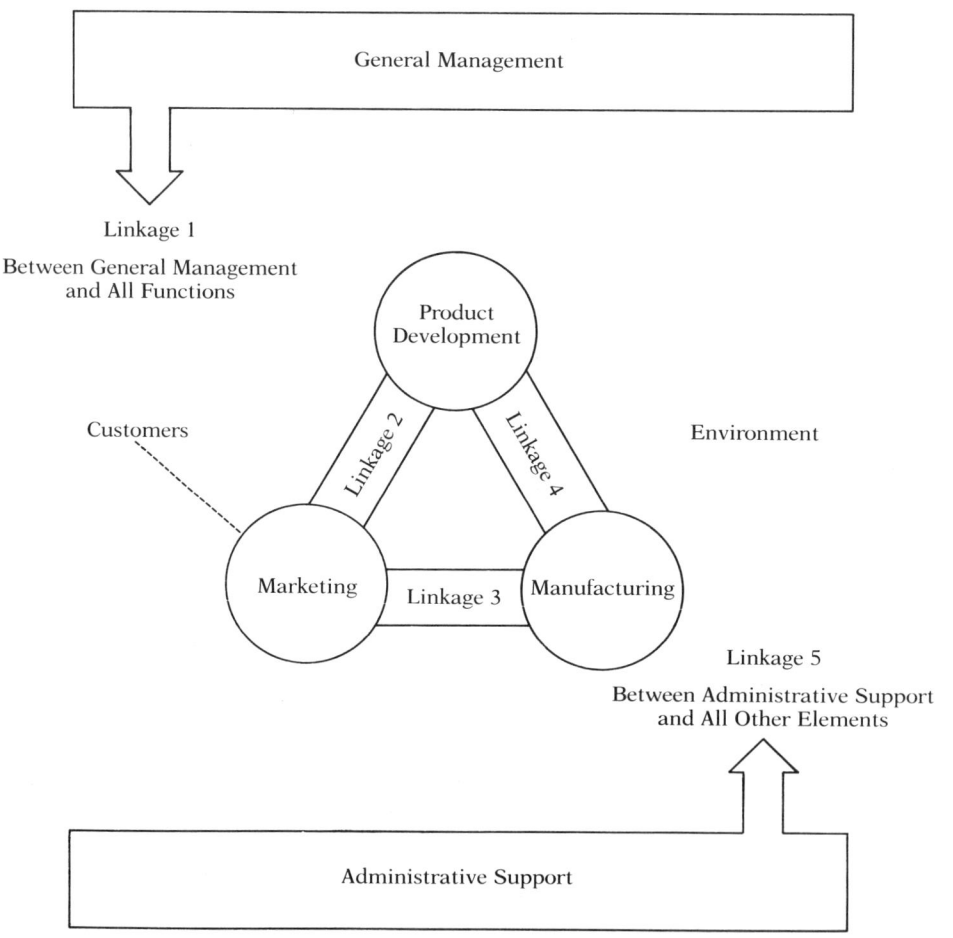

Strategy Execution: A Functional Model

Each functional element in the model is charged with implementing the organization's business strategy through interlocking functional strategies and tactical plans. The primary operating functions of the business have the following major objectives.

Product development's primary role is to

- Formulate a new product development strategy consistent with overall business goals;
- Design and develop new products for effective manufacturing and marketing;
- Apply advanced technologies to new product design;
- Provide technical support to the other functions of the business.

Marketing's primary responsibilities include

- Understanding the needs of customers in the firm's fields of interest and, working with product development, developing a marketing strategy that couples the firm's products and services to these needs;
- Developing and implementing strategies to maximize sales of existing products and services at an optimal level of profit;
- Developing and implementing strategies for new product introduction;
- Providing effective presale and postsale service and support to customers;
- Providing accurate forecasts of product sales to manufacturing.

Manufacturing's primary role is to

- Provide products to fill customer orders at competitive prices and delivery dates, at the highest possible quality, while meeting the company's profit objectives;

- Bring new products successfully into production;
- Maintain inventory levels at a minimum consistent with competitive delivery dates;
- Keep abreast of and apply new developments in manufacturing technology.

These three functional elements in the model have the primary responsibility for strategy execution and, in Figure 5–1, are shown linked closely together. The customers that the organization serves and the environment in which it operates are critical factors to successful strategy execution. Although external to the firm itself, customers and environment are included in the model. For example, marketing is closely linked to the firm's customers, and consequently continuous feedback on how well the firm's strategy is working comes through this linkage. The functions that make up the administrative support element provide the necessary financial, personnel, and quality management services for the operating elements, general management, and each other.

There are five major linkages between elements of the functional model:

- Between general management and all functions;
- Between product development and marketing;
- Between marketing and manufacturing;
- Between product development and manufacturing;
- Between administrative support and all functions.

A *linkage* is defined as an essential information exchange between elements. For example, a critical linkage between marketing and manufacturing is the sales forecast. Without this information, manufacturing has little on which to base a production plan. Figure 5–2 lists some of the major linkages that exist between elements in the functional model.

Strategy Execution: A Functional Model

Figure 5-2   Major Interfunctional Linkages

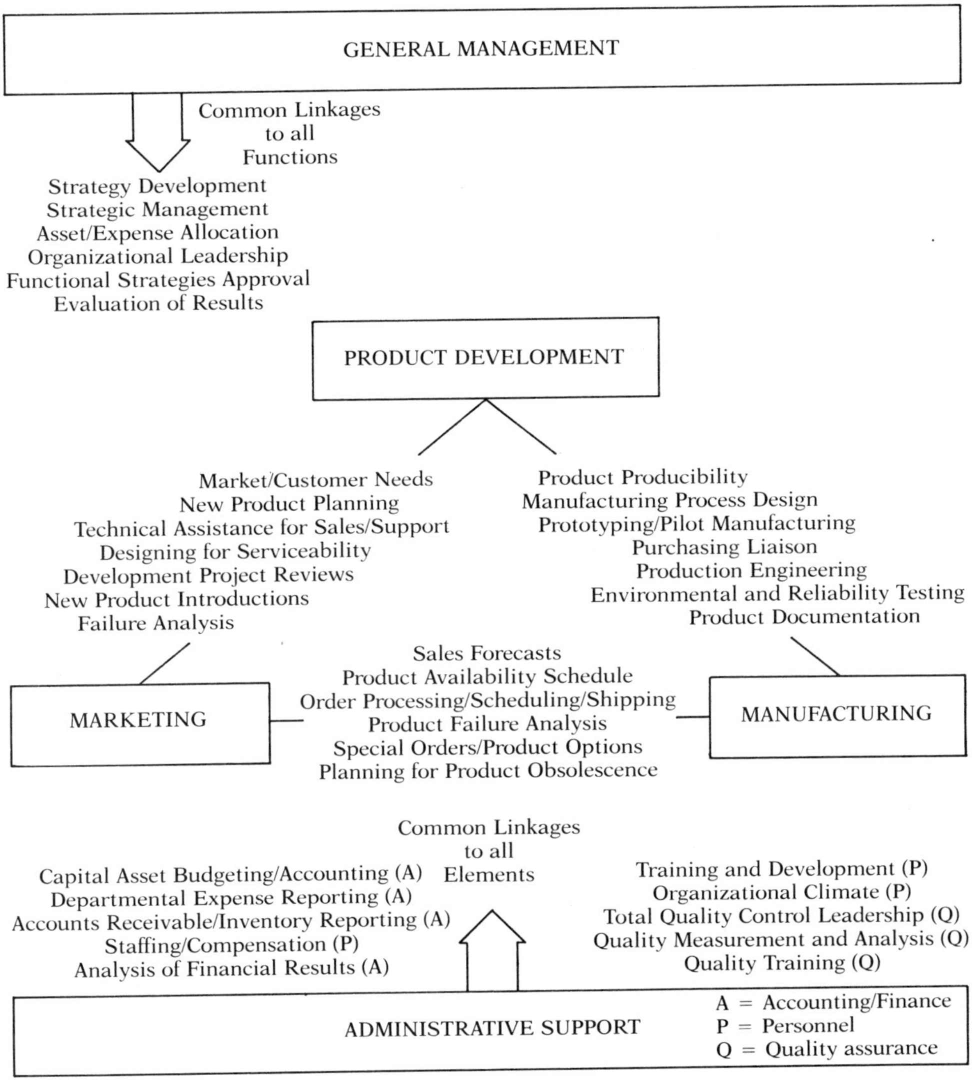

```
┌─────────────────────────────────────────────────────────────────┐
│                      GENERAL MANAGEMENT                          │
└─────────────────────────────────────────────────────────────────┘
         ↓ Common Linkages
           to all
           Functions
   Strategy Development
   Strategic Management
   Asset/Expense Allocation
   Organizational Leadership
   Functional Strategies Approval
   Evaluation of Results

                    ┌─────────────────────────┐
                    │   PRODUCT DEVELOPMENT   │
                    └─────────────────────────┘

         Market/Customer Needs              Product Producibility
         New Product Planning               Manufacturing Process Design
         Technical Assistance for Sales/Support   Prototyping/Pilot Manufacturing
         Designing for Serviceability            Purchasing Liaison
         Development Project Reviews             Production Engineering
         New Product Introductions         Environmental and Reliability Testing
         Failure Analysis                        Product Documentation

                              Sales Forecasts
                         Product Availability Schedule
                      Order Processing/Scheduling/Shipping
┌───────────────┐        Product Failure Analysis        ┌───────────────┐
│   MARKETING   │──    Special Orders/Product Options   ──│ MANUFACTURING │
└───────────────┘      Planning for Product Obsolescence  └───────────────┘

                           Common Linkages
                               to all
  Capital Asset Budgeting/Accounting (A)   Elements    Training and Development (P)
  Departmental Expense Reporting (A)                   Organizational Climate (P)
  Accounts Receivable/Inventory Reporting (A)         Total Quality Control Leadership (Q)
  Staffing/Compensation (P)                           Quality Measurement and Analysis (Q)
  Analysis of Financial Results (A)                   Quality Training (Q)

                                                   ┌──────────────────────────┐
┌─────────────────────────────────────────────┐    │ A = Accounting/Finance   │
│          ADMINISTRATIVE SUPPORT             │    │ P = Personnel            │
└─────────────────────────────────────────────┘    │ Q = Quality assurance    │
                                                   └──────────────────────────┘
```

General management has six major linkages that are common to each function in the firm. Strategy development and strategic management set the overall direction for the organization. Additional linkages are resource allocation, organizational leadership, and approval of the individual functional strategies. Evaluation of the firm's performance rounds out the major linkages between general management and the functions.

The primary linkages between product development, marketing, and manufacturing are shown in the center of Figure 5–2. For example, a critical link between product development and marketing is the understanding of market and customer needs. Similarly an important link between manufacturing and product development is manufacturing process design.

The administrative support element of the model includes the functions of accounting and finance, personnel, and quality assurance. They are combined in the same element of the model because each has common links to the other elements as well as to each other. For example, the administrative support element, via the accounting and finance function, is linked to each function and to general management for capital asset budgeting and accounting. For this reason, that linkage is denoted by the letter A, signifying accounting and finance. Another link to each function and to general management is training and development, an activity provided by the personnel function.

An example will illustrate the importance of these interfunctional linkages. In the early 1970s I was a member of a Hewlett-Packard management team that was responsible for introducing a major new product. The product had been under development for three years, and a product introduction date had been set for a year ahead of anticipated completion of product development. The product development department had provided marketing with a set of specifications for the product and encouraged an early introduction to secure an order backlog. Many early orders were received. When the new product was nearing production, it was discovered that some specifications promised to customers could not yet be met. A subsequent analysis revealed unrealistic optimism on the part of the product development department and overzealous sales efforts by marketing. The only course of action was to put the product on hold in order to do some necessary redesign. Several of us on the management team had the embarrassing duty of informing customers of the situation and suggesting that they withdraw their orders until a time when specifications could be proven through actual testing.

This example shows an obvious breakdown in the marketing/product development linkage. When weaknesses appear in any of these critical interfunctional linkages, things nearly always go wrong. In the case of the marketing and product development linkage, it is likely that marketing will want to sell the product early. No one wants a marketing organization that lacks aggressive enthusiasm. The management challenge is to get both marketing and product development executives to commit to a realistic product introduction plan. This requires an appreciation for the management responsibilities of both functional areas. Unfortunately, few management and executive development efforts devote enough attention to interfunctional relationships.

Executive development for general and functional managers must address the skills and knowledge required for developing effective linkages. For example, marketing managers need to be trained in sales forecasting techniques, and accounting managers in personnel hiring practices. This is the easy part. Strong linkages are not developed unless managers in one element really understand the management problems of managers in the other elements. Marketing managers need to be able to internalize the problems caused for the manufacturing manager when a sales forecast is done poorly. Likewise, the accounting manager who wants to hire a new person without considering equal employment opportunity procedures needs to appreciate the potential human and legal problems created for the personnel manager. Management and executive development efforts need to address not only the skills and knowledge appropriate to the linkage but also the effects on the managers at the receiving end.

THE IMPORTANCE OF INTERFUNCTIONAL TEAMWORK

The top management team has the major responsibility for developing a sense of teamwork between the functions of the organization that will encourage the building of communication channels of high fidelity. A system of optimal teamwork is critical to successful strategy execution.

This is sometimes a very difficult process because much of our culture is oriented toward individual contribution. Except in athletics and music, I know of no strong incentives in our educational systems for developing effective teamwork. There are no SAT scores for college-bound students to indicate how well they contribute to achieving team goals. At Hewlett-Packard we found that the majority of our new employees, regardless of their formal and informal education, required training in how to work effectively in groups. This training was particularly important for new managers because effective teamwork requires leaders with good group facilitation skills who can set the example for the people they lead. Excellent groups need excellent leaders.

Current management literature is awash with books, articles, and anecdotes on the subject of leadership. I recently was a speaker at a management training and development conference in New York City sponsored by The Conference Board. I was surprised by how much attention was being paid to the attempt to draw a distinction between a manager and a leader. I believe that you cannot be a good manager without also being a good leader.

John Doyle, an executive vice-president at Hewlett-Packard, offered an excellent definition of the characteristics of an effective manager several years ago to a group of us who reported to him. He drew a triangle and labeled the sides as follows:

- Ability to manage people;
- Ability to manage things;
- Technical knowledge of the activity being managed.

To be effective, a manager needs a balance of all three characteristics. Equate the total effectiveness of a manager as proportional to the area of the triangle. When a manager is deficient in one of the characteristics, the triangle collapses a bit. The area corresponding to effectiveness is smaller. Characteristic number 1 is leadership. Number 2 is skill in handling the ever-present administrative tasks — for example, budgeting and expense analysis. The third characteristic of an excellent manager is having a good grasp of the technical aspects of what is being managed. A general manager must know enough about each function to be able to evaluate the performance of the functional management team. The characteristics also interrelate; it is difficult to be out in front leading your team when you lack the technical knowledge on which the team depends.

There is another characteristic that is difficult to include in Doyle's triangle. Caught up in leading their own teams, I think that many potentially excellent managers sometimes tend to lose sight of the importance of being an effective team player. Interfunctional teamwork cannot exist when any of the functional managers are reluctant team members. Making sure that this teamwork happens is the responsibility of the general manager, but it also deserves the attention of the people designing management and executive training programs.

SOME PROCESSES FOR DEVELOPING INTERFUNCTIONAL TEAMWORK

The trifunctions of product development, marketing, and manufacturing are shown in the center of the functional model of Figure 5–1 because teamwork between these functions is particularly critical to a firm's success. At HP we devoted great effort to nourishing this teamwork. For instance, new product development teams included members from marketing and manufacturing who joined the product development effort for the life of the project. These marketing, manufacturing, and product development *triads*, as they became known, were a major factor for the successful new product introductions of the 1970s and 80s.

One of the outgrowths of the teamwork provided by the triad process was the concept of concurrent new product development. At the same time as the product is being developed, manufacturing must design the processes to make the product, and marketing must design the processes for bringing the product to customers. This all seems obvious, but getting these three functions to work closely together to design the product, develop methods for producing it, and create a marketing program to launch it successfully takes time and patience. Most of all, it needs the commitment and leadership of the top management team.[5]

Another effective tool for developing teamwork is the task force. All organizations have problems where solutions require a cooperative effort among several functions. A short-duration task force consisting of members from all affected functions is often an excellent way to reach an optimal solution that is readily implemented throughout the organization. Task forces give managers an understanding of the problems and concerns of other functions and help develop a feeling for the important issues facing the firm. They develop a sense of ownership, not only for the problem but also for the solution generated.

Several years ago I chaired a task force that was chartered to revise Hewlett-Packard's performance evaluation system. I used this as a developmental opportunity for a recently hired MBA graduate to see how some of the senior managers of the company functioned as a team. The time spent by this individual as an active member of the task force was worth much more than mere experience as an onlooker. This assignment was also beneficial to the senior managers because they received some fresh ideas.

Strategy Execution: A Functional Model

THE NEED FOR CONCURRENT EXECUTIVE DEVELOPMENT

The theme of this chapter has been that effective strategy execution depends on close communication, cooperation, and coordination between the functional departments of an organization. To achieve this teamwork, managers and executives in each function need to understand the basic operations that are closely linked to their own functions, as suggested in Figure 5–2. For this reason the training and development of managers and executives must include interfunctional relationships. Managers whose experience spans only one function must be trained in the basics of other functions and, if possible, spend some time "walking in the shoes" of other functional managers through direct experience or via a well-structured management simulation.

Equally important is the need for concurrent executive development. By this I mean that when you conduct a program in marketing management for your marketing team, run a condensed version of the program for managers in other functions. If the training need is important for one function, it is equally important that other functions experience the program. This is the only way that critical interfunctional linkages can remain healthy.

MEASURES OF PERFORMANCE

How does an organization with excellent teamwork, with managers who are well trained in functions other than their own, and with well-developed interfunctional linkages know when things are going well? Perhaps even more important, how will they know when danger is just around the corner? Management at the general and functional levels is a series of closely linked processes. These processes include product development, manufacturing, marketing, and all of the administrative tasks that support the line operations. The effectiveness of each of these processes needs to be measured because this is the only way that executives can get an indication of where they are relative to their plans. This measurement process, when linked to specific corrective actions, can lead to the course corrections that are necessary for excellence in strategy execution. The next chapter introduces a system for the measurement of management and executive processes.

REFERENCES

1. Peter F. Drucker, *Management: Tasks, Responsibilities, Practices*, New York, Harper & Row, 1973, pp. 45–46.
2. See "And Now, The Post-Industrial Corporation," *Business Week*, March 3, 1986, pp. 64–71.
3. Michael E. Porter, *Competitive Advantage*, New York, The Free Press, 1985.
4. Michael E. Porter, "Changing Patterns of International Competition," *California Management Review*, vol. 28, no. 2, Winter 1986.
5. For another view of product development linkages to other functions, see Hirotaka Takeuchi and Ikujiro Nonaka, "The New, New Product Development Game," *Harvard Business Review*, January/February 1986.

CHAPTER 6

TOTAL QUALITY CONTROL: A TOOL FOR IMPROVING THE QUALITY OF MANAGEMENT

This chapter provides an overview of total quality control (TQC), a powerful tool for executive development strategy formulation. TQC first found wide application in Japan as a way to enlist an entire organization in product quality improvement, although the original term comes from the American, Armand V. Feigenbaum.[1] Total quality control is a management philosophy that addresses product and service quality by focusing on the processes used to produce the product or service. The goal is total commitment to quality by all employees at all levels through attention to continuous process improvement. Because management itself is a process, the principles of TQC can be applied to the continuous improvement of the management and executive processes.

The implementation of TQC in an organization requires top management commitment, comprehensive training for all employees, and a champion within the organization to get TQC started and to keep it going. This chapter is not intended to cover the detailed steps necessary to install TQC in a firm but only to introduce the concept. It is hoped that this introduction will entice you to make a thorough investigation into how TQC can be applied in your organization, particularly in management and executive training.[2]

TQC BASICS

Historically quality control efforts have been based on exhaustive inspection procedures to find defects. Inspection might occur during any phase of product manufacture and almost always before the product was shipped to a customer or put into finished goods inventory. In many firms 100 percent inspection of purchased components and materials is also employed. Quality control under this philosophy is based on preventing defective products from reaching the customer. It makes the assumption that a certain number of products will be produced improperly. To improve quality, do more inspection.

The search for defective products does not come cheap. The high cost of inspection has led to the commonly held belief that high-quality products always cost more to produce. Yet the total costs of a quality control system based on inspection are not just in the cost of the inspection process. The major costs occur in reworking defective products, in scrapage, in the additional inventory needed to replace the defects being reworked, and in the extra manufacturing space needed for correcting quality problems.

In 1982 Hewlett-Packard estimated that about one-fourth of all manufacturing costs were attributable to not making the product right the first time. If products were manufactured properly to begin with, the costs associated with inspection and rework would disappear. An aggressive total quality control program has helped HP reduce product failure rates by 25 percent per year over the past five years, and inventories as a percentage of sales were reduced by 3 percent over the same period. The savings in inventory alone made $195 million available for productive investment purposes.[3]

Compared to most U.S. companies, Japanese firms have taken a different approach to product quality. First, they assume that all employees want to take responsibility for the quality of their products. When employees are given adequate training in processes for which they are responsible and lessons in how to use some basic quality tools, a quantum increase in product quality will take place. Second, they realize the contribution that a thinking employee can make. Unlike the common practice of telling employees, "You do the work and we'll do the thinking," the Japanese encourage their people to come up with ways to do their jobs better. Quality circles have focused employee efforts on quality and productivity improvement. Third, most Japanese managers realize that quality products result from getting everyone in the organization to believe in quality and have it as their prime goal. This is particularly true for top management in Japanese companies. Total quality control in Japan means just that — everyone is involved in the quality effort. Fourth, quality control activity focuses on all of the processes that go into a product, including research and product development, marketing, and administration.

The central idea behind TQC is that product quality is achieved not by product inspection or other product-centered activity, but by an understanding of all the processes that go into making the product. Once these processes are understood, clearly defined, and appropriately measured, attention is paid to continuously monitoring and improving each process. Processes are generally understood best by the operating employees who actually work with the process, and the involvement of these employees is a fundamental part of TQC. Employees responsible for carrying out a process should "own" that process and be responsible for its continuous improvement.

Another basic TQC concept is the achievement of total customer satisfaction. Customer expectations must set quality standards. The definition of *customer* includes every individual, inside as well as outside the firm, who depends on the product or service provided by the process. In a manufacturing system the people involved in the next process down the line are the customers for the current process. Appropriate performance measures for all processes should result from a careful analysis of customer expectations.

Based on the experience of Japanese companies, the most important ingredients for successful total quality control efforts are (1) top management commitment and involvement in the TQC program and (2) management and employee training in quality control principles. Total quality control represents a change in management philosophy, and management teams must work hard to implant the TQC philosophy in their organization. All employees need to understand the basic principles of process analysis, simple statistical methods, measurement of critical process performance factors, working successfully in groups, and problem-solving techniques. TQC training needs to be done on a continuing basis, and classroom training needs to be reinforced through experience on the job. Some companies do this training as part of their quality control circle program.[4]

THE DEMING PRIZE AND THE DEMING CYCLE

Many of the quality control techniques used by the Japanese were originally developed in the United States, and these techniques were introduced to Japan after World War II by two Americans, Dr. W. Edwards Deming and Dr. J. Juran. Deming was invited to Japan in 1950 to lecture on statistical quality control techniques, and his teachings were rapidly adopted. He has been a frequent visitor ever since, and to honor his contribution to their quality success, the Japanese created a prestigious award, the Deming Prize, that is awarded each year to Japanese companies with exemplary quality improvement records.[5] To illustrate his approach to quality control, Deming used a cycle of planning, doing, checking, and acting as the key steps in the quality assurance process. This cycle, now commonly referred to as the Deming cycle, is shown in Figure 6–1. The steps in the Deming cycle are

> *Plan.* The initial step in the cycle establishes specific goals for a process and a plan to achieve these goals. In a manufacturing process it would include target specifications and tolerances and the procedures to attain them. In a management process it would include desired outcomes and the action plans to achieve these outcomes. Examples might include sales targets and expense levels. In addressing a quality problem, a plan must be developed to correct the discrepancies.[6]

Do. This is the execution of planning. It includes all activities required to accomplish the planned task, including the training of employees in necessary job skills. More generally, *Do* consists of all actions to implement strategy.

Check. The third step compares actual performance against planned results. It is an obvious step but one that is often missing in practice. *Check* should not be associated with traditional quality control inspection. This checking is done by the people responsible for running the process, using specific measures of process performance that were established in the *Plan* step. A critical element for checking a process is the gathering and analysis of data. The data provides information for solving any problems that are found.

Act. This step provides the necessary feedback to correct the discrepancies that are found during *Check*. Before changing the process, however, careful study of discrep-

Figure 6-1   The Deming Cycle

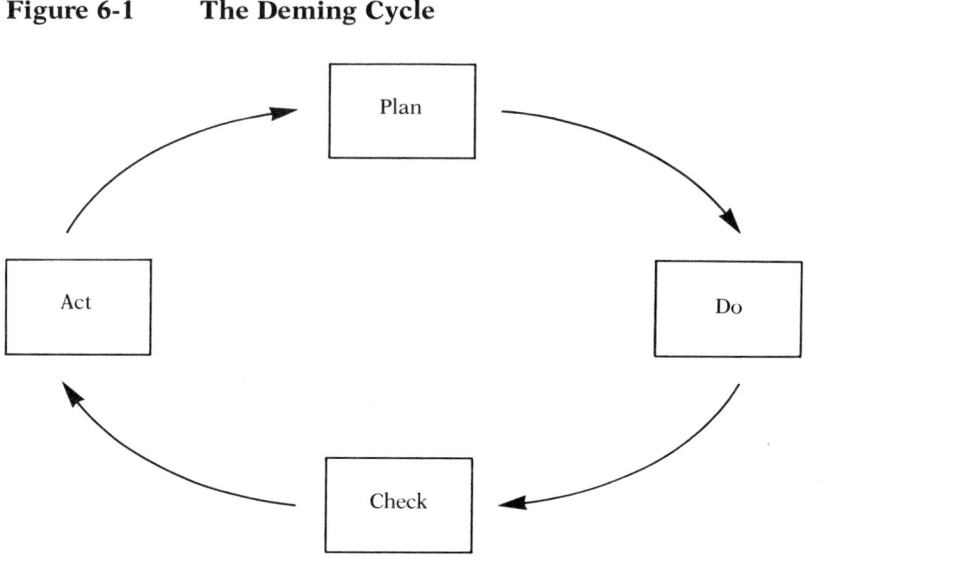

Operations

ancies and their causes is necessary. The best solution is implemented by careful *Planning*, and the cycle starts all over again. The solution to be tried is implemented in the *Do* step, results are *Checked* against desired outcomes, and further *Action* is taken as necessary. The objective of TQC training is to etch the cycle of *Plan, Do, Check, Act* in the minds of all employees.

The *Check* and *Act* steps are in many ways analogous to a simple feedback control system, such as a thermostat on a heating system or the speed control option (cruise control) on many automobiles. Figure 6–2 is a general diagram for a simple closed-loop feedback control system. It is a closed loop because a measurement of the process output, or result, is compared with process goals, and any discrepancy is fed back to correct the process.

In a heating system the measurement device is a thermostat that determines whether the temperature in the room is at the desired, or planned, level. If not, a signal (feedback)

Figure 6-2   **The Deming Cycle as a Closed-Loop Feedback Control System**

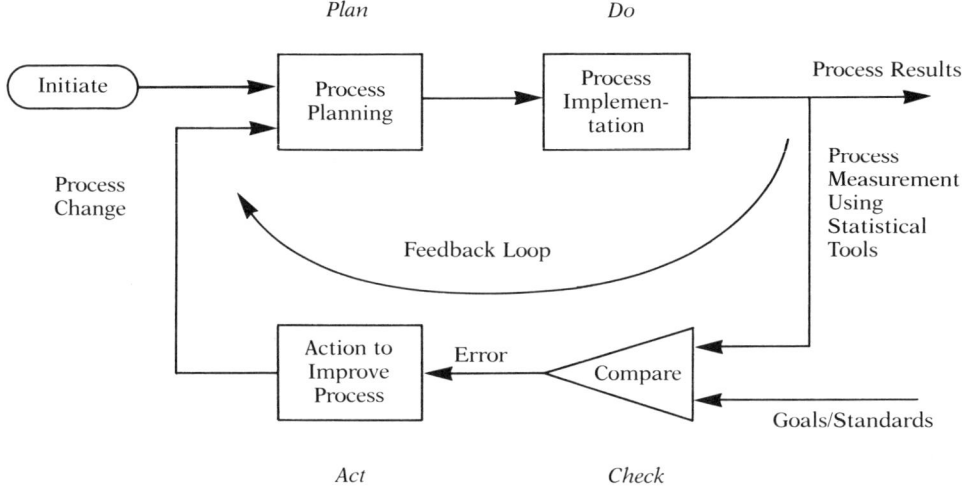

is sent to the heating device to increase or decrease heat output until the thermostat no longer measures a discrepancy between actual and planned temperature. In a speed control system for a car, a measuring device, the speedometer, determines whether the car is going at the planned speed, and a signal is fed back to the car's engine to increase or decrease speed accordingly.

In any control system the object is to get the output, or process results, to match the goal or desired results. In a perfectly behaving control system the output, or process results, will always equal the desired goal. Likewise, in any process that functions in accordance with planned objectives, the outcomes of the process will track the objectives. Any error (that is, the discrepancy between the measured process output and the goals or standards for the process) results in action to correct the process. A control system cannot function without measurement of results that leads to corrective feedback to the system. Likewise, total quality control cannot work without measurement of critical process performance factors and corrective feedback to improve the process.

PROCESS ANALYSIS

To make effective use of the Deming cycle, the process being studied must be adequately described and specific measures of process performance established. The starting point is to make a flowchart of the process. The process under study is analyzed and broken down into a series of sequential steps. Each process step should be labeled and arranged into a flowchart using appropriate symbols. Figure 6–3 shows the symbols that are frequently used for flowcharting.

The Deming cycle itself is a simple process and can be flowcharted in sequential steps as shown in the example in Figure 6–4.

The first step in the Deming cycle example is to develop a plan for the process under consideration, or for an intervention in a process. After planning, a decision is made on whether training is needed for the people who will implement the process or intervention. If training is needed, it becomes the next step in the flow diagram. Otherwise, the process is implemented directly. This is the *Do* step in the Deming cycle. The results of the process are measured and compared against goals or standards that were developed during the planning phase. In the unlikely event that the performance is already perfect, no further action occurs until the process is initiated again. In the more frequent case of a discrepancy in performance, corrective action is initiated to improve the process. The cycle then repeats, and, in this way, continuous process improvement is achieved.

Figure 6-3 **Common Flowchart Symbols**

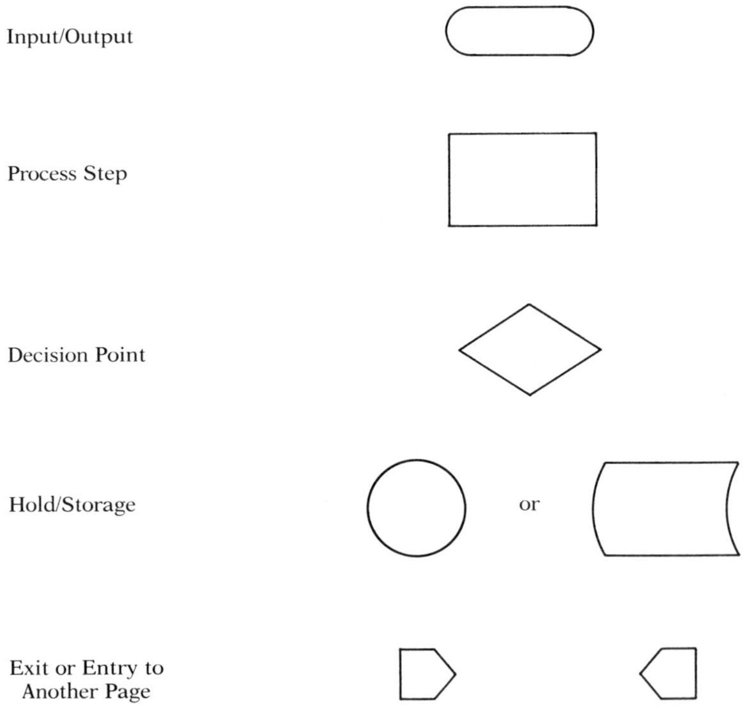

Input/Output

Process Step

Decision Point

Hold/Storage   or

Exit or Entry to
Another Page

Figure 6-4 **The Deming Cycle as a Process**

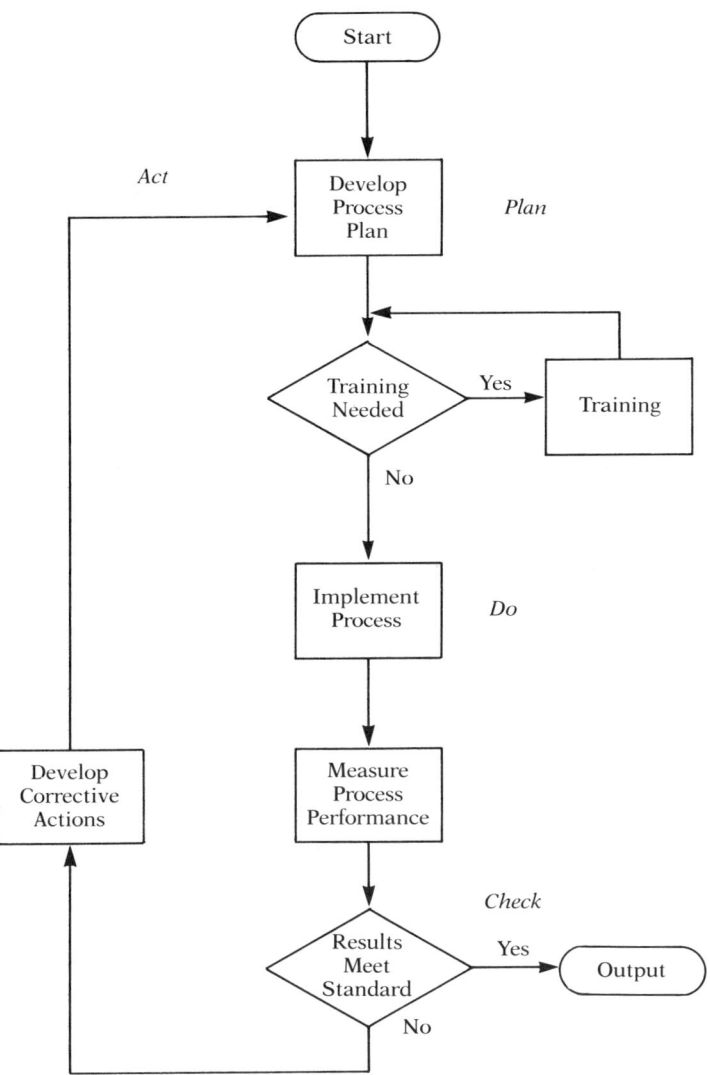

Figure 6–5 is a flowchart for the common process of selecting your own airline flight. The chart was developed using the following process steps:

1. Determine destination.
2. Establish a satisfactory time window around the desired time for arrival.
3. Review personal preferences and list criteria.
   - Nonstop?
   - Airline?
   - Aircraft type?
   - Class of service?
   - Seating preference?
4. Review your organization's travel policy.
5. Obtain an airline flight guide.
6. List all available flights to your destination.
7. Test available flights against criteria in steps 1 through 4.
8. Make reservations.
9. Obtain confirmation.
10. If necessary, compromise criteria.

The first six steps of the process are straightforward and follow the listing above. If the class of service on available flights conflicts with the firm's travel policy, special approval is requested. The next two comparisons are against personal criteria — for example, airline and type of aircraft, and desired departure and arrival times. Should the criteria not be met, they must be changed as indicated in the side loops to the process flow. After these three tests, reservations are made, and, if confirmed, the process is completed. Otherwise, an alternative flight is selected.

After the process has been charted, the flowchart should be tested to ensure that it is a faithful representation of the

Total Quality Control: A Tool For Improving The Quality of Management

Figure 6-5   **Process for Selecting Your Own Airline Flight**

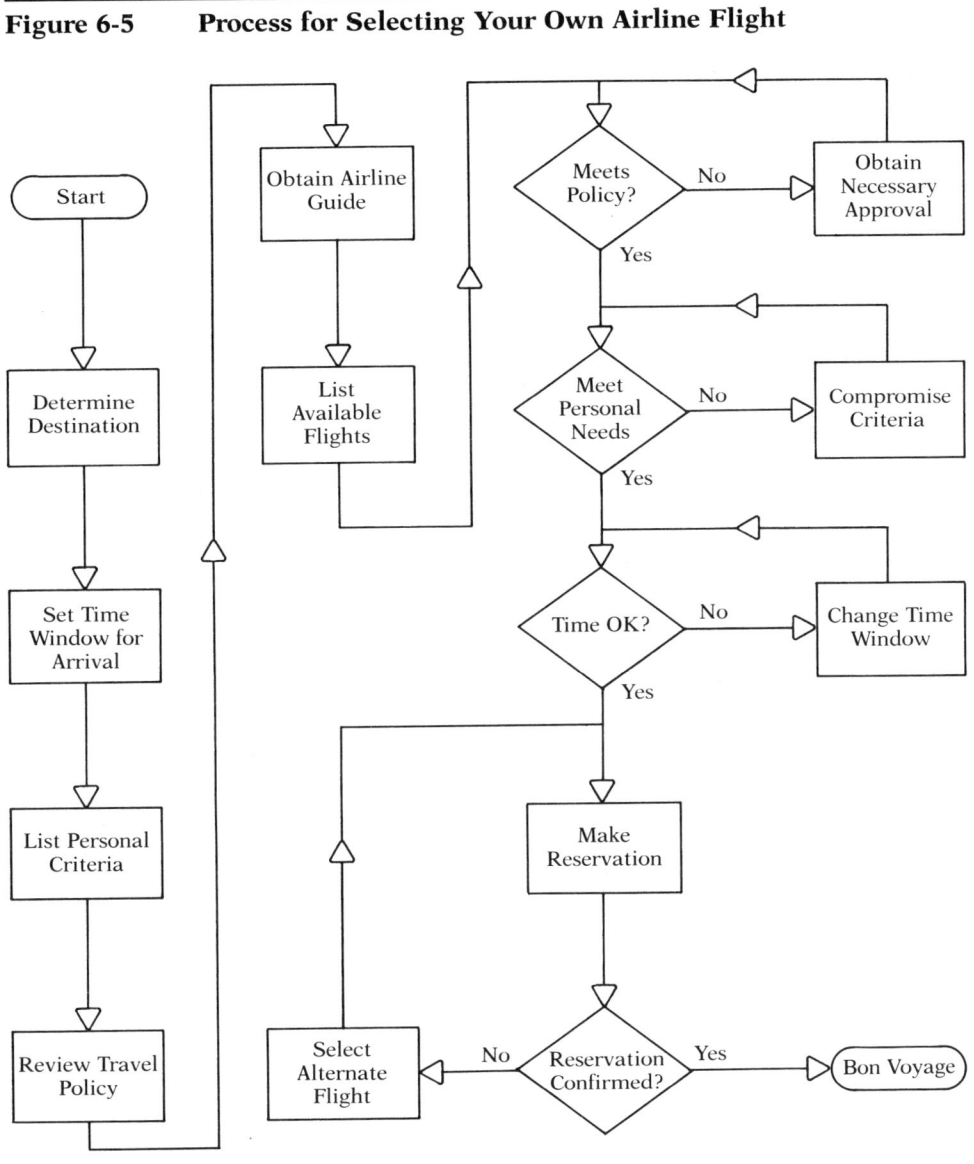

process. The diagram should also be well annotated, so that anyone could become familiar with the process by simply studying the flowchart.

Thus far we have only considered the analysis of simple processes; most processes encountered in the real world are more complex. However, even the most complex process can generally be broken down into a series of processes within processes, so that with some diligence the analysis tools covered in this chapter are applicable. Analyzing more complex processes is facilitated by looking at the whole process as a series of smaller processes nested together. For example, the process of selecting an airline flight illustrated in Figure 6–5 can be looked on as a process nested within the larger process of planning a business trip to Singapore. Planning this trip would also involve other nested processes for hotel selection, airport transportation, currency exchange, setting up business appointments, and so forth. Likewise, there are additional subprocesses nested within the flight selection example. One of these might be finding a copy of the airline guide, which in some offices is no simple task. The point is that processes tend to be hierarchical and can usually be analyzed most efficiently by starting with one piece of the process with which you feel comfortable and moving to the subprocesses nested within. Also, most processes are linked serially — that is, the input to one process is the output for still another process. This needs to be considered when analyzing complex operations.

MEASURING PROCESS PERFORMANCE

The third step in the Deming cycle and an important principle in total quality control is checking the output of a process against established objectives or standards. To do this, specific measures of process performance need to be identified. This step is frequently neglected in the rush to implement strategies. The *Plan* and *Do* steps tend to get most of the attention, but a systematic *Check* of the process is critical for continuous improvement.

In developing appropriate measures it is important to consider the expectations of customers, whether they be external or internal to the organization. What do they expect from the output of your process? How can these expectations be quantified? How can they be regularly measured?

In 1984 I visited HP's Japanese subsidiary, Yokogawa Hewlett-Packard Ltd. in Tokyo. YHP had won the Deming Prize in 1982, and I was particularly interested in learning how their management team had successfully implemented TQC throughout the organization. During a meeting with Kenzo Sasaoka, YHP's president, I was briefed on applying TQC to the achievement of customer satisfaction. To achieve customer satisfaction, it is necessary to eliminate all causes of customer dissatisfaction. Consequently, a number of measures of customer dissatisfaction were established, including late delivery of products, difficulty in understanding instruction manuals, and premature product failures. A systematic method for recording incidents of customer dissatisfaction was instituted, and a goal to eliminate these incidents was established. The data that I was shown was convincing proof of the progress that they had already made. The keys to their success were the performance measures that they had established.

What might be some appropriate performance measures for the airline flight selection process illustrated in Figure 6–5? Three possible measures are

- Total flight time;
- Airfare;
- On-time performance of the airline selected.

Because most destinations are served by competing airlines, the measurement of these performance factors will provide some guidance on which airline and flight to choose in the future. Other factors — such as contribution to the passenger's frequent flyer program flight activity — could also be considered a measure, depending on the traveler's priorities.

The success of process performance measurement and subsequent analysis is highly dependent on the use of relatively simple statistical tools. Data must be put into a useful form for analysis before it becomes information that can be used in problem solving. In his book *The Knowledge Executive*, Harlan Cleveland refers to data as "undigested observations" and information as "organized data."[7] Statistical tools provide a means to digest and organize the process performance measurements.

Because a basic premise of TQC is the involvement of employees in continually improving their work processes, organizations must invest in training all their employees in basic data gathering and statistical quality control techniques. Many of these techniques are covered in the curriculum for quality circle training programs — for example, working effectively in groups, brainstorming, basic problem-solving skills, flowcharting, the Pareto principle, and methods for gathering and analyzing measurement data. Executives should not underestimate the importance of this training requirement.[8]

CAUSE AND EFFECT ANALYSIS

When discrepancies in performance are discovered, not much can be done until the cause of the discrepancy is known. A useful tool for cause-and-effect analysis has been developed by Kaoru Ishikawa, president of Musashi Institute of Technology in Tokyo.[9] The tool is the Ishikawa diagram or, as it is sometimes called in western countries, the fishbone diagram. Causes are determined and systematically plotted on an Ishikawa diagram as shown in Figure 6–6.

Figure 6–6A shows the general format of the diagram. The main branch of the diagram (the spine of the fishbone) is an arrow pointing to the right with the effect or discrepancy to be analyzed labeled at the arrow tip. Potential causes are divided into general categories, and each general category corresponds to a series of arrows drawn toward the main branch at an angle of sixty degrees. Major potential causes in each category are arrows drawn parallel to the main branch, and these main cause arrows point to the right. Potential sub-

Total Quality Control: A Tool For Improving The Quality of Management

Figure 6-6   **The Cause and Effect Diagram**

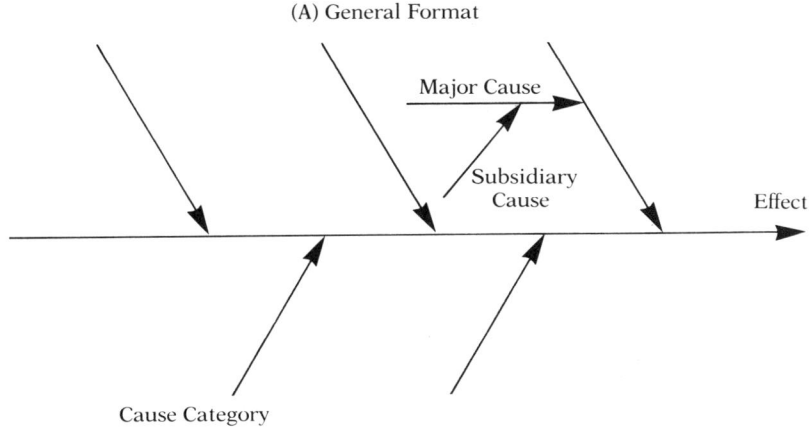

(A) General Format

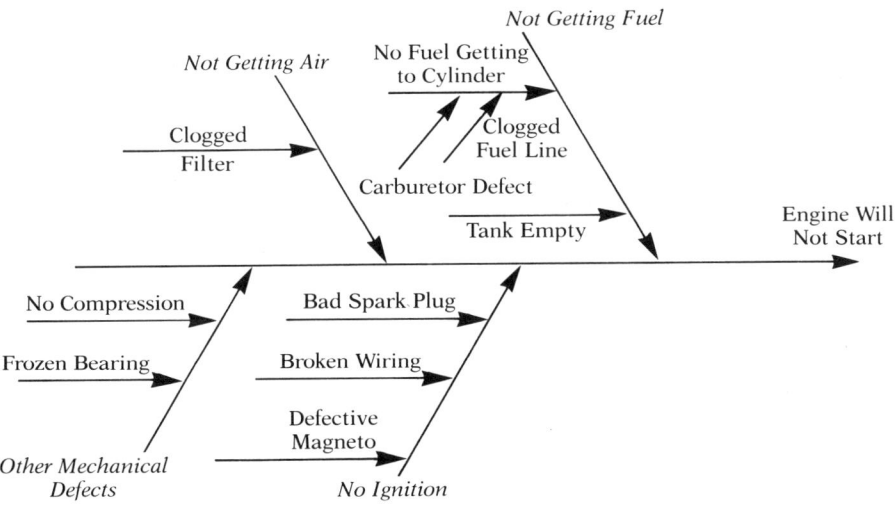

(B) Example — Gasoline Engine

sidiary causes are drawn as additional arrows at an angle of thirty degrees to the appropriate cause.

To complete an Ishikawa diagram all potential causes must be identified. One of the most effective methods used to identify causes is a group brainstorming session by the employees responsible for the process. The leader of the brainstorming session should follow this general outline:

1. Idea generation phase
   - Any ideas are OK, no judgment or evaluation;
   - Record all ideas on blackboard or flip chart;
   - Stimulate imagination;
   - Maximize number of ideas;
   - Add to or further develop the ideas of others;
   - Use who, what, when, where, why, how, how much questions.

2. Evaluation/categorization phase;
   - Evaluate each idea objectively;
   - Don't prematurely discard ideas that might have value;
   - Look for common characteristics and gather into categories;
   - Prepare revised list.

Don't underestimate the importance of an open session where all ideas are considered no matter how wild or irrelevant they may seem at first. The objective is to spread a wide net to capture any idea that may have a bearing on the problem. Evaluation of ideas should be attempted only after all team members are convinced that all ideas are on the table. Even then, it may be worthwhile to temporarily end the session before evaluation and reconvene when some new ideas may result from a day's recess.

Once a list of potential causes has been developed, an Ishikawa diagram can be used to display each cause in major categories and subcategories. Figure 6–6B is an example of a diagram listing the causes for the failure of a small gasoline engine to start. Note that the cause categories are

- Not getting enough fuel;
- No ignition;
- An insufficient air supply to the engine intake;
- Other mechanical defects.

Major potential causes within each category are shown along with any subsidiary causes.

CORRECTIVE ACTION

The final step in the Deming cycle, *Act*, can begin once potential causes are analyzed and a decision is made about the first causes to attack. It is important that the right problem be addressed, and this requires a familiarity with basic problem-solving methods. Readers should consider a formal training program in problem-solving skills for their organization. The following outline will illustrate one approach to deciding on appropriate corrective action and summarize the main components of the *Act* step in the Deming cycle:

1. Define the problem.
2. Describe the effect of the problem.
    - What?
    - Where?
    - When?
    - How?
    - How much?
    - Why?
    - Who?
3. Develop probable causes.

4. Categorize causes and identify the most probable cause.

5. Decide on the objectives for the solution. Differentiate between essential requirements and desirables.

6. Generate possible solutions.

7. Evaluate solution alternatives.

8. Decide.

9. Develop implementation plan for decided action.

10. Anticipate potential problems. (Cycle repeats. *Plan*)

11. Implement decided action. (*Do*)

12. Evaluate effectiveness. (*Check*)

13. Modify implementation as appropriate. (*Act*)

APPLICATION OF TQC TO THE PROCESS OF MANAGEMENT

The majority of problems facing companies today are management problems. By better understanding the process of management, executives can focus their efforts on activities that continually improve the effectiveness of their organizations. This is total quality control applied to the management of the company. To be successful, however, specific measures of management and executive performance must be identified and monitored continuously. Deviations from objectives must be understood and eliminated.

TQC is unlikely to work when the executives of the firm are not actively involved in the TQC process themselves. They need to establish the performance measures and analyze deviations from standards and objectives. Equally important, executives need to develop the actions required for continuous management improvement.

Management is a complex process; constructing a flowchart to accurately represent the complete process would be an extremely difficult task. Moreover, management is as much an art as a science, and this makes process analysis complex. Yet there are some subprocesses in management that can be readily flowcharted, and performance measures for these subprocesses can be developed. To the extent possible, TQC must be applied to management if we are to continue to improve the management process.

In the next chapter, TQC will be applied to the general and functional management processes as a tool to develop an effective executive development strategy.

REFERENCES

1. Armand V. Feigenbaum, *Total Quality Control*, 3d ed., New York, McGraw-Hill, 1983 (originally published in 1951).
2. For more details on total quality control, see Kaoru Ishikawa, *What Is Total Quality Control?*, Englewood Cliffs, N.J., Prentice-Hall, 1985 (translated by David J. Lu.), and Richard J. Schonberger, *Japanese Manufacturing Techniques*, New York, The Free Press, 1982, ch. 3.
3. For a discussion of HP's experience, see "One Company's Quest for Improved Quality," *The Wall Street Journal*, July 25, 1983. Results through 1985 are summarized on page 7 of Hewlett-Packard's *1985 Annual Report* to shareholders.
4. Quality control circles, or as they are more commonly called, quality circles, are small groups of employees who meet regularly with their supervisor to identify, analyze, and solve work-related problems in their areas of responsibility. Solutions are presented to management for approval, and the circle members implement the solutions. For an in-depth description of quality circles, see William L. Mohr and Harriet Mohr, *Quality Circles*, Reading, Mass., Addison-Wesley, 1983.
5. For a description of the contribution that Drs. Deming and Juran and others have made to quality control, see Jeremy Main, "The Curmudgeon Who Talks Tough on Quality," *Fortune*, June 25, 1984, and "Quality — The U.S. Drives to Catch Up," *Business Week*, November 1, 1982.
6. In discussions on TQC the application of the Deming cycle is often focused exclusively on procedures to correct discrepancies. I have chosen to apply the cycle more generally to all processes, treating procedures for discrepancy correction as a special case.

7. Harlan Cleveland, *The Knowledge Executive*, New York, E. P. Dutton, 1985, p. 22.
8. For a discussion of statistical quality control methods, see Kaoru Ishikawa, *Guide to Quality Control*, 2d rev. ed., Tokyo, Asian Productivity Organization, 1982, and Dale H. Besterfield, *Quality Control*, 2d ed., Englewood Cliffs, N.J., Prentice-Hall, 1986. For a discussion on the general subject of problem analysis and problem solving, see Charles H. Kepner and Benjamin B. Tregoe, *The New Rational Manager*, Princeton, N.J., Princeton Research Press, 1981.
9. Dr. Kaoru Ishikawa is a worldwide authority on quality control and a strong advocate of TQC. See Kaoru Ishikawa, *What Is Total Quality Control?*, Englewood Cliffs, N.J., Prentice-Hall, 1985 (translated by David J. Lu).

CHAPTER 7

PROCESS IMPROVEMENT AND EXECUTIVE DEVELOPMENT

In this chapter we will apply the fundamentals of total quality control to the process of general and functional management and develop a TQC model for the continuous improvement of this management process. In Chapter 6 the Deming cycle was used to define the basic TQC functions of *Plan, Do, Check,* and *Act.* This cycle is again shown in Figure 7–1.

Process improvement comes about through the *Act* step. For the process of management, management development activity is frequently the *Act* step. A management development program, correctly chosen, will improve the process of management. Taking the right action depends on the previous steps in the cycle. For example, sending a manager to a management development program will address only performance discrepancies that are caused by a lack of knowledge or skills.

Frequently, executives do not take the necessary time to complete the *Check* step — that is, a cause-and-effect analysis to really understand the cause for a discrepancy. Correct action is possible only if you understand the steps of *Plan, Do,* and *Check.* The first six chapters of this book are related to the *Plan* and *Do* steps in the Deming cycle, which is why I have devoted so much time to strategy development and execution. This chapter deals with the *Check* step. The remainder of the book is devoted to executive development strategy formulation, program development, and implementation — that is, the *Act* step.

The Deming cycle can be relabeled to illustrate the principal linkages between executive development and business strategy, and this adaptation is shown in Figure 7–2. Developing the firm's strategy (doing the right things) is the *Plan* step, and execution of the strategy (doing things right) is the *Do* step. In the *Check* step management performance is measured and compared against previously established goals. For this to work it is necessary to establish some specific, measurable goals, and a procedure for making the measurements. In the case of financial, sales, and production goals, the measurement is relatively easy. The measurement of people management goals (such as leadership) is not as straightforward. Note that management and executive development efforts are not the only interventions that can be associated with the *Act* step. For example, when a strategy is wrong, it needs to be revised. In this case executive development, except on the subject of strategic management, is probably a waste of time. Other interventions may include clarifying objectives, adding human or physical resources, and removing barriers to strategy execution. This book emphasizes the application of the

Figure 7-1   The Deming Cycle

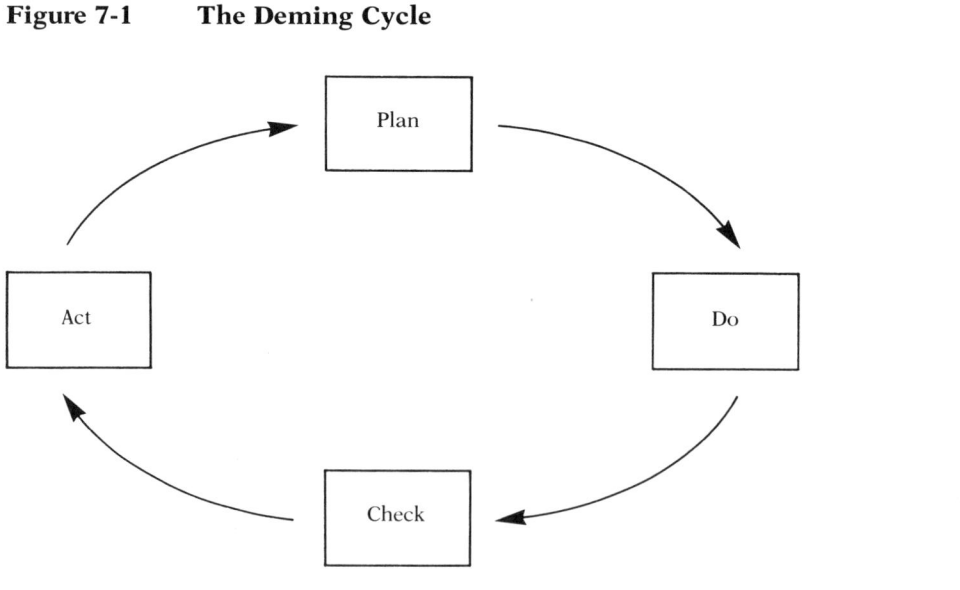

Process Improvement And Executive Development

TQC model to executive development as a tool for continuous improvement in the management process, and nondevelopmental interventions will not be broadly considered.

THE GENERAL AND FUNCTIONAL MANAGEMENT PROCESSES

Is it possible to precisely define and flowchart the processes of management at the general and functional management levels? I think the answer depends on the detail expected. A rigorous analysis that accommodates every activity of an executive would be difficult — perhaps requiring an effort be-

Figure 7-2 Adding Strategy, Strategy Execution, and Executive Development to the Deming Cycle

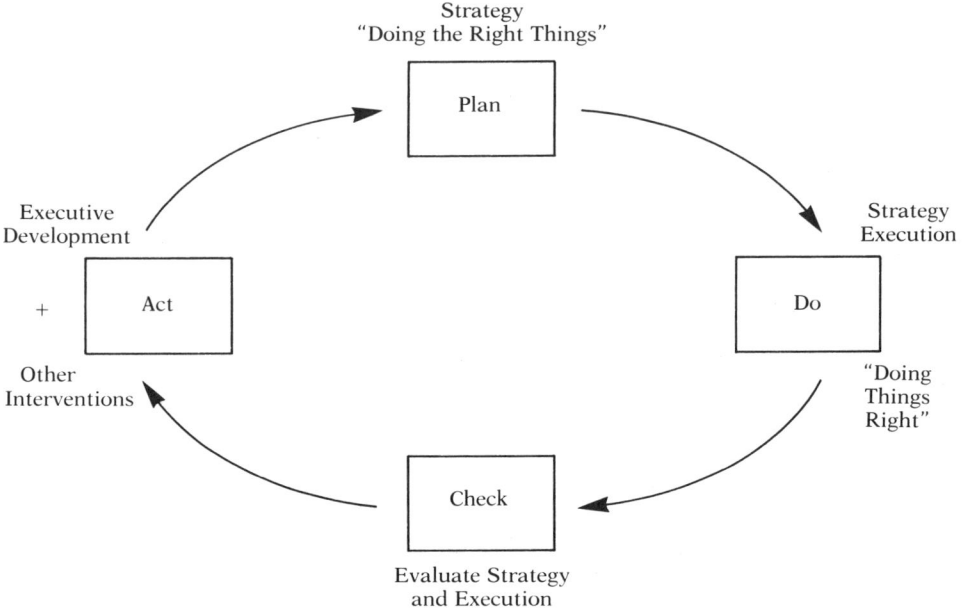

yond the point of diminishing returns. It is also necessary to consider that effective management has many of the characteristics of an art, and precise definition is difficult. Nevertheless, if one's objective is to define the five or six key steps in a particular management process with a few key performance measures specified, a useful process definition can be developed and flowcharted. TQC can then be applied to the process.

A simplified generic flowchart for the executive process is shown in Figure 7–3. Specific objectives for executive actions are derived from the organization's values and capabilities, its strategic goals and strategy to reach these goals, and the tactical plan for the current fiscal year. The results of executive actions are compared against these objectives. Results that do not meet objectives are discrepancies, and causes are analyzed to see which of the following categories they fit:

- A discrepancy in knowledge or skills required by the executives to do the job;
- A structural problem — that is, something getting in the way of effective implementation;
- Environmental factors — such as governmental actions, moves by competitors, and economic shocks.

The objectives that are established and their measurability are the keys to the flowchart being an effective model. Let's look first at objectives for executive action.

Management literature offers many standards by which general and functional managers may be evaluated. A very useful definition is offered by John Kotter in his *Harvard Business Review* article on what effective general managers actually do.[1] Kotter concludes that general management activities fall into two broad categories — (1) agenda setting and (2) networking. Agenda setting would include the generation of a vision for the firm and a strategy to reach the objectives associated with this vision. Objectives are reached through the coordinated efforts of many people throughout the orga-

Figure 7-3 A Generic Flowchart for the Executive Process

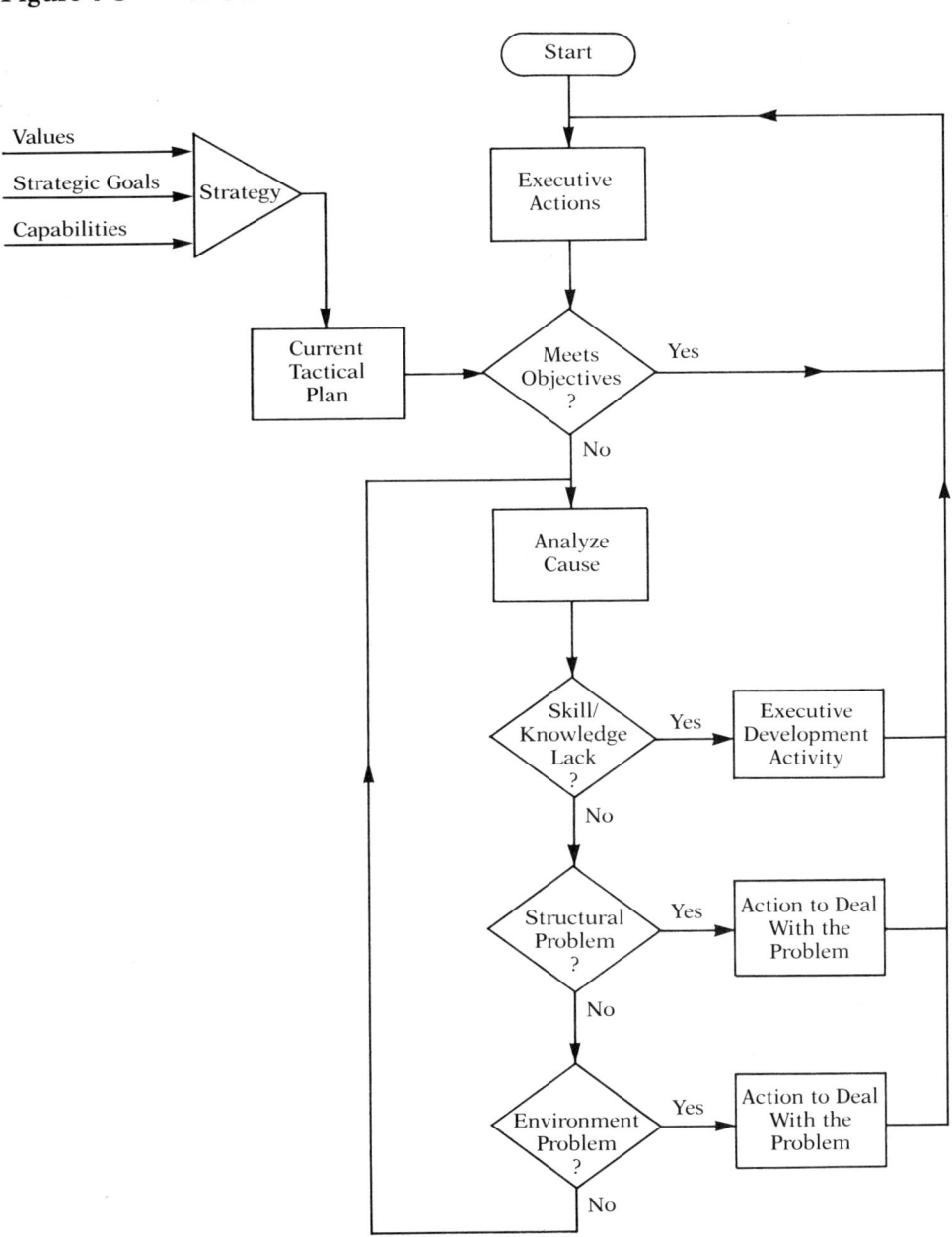

nization, and an important step in achieving objectives is to get these people to share the vision and work toward making it a reality. Networking is the activity of creating cooperative relationships among the people who will implement the agenda. Vision sharing and commitment result from effective use of networks. Regardless of how one defines management activities or how one establishes objectives for these activities, executives and executive development managers who want to tailor Figure 7–3 to their own organization must select appropriate objectives to fit their firm.

My experience at Hewlett-Packard convinces me that general and functional managers should be evaluated on how well they perform the following three tasks:

- Their ability to formulate and execute *strategy*, particularly strategies to develop, manufacture, and market new products;
- Their *people management* effectiveness;
- Their ability to manage their *expenses*, capital *assets*, and *profit* targets.

In Figure 7–4 these criteria for the executive management process have been added to the generic flowchart. The specific objectives for executive action are to

- Develop and execute an effective strategy for achieving the firm's strategic goals, including the setting of an appropriate agenda and the development of the necessary implementation networks;
- Provide effective people management;
- Provide effective management of expenses and capital assets and the achievement of profit targets.

A more detailed listing of these objectives would include quantitative and qualitative measures.

Figure 7-4   **Flowchart for the Executive Process with Three Specific Goals**

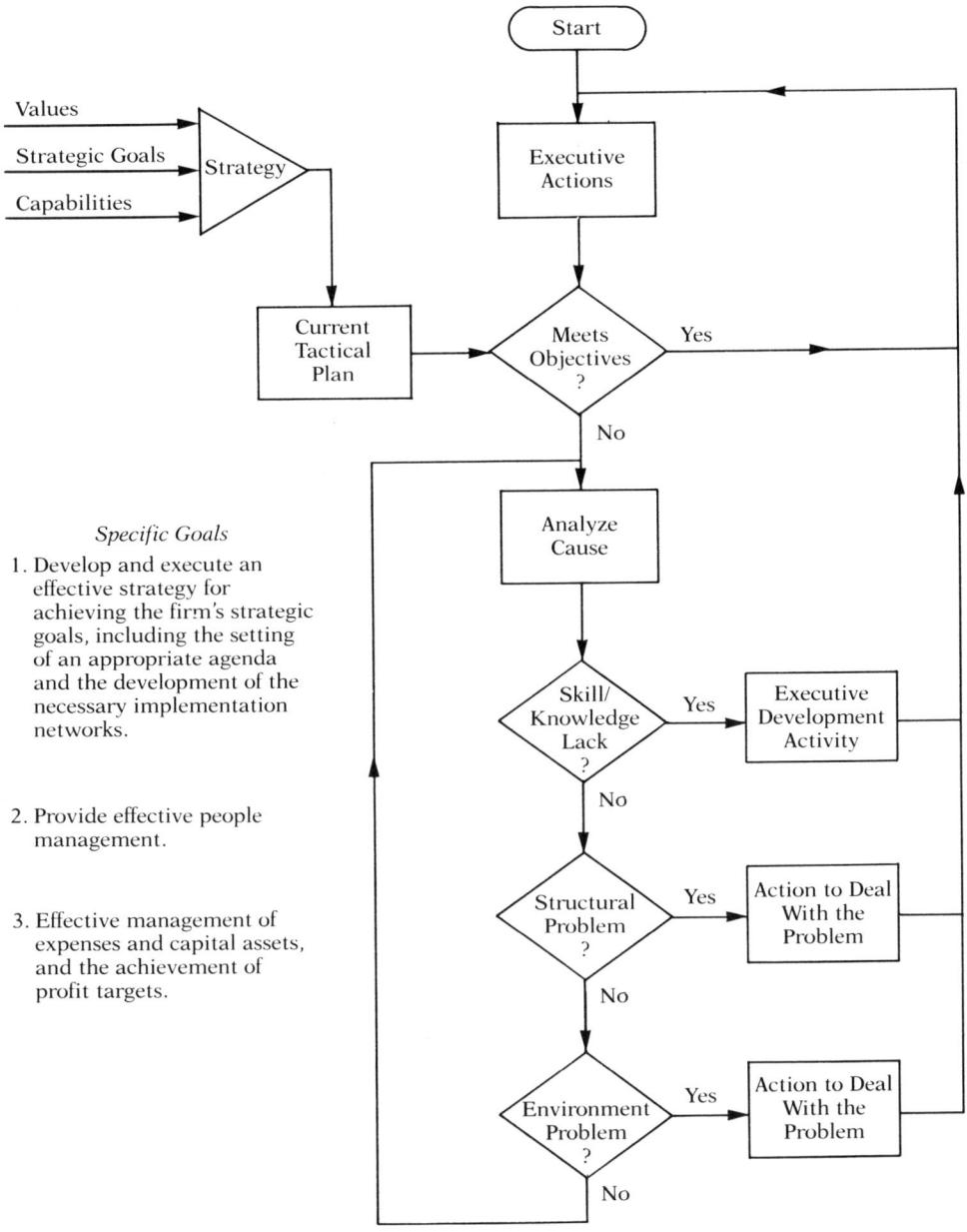

EVALUATING THE EFFECTIVENESS OF EXECUTIVE PROCESSES

What are the appropriate measures of process performance for the executive process in Figure 7–4? How can these measurements be made? The answers to these questions are critical to the application of TQC to executive actions. Objectives that can be stated in very specific goal statements will have the measure built into the statement. For example, the first objective is to develop and execute a strategy to achieve strategic goals. One of these goals is a certain level of after-tax profit — let's assume 8 percent. When the objective is stated in a way that includes the 8 percent figure, one of the measures for executive performance becomes obvious. Other measures that might be applicable to a firm's objectives are sales figures, earnings growth rates, market share, number of customer complaints, and so forth. These quantitative measures leave little doubt as to whether the objective has been achieved.

Some objectives, such as people leadership effectiveness, are difficult or impossible to quantify. Qualitative or subjective measures must be used for these objectives. In applying these measures, the critical thing is for executives to know how they are being evaluated. Some possible measures for people leadership are employee turnover rates, the enthusiasm displayed by employees, frequency of oral or written expressions of dissatisfaction, and so forth. Many companies use formal employee attitude surveys to measure organizational climate. Others make more subjective measurements by one of the personnel staff or a line manager conducting interviews on an informal basis — an example of managing by wandering around.[2]

I think it is important to have a few good measures rather than the twenty-five, fifty, or 100 that you often see on formal management performance appraisals. A few meaningful measures are much easier to monitor continuously and are more compatible with the TQC approach to continuous improvement. Decide on five or six measures, how often they are to be made, and who is to be responsible for the measurement.

Let's take a further look at the example of Figure 7–4 applied to the general management of an industrial organization. Figure 7–5 lists some typical goals for an organization and how the goals might be measured. The example lists

Figure 7-5   An Example of General Management Goals and Performance Measures

Goal	Measure	Source/Frequency
1. Develop and Implement an Overall Strategy to Achieve the Firm's Principal Objectives:		
A. Sales Volume Increase of 20 Percent While Achieving Profit Goal	Sales Statistics	Marketing/Monthly
B. Increase R&D Spending to a Level of 10 Percent of Sales	R&D Expense Reports	Accounting/Monthly
C. Introduce Ten New Products During the Next Twelve Months	Actual Number of New Products Released	Manufacturing/Monthly
D. Achieve a Significant Increase in Customer Satisfaction	Phone Calls/Letters Expressing Dissatisfaction	Marketing/Weekly
	Number of Warranty Failures	Marketing/Monthly
	Customer Attitudes	Marketing/Semiannually Sales Force/Continually
2. Provide a Leadership Environment That Engenders Enthusiasm, Pride in Achievement, and Rewards for Contribution	Employee Attitudes Formal Surveys Informal Feedback	Personnel/Annually Management Team/Continually
	Absenteeism	Personnel/Monthly
	Employee Turnover	Personnel/Monthly
3. Effective Management of Expenses, Assets, and Profit		
A. Manage Expense Levels Not to Exceed Target	Department Expense Reports	Accounting/Monthly
B. Achieve After Tax Profit of 8 Percent	Monthly Earnings Statement	Accounting/Monthly
C. Reduce Inventory Levels to 15 Percent of Sales	Value of Finished Goods, Work in Process, and Materials Inventory	Accounting/Monthly

three major goals that are further divided into specific numerical objectives where possible. The goal concerning leadership will require qualitative measures.

The measures for goals 1 and 3 are primarily numeric, and the firm's normal accounting and financial systems can make the measurements on a monthly basis. Customer satisfaction can be measured through surveys, product warranty failure statistics, letters and telephone calls from customers, and feedback from the sales force and distributors. The second goal, leadership, presents a more difficult measurement problem. The executive team must decide on some measures and the approach to making these measurements. A good place to start is by going out and asking the people in the organization how they feel about the organization, the direction it is heading, their level of contribution, whether their personal career goals are being met, and so forth. Any quantitative measures that reflect employee attitude should also be used — for example, absenteeism and employee resignations. The important thing is to decide on the measures and begin the process.

This approach to executive process performance measurement is also applicable to executives at the functional management level. Figure 7–6 shows the goals, measures, and measurement sources for a typical marketing manager. There are three overall goals that are similar to those of the general manager in Figure 7–5. The measures for the first goal are straightforward. The measure chosen for the effectiveness of new product introduction is the growth rate in orders for that product compared to estimates made during the product's development. Customer satisfaction is achieved by eliminating customer dissatisfaction, and one measure of this is the number of customer complaints.

The second goal, leadership, requires some subjective measurement, although the marketing manager's goal of leading by going out into the field can be quantified and measured.

The administration goals are all quantifiable, and the measures would already be available in most marketing departments.

Figure 7-6 An Example of Marketing Management Goals and Performance Measures

Goal	Measure	Source/Frequency
1. Develop and Implement a Strategy to Achieve the Company's Marketing and Sales Objectives		
A. Sales Volume Increase of 20 Percent with Half from New Accounts	Sales Statistics	Marketing/Weekly
B. Effectively Introduce New Products	New Product Sales Growth Versus Target	Marketing/Weekly
C. Concentrate Promotion Efforts to Increase Lead Generation by 25 Percent	Ad Inquiry Count	Marketing/Monthly
D. Achieve Total Customer Satisfaction	Number of Customer Complaints	Marketing and Field Offices/Monthly
2. Provide Effective Marketing Leadership for Factory and Field Marketing Personnel		
A. Marketing Manager to Spend 40 Percent of the Time in the Field Talking to Customers Including Visits to the Top Fifty Customers During Next Twelve Months	Trip Records	Marketing Manager/ Monthly
B. Set an Example for the Rest of the Company for Employee Morale and Enthusiasm	Employee Attitude Surveys	Personnel/Annually
	Absenteeism	Personnel/Monthly
	Employee Turnover	Personnel/Monthly
3. Provide Effective Management of Marketing Expense, Capital Assets, and Administration		
A. Process and Acknowledge Orders within One Working Day	Actual Acknowledgement	Marketing/Weekly
B. Ship Customer Orders on or Before Acknowledged Delivery Date	Shipping Document	Marketing/Weekly
C. Maintain Marketing Expense Under 18 Percent of Revenues	Department Expense Reports	Accounting/Monthly
D. Increase Accuracy of Forecasts by 25 Percent	Actual Orders Versus Forecast	Marketing/Monthly

Operations

CAUSE AND EFFECT ANALYSIS

In order for data to be useful, it must be organized for analysis and, through analysis, turned into information that can help to improve the process. For instance, knowing that you have had six months of steadily declining profit levels is useful only to the extent that the information triggers appropriate action to solve the underlying problem for the profit decline. An analysis of monthly earnings statements may reveal that manufacturing overhead costs have steadily increased, and the manufacturing manager may already be analyzing overhead costs.

To effectively deal with results that do not meet objectives, you must explore all factors that could influence the outcome. Brainstorming may help identify potential causes. Causes for discrepancies can be gathered into major categories, using the procedures outlined in Chapter 6. As suggested earlier, management performance discrepancies generally fall into three categories:

- Skill or knowledge causes;
- Structural causes;
- Environmental causes.

Figure 7–7 illustrates cause categories and potential major causes on a fishbone diagram. The three main branches on the diagram correspond to the major cause categories of skill or knowledge, structural, and environmental problems. Secondary causes are shown for each main category — for example, a skill or knowledge problem can be due to poor selection of the manager in the first place, insufficient experience, or a lack of understanding of the task to be accomplished. Similar secondary causes are shown on the two other branches of the diagram.

Process Improvement And Executive Development

PROCESS PERFORMANCE MEASUREMENT COMPARED TO PERFORMANCE APPRAISAL

What is the difference between the process performance measurement procedure being suggested and the executive performance evaluation systems used by most firms? Ideally, they should measure the same achievement — that is, the

Figure 7-7   A Generalized Cause and Effect Diagram for a Management Performance Discrepancy

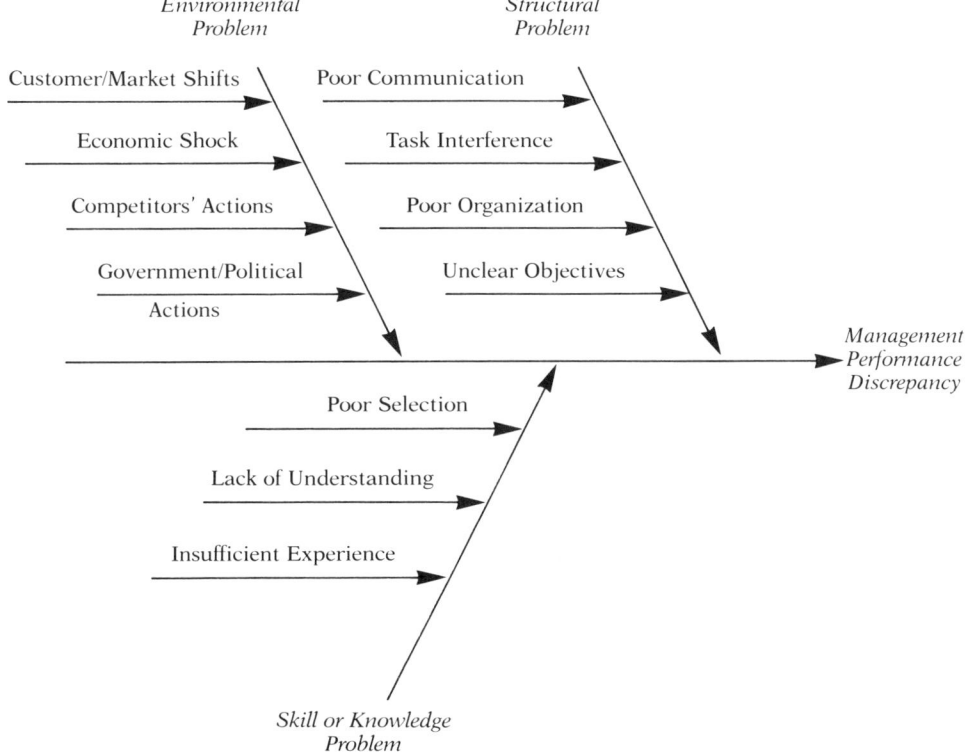

goals achieved and the methods used to achieve these goals. There are several differences, however. Executive performance appraisal is normally done by the executive's superior. It is highly subjective and is usually done on a formal basis only once each year. The measurement of executive process performance using the TQC model is a continuous activity with the executive directly involved in the measurement. The only objective of the TQC measurement process is to identify ways to improve performance. The approach focuses on the half dozen or so key measures that really signify executive management excellence.

ALTERNATIVES FOR EXECUTIVE PROCESS IMPROVEMENT

One of the advantages of careful analysis of cause-and-effect data is that the steps necessary for process improvement are often obvious from the analysis. For example, when the primary cause for missing sales targets is insufficient sales representatives in the field, a fairly obvious solution is to hire and train additional representatives.

Structural and environmental causes are not generally removed by executive development activity. There are, however, situations where executive training can help managers cope more successfully with things over which they have little control — such as economic shocks and adverse governmental actions. Often the best way to cope with these situations is to modify the firm's strategy, and executive development may help this process. Also, top management may want to create a higher sense of awareness among executives on a particular matter that may fall into the structural or environmental area. A focused executive development program can help create this awareness.

For discrepancies that are clearly caused by executives lacking knowledge or particular skills, there are several alternatives for action. A determination should be made as to whether the executive or manager has an adequate understanding of the tools and techniques for his or her job. If not, attendance in a formal class or seminar in the particular subject can be scheduled. To apply knowledge to the job itself, executives and managers need to gain additional skills on the job. The active coaching of the boss is critical to this successful transfer.

Job rotation is another method for achieving on-the-job experience, and this is usually done early in the executive's career. For example, engineering project managers at Hewlett-Packard are frequently assigned to manufacturing and marketing for a period as part of their development. These rotations are often self-initiated.

Occasionally top management must decide that a struggling executive is simply not capable of achieving the desired results. This is particularly true with individuals who have not paid attention to their own career development by keeping up with changing job requirements. Reassignment or outplacement of the executive is the only logical alternative.

SUMMARY OF PART II

An understanding of how the operations of a business contribute to strategy implementation is fundamental to the development of an effective executive development program. The discussion in Chapter 5 focused on a functional model of the major elements of a business unit. These elements are general management; the three line functions of product development, marketing, and manufacturing; and the supporting staff departments. The major linkages between these elements were outlined. The activities in these linkages must be carefully managed in order to successfully execute a strategy. Executive development must address any weaknesses in these linkages as well as interfunctional teamwork.

Chapter 6 described total quality control as an effective tool for gaining continuous process improvement in all of the processes going into a product or service. Management is one of these processes. A model for process improvement, the Deming cycle of *Plan, Do, Check, Act,* was introduced. The principles of TQC include methods for measuring process performance and for using the data to plan action for process improvement.

In Chapter 7 the basic principles of TQC were applied to the general and functional management processes, and performance measures were established for the major goals of these processes. Measurement data is analyzed and used to plan improvement activity. Executive development is a central activity for process improvement and is most effective when it is an ongoing activity and part of the firm's strategic management process. Total quality control provides a framework for identifying the issues that executive development activity should address — that is, the causes of executive performance discrepancies. This has been the focus of the book for the first seven chapters.

We now turn our attention to planning and implementing executive development activity. TQC serves as a good model for this topic. Chapter 8 covers the formulation of executive development strategy — the *Plan* step. *Doing* executive development is addressed in Chapters 9, 10, 11, and the first part of Chapter 12. The remainder of Chapter 12 covers the evaluation (*Check*) and improvement (*Act*) of executive development efforts.

REFERENCES

1. John P. Kotter, "What Effective General Managers Really Do," *Harvard Business Review*, November/December 1982.
2. The concept of management by wandering around (MBWA) has been popularized in recent books and articles. I believe that the origin of this phrase comes from a title of a presentation made by John Doyle, an executive vice-president at Hewlett-Packard, at a general management meeting in the mid-1960s.

PART 3
EXECUTIVE DEVELOPMENT

CHAPTER 8
EXECUTIVE DEVELOPMENT STRATEGY FORMULATION

This chapter outlines the starting point for executive development activity — establishing specific objectives and formulating a strategy to achieve them. To be an effective tool for business strategy implementation, the executive development strategy must address the needs of the firm. For this reason, top management and the firm's executive team need to play a major role in training strategy development. Moreover, to achieve maximum effectiveness, the strategy needs to be jointly owned by top management, the executive team, and the executive training function.

BASIC RESPONSIBILITIES

The major responsibilities for the training director, the top management team, and the executive team are outlined below and summarized in Figure 8-1. A first responsibility for all parties involved in strategy formulation is to recognize that executive development is a continuous process that requires active participation and commitment. All too often, an executive development strategy is equated to attendance at company-sponsored or university executive seminars. Executives may be inclined to think that development is something that you go elsewhere to obtain. Training seminars are an important executive development activity, but the primary focus for executive development must be one of continuous process improvement.

The framework for an effective strategy should be a synthesis of the things that executives need to work on in order to do a better job of business strategy execution. What can

Figure 8-1 **Executive Development Strategy Formulation — Major Responsibilities**

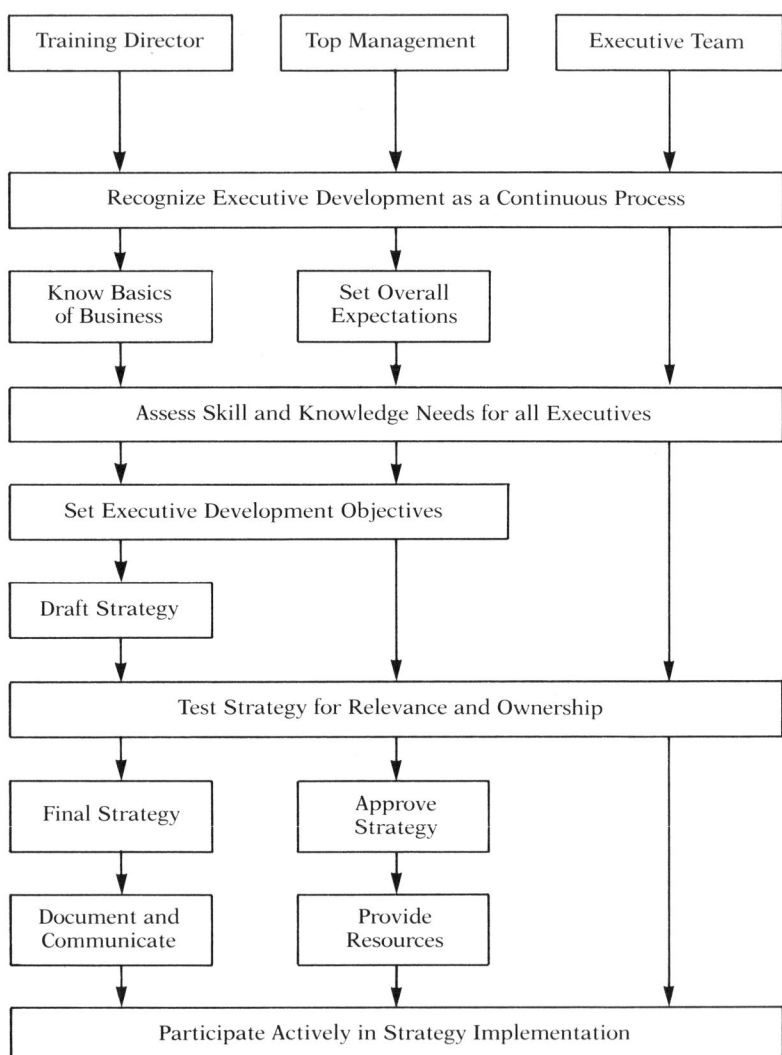

they do to outperform their competitors? How can they continue to achieve superior performance? The basic principles of TQC apply to the processes of executive action.

Training Director Responsibilities

The training director's first responsibility is a thorough understanding of the firm's businesses and the strategies that are being followed to succeed in these businesses. What are the strategic issues that need to be addressed? What actions are planned for dealing with these issues? Without this understanding it would be impossible to develop an effective executive development agenda for doing a better job of achieving strategic goals.

One of the best ways to acquire this knowledge of the business is to talk to the managers responsible for each function in the company. Wander around their work areas, and ask questions. Get the managers to outline their tactical plans and describe their own strategic issues. Develop an understanding for the important relationships between their functions and the other functions in the firm. This interaction must take place on a regular basis and become a part of the training director's day. It also contributes to building the network of management support that will be needed later for program implementation.

The training director also needs to understand the organizational context in which the firm's executives manage. This context includes all the factors that influence the organization, including customer needs, product applications, competitor strengths and weaknesses, the technologies critical to the industry, and the economic and regulatory environment. All executive and management development must be framed within this organizational context.

Once the business is well understood, the training director must assess the skill and knowledge needs for the firm's executives. This assessment should be done on a macro basis for the firm as a whole as well as for individual executives. The top management team, particularly the chief executive officer, needs to play a major role in this assessment.

Most organizations have distinctive competencies — the skills that have made the firm successful. For example, many high technology companies owe much of their success to the scientific and engineering expertise of their founders. The development of marketing skills is often neglected. In assessing executive development needs, look for gaps in knowledge and experience for the firm as a whole.

Individual needs are best identified through a meeting with the CEO. Ask for a brief appraisal of each executive. What skill and knowledge areas need strengthening? I think it is important to gather this data for the two levels immediately under the chief executive officer, but don't forget the needs of the CEO. Most CEOs can be quite objective about their own developmental needs.

A preliminary understanding of overall executive development needs will form the basis for establishing some specific objectives for the executive development activity. Top management should again be involved in setting these goals. The most critical needs should head a prioritized list. The focus should be on the results expected by top management from its investment in time and resources for executive training.

During the process of understanding the firm's business strategy and operating environment, and while assessing executive development needs and objectives, the training director should begin to identify some specific actions that will be possible options for a development strategy. These early ideas should be organized into a strategy draft that can be discussed with top management and the executive team. It is important to establish early ownership of the strategy by top management and the firm's executives. To be effective, it must be their strategy — one that they participated in developing and one that expressly meets their needs.

An effective technique that can be used to build ownership of the executive development strategy by top management and the executive team is to form an advisory board to provide ongoing guidance to the training and development staff. The advisory board can be chaired by a member of the top management team. In addition to the training director, other members of the board can be selected to represent a cross-section of the executive team. The board can meet quarterly or semiannually to review major projects, update the executive development strategy, and reset priorities as necessary.

The final strategy draft should be presented to a meeting of the top management team for endorsement and approval. Once approved, it should be documented and communicated to all executives in the company. Like other effective business strategies, the strategy for executive development will need to change to meet changes in the company's operations. For this reason it is vital to keep open those communication links with the firm's executives that are created during strategy development.

The practice of executive development is dynamic, and training directors need to stay current with new methods and ideas. A number of means are available for staying up to date, but I found the best method to be frequent discussions with executive development specialists in other companies and in the academic community. Take time to build these networks. In addition, articles in business journals, particularly the *Harvard Business Review*, the *Sloan Management Review*, and the *California Management Review*, contain numerous ideas for curriculum content and executive development processes. *Stanford GSB* includes timely articles as well as listings of pertinent research papers by Stanford Business School faculty.

Top Management Responsibilities

Andy Grove in an article in *Fortune* magazine stated, "Training is, quite simply, one of the highest leverage activities a manager can perform." He describes the article as the chapter inadvertently left out of his best-selling book *High Output Management*. Grove also comments in the *Fortune* article, "For training to be effective, it has to be closely tied to how things are actually done in your organization."[1]

Top management should set the overall direction for executive development strategy and ensure that it is congruent with business strategy and the operational style of the company. As stated earlier, top management must support the philosophy of executive development as a continuous process. Overall expectations for executive development must come from the CEO. The CEO must also devote time to helping the training director assess the overall skill and knowledge needs of the executive team and formulating specific objectives for development activity.

Once a draft strategy exists, top management needs to offer counsel on the strategy's relevance and suggestions for refinement. The objective should be a final strategy that the CEO and top management team can own. Final approval should be clearly indicated and implementation support should be made obvious, particularly the allocation of necessary resources. Top management exerts a tremendous influence on how well the strategy is implemented; active involvement must be routine.

At Hewlett-Packard the top management team reviewed management and executive development activity during frequent formal meetings and offered not only suggestions for improvement but also strong encouragement and support. This level of support is particularly critical during the development of executive training programs. A visit to the training department by a senior manager can work wonders for the morale of the project team.

Members of top management can have significant influence on their organization's executive development process by setting an example through their participation in development activities, including paying attention to their own self-development. Participation in executive seminars by serving as an instructor or a luncheon or dinner speaker will contribute to a program's effectiveness and to the executive's own development. A member of the top management team attending a seminar as a student is a valuable resource during class and small group discussions. The executive's experiences can add much to the learning process. At HP the value of many of these discussion sessions involving top management often exceeded the original objectives for these seminar segments. In the early days of the first HP general management seminar, I invited Bill Hewlett to speak at a seminar luncheon and provided him with a fairly structured outline on what I thought he might say. After getting up to speak, he quickly displayed the outline and mentioned that he wasn't going to use it. Instead he gave an informal talk about the philosophies that he and Dave Packard followed when they started the company in 1939. The ensuing discussion was more valuable than any formal session that I could have planned for this occasion. It established a format for succeeding luncheon discussions with top management.

Executive Team

The company's executives are important resources for executive development strategy formulation. First, if executive development is to be a continuous process in your firm, it starts by executives believing in this approach and becoming committed to it. Second, executives can describe their needs. Third, the executive team can help mold the initial strategy draft into one that will precisely meet their needs and one that they can own. Fourth, executives are the key players in strategy implementation, and their involvement must be designed into the strategy. The effectiveness of executive training programs is quite dependent on the involvement of executives as instructors and their subsequent coaching efforts. This involvement is much easier to achieve when they feel ownership for the strategy guiding these programs. The rest of this chapter provides more details on formulating an executive development strategy for a business organization.

DETERMINING OVERALL NEEDS

The training director starts the strategy development process by meeting with the CEO and other members of top management to discuss the development needs of executives individually and as a group. Pay attention to both generic business management knowledge and skills as well as those that are specific to the implementation of the company strategy. An inventory of existing skills should be made, noting the educational backgrounds of executives as well as management training courses completed. Trends will often appear while taking this inventory. For example, in many high technology companies, a majority of executives have their formal education in science and engineering, and a common need exists for business management skills.

A representative sample of the company's executives should be interviewed individually to ascertain how they perceive their developmental needs. To ensure consistency, a brief questionnaire should be designed and used as an interview guide.

After completing the discussions with top management and interviews with executives, the training director may possess conflicting data. Some way is needed to sort the data into information that can lead to a development strategy. It is helpful to establish some broad categories for sorting the data. Figure 8–2 illustrates a method for dividing executive

Figure 8-2   Executive and Management Development — Categories of Curriculum Emphasis

1. Getting the Basics Right
   (Blocking and Tackling)

   A. Philosophy
      The underlying philosophy and principles for managing the organization — the value set — needs to be shared throughout the organization

   B. Generic Business Management
      Basic knowledge and skills for management, e.g., strategic management, finance, customer satisfaction, computers as management tools, quality assurance

   C. Functional Knowledge and Skills
      Specific functional skills, e.g., marketing, manufacturing, product development, human resources management

2. Strategy Specific
   (Preparing the Game Plan)

   Acquiring Knowledge and Skills to Implement a Specific Strategy development needs into two categories — (1) getting the basics right and (2) training that is strategy specific.

This method is somewhat analogous to the approach that an athletic team takes to training and game preparation. Basics, such as blocking and tackling in U.S. football, need to be developed in the preseason prior to any games. It would be premature to spend much effort preparing for a specific game at this stage of the team's development. After the basics are mastered, serious game preparation can begin. In business, basic management principles must be mastered as a necessary foundation on which to build strategy implementation skills.

Getting the Basics Right

This category is further divided into three components:

> *Philosophy.* It is difficult for an organization to execute strategy without a general understanding of the organization's management philosophy. This philosophy includes the general principles for managing the company and the values that shape strategy and operations. The philosophy needs to be shared and understood throughout the organization, but executives have a special role in its perpetuation by virtue of their leadership position. Many companies, including IBM and Hewlett-Packard, place great emphasis on including their management philosophy in management and executive training curriculum for all organization levels.
>
> A number of educational institutions offer seminars in the humanities for senior executives. Although this topic does not come under my usual definition of a firm's management philosophy, it is somewhat related. Providing leadership for organizations that face incredible complexities in a changing environment requires an understanding of the forces in society that shape the environment. One can debate whether the shareholders of a business should underwrite the education of execu-

tives in the humanities, but the fact remains that this topic needs to be addressed. A very successful two-week program has been run at Stanford for a number of years.

Generic business management. This component includes business management knowledge and skills that cut across all functional areas. Examples include basic management and leadership skills, accounting and finance, strategic management, customer satisfaction, computers as management tools, and business law. It is usually assumed that executives already have these skills, but assumptions like this are often wrong. I once included a very simple accounting question — a sources and uses of funds problem — on an examination given at the conclusion of a general management training program. I was surprised at the number of individuals who had difficulty calculating the correct answer.

Functional knowledge and skills. Included in this component is curriculum based entirely on one of the major functions, including marketing, manufacturing, product development, finance, quality assurance, and personnel. Most executives are promoted after success in one or two functions. They frequently do not thoroughly understand the key elements of other functions. It is a good idea to include basic functional training for all new executives. All executives also need training on new developments and techniques for managing their function.[2]

In Chapter 5, I described a triangle model of management that suggests that to be effective a manager needs to be able to manage people, manage things, and understand the technical side of what is being managed. Leadership and managing things (that is, administration) are examples of generic management skills that need to be part of any executive and management development strategy. The technical side of the triangle corresponds to the functional knowledge and skills category in Figure 8–2.

Strategy Specific Training

Strategy specific training, the other major category in Figure 8–2, should be the principal focus for executive development, assuming that the basics are well in place. This category is the major theme of this book, and the curriculum must be derived directly from the strategic issues facing the firm. To again use the football analogy, this activity prepares the executive team to execute right the first time when the score counts.

At this stage of strategy development it is possible to get bogged down in trying to define executive development needs in too much detail. Leave this detail for a formal needs analysis for a specific program (methods for doing this will be discussed in Chapter 9). The important thing in developing a strategy is to define a meaningful framework that can later support the detail.

Considerable attention has been paid recently to competency-based management training.[3] Identifying the competencies that effective executives possess, and using these competencies as the basis for executive training, is a generally sound process. There is a fair amount of evidence, however, that management is just as much an art as a science, and executive training directors need to recognize this. Management is situational in nature, and managers can't always reach into their bag of competencies for an answer. This is why training on management philosophy is so important. When managers and executives have a solid foundation in the values and philosophies of the firm, they will be able to deal with the hundreds of situations that a list of competencies can't foresee. When faced with a number of decision choices, the alternative that maps most consistently with the philosophy of the organization will normally be optimal.

An important responsibility for all executives is paying attention to their own self-development. Peter Drucker has wisely observed that "Development is always self development. No business enterprise is competent, let alone obligated, to substitute its efforts for the self-development efforts of the individual."[4] Yet few executive development strategies pay attention to self-development, and this is unfortunate. Self-development requires few resources and little expense. Strategies can include some relatively simple actions to encourage these efforts by the firm's executives. Years ago, Bill Hewlett started a practice of sending relevant management books to the firm's senior managers. In this era of computer desktop publishing, training directors can easily send out newsletters to managers and executives recommending recent articles in business and management journals. When new resources are used in ongoing executive training programs, these resources can also be shared with past participants.

For self-development to be effective, executives need a framework for their self-directed efforts. This is why getting the basics right first is so important. It is also necessary for executives to be able to visualize how their self-development activity links to the organization's business strategy. The list of strategic issues is an excellent tool for clearly establishing this linkage. Recent research in education suggests that the human mind can more readily accommodate new information into its long-term memory when the information is organized into a relatively small number of chunks and when these chunks fit into a previously established framework.[5] Executive development strategies should provide for building these frameworks that facilitate self-development of executives.

DEVELOPING THE STRATEGY

Once an inventory of needs has been categorized, some choices for meeting these needs can be developed. The odds always seem to favor a list of needs far in excess of available time and resources, and a first step is to establish priorities. This process should result in a one-page list of executive development priority issues, and this list should drive subsequent strategy formulation activity. The list should be reviewed by top management for endorsement. Training needs on the list that fall into generic business management and functional training categories (categories 1B and 1C in Figure 8–2) can often be met by existing educational programs offered by colleges, universities, or outside training organizations. When a need can be satisfactorily met by one of these resources, effort spent on in-house development is wasted. Needs in the categories of management philosophy and acquiring knowledge and skills to implement a specific strategy (categories 1A and 2) must generally be met by programs conducted in house, and the firm can make the decision either to design and develop the program inside the organization or to subcontract this effort to a consulting organization willing to work closely with the training director and top management.

Formulation of the executive development strategy can become quite specific once a list of priorities exists. Focus attention on the choices available for meeting the prioritized needs. In addition to training programs, a variety of developmental methods are available including on-the-job training, rotational assignments, orienting and integrating new executives hired from outside the firm, involvement in task forces, and needs-focused performance evaluation. These methods all have in common the acquisition of job-related knowledge and skills and share the reality that they will not work unless a way is found to transfer acquired knowledge and skills to the executive's job.

A model is a very useful device to illustrate and communicate executive development strategy. It defines the development agenda and focuses resources on priority items. An example of a model is shown in Figure 8–3. There are three dimensions to this particular model. The X axis defines the categories of curriculum emphasis and in this case uses the same categories described in Figure 8–2 — the philosophy of management in this particular organization, generic management knowledge and skills, functional knowledge and skills, and curriculum designed for acquiring the knowledge and skills to implement the organization's specific strategy. The first three categories represent basic skills and knowledge that must be in place for success in achieving strategic objectives. The model's Y axis defines three executive levels —

corporate, general management, and functional management. The model is intended to recognize the individual developmental needs of executives at these three levels. The Z axis defines more detailed curriculum topics — such as manufacturing knowledge and skills. This model includes the major functional areas for a typical manufacturing business as well as leadership, environmental, and political topics. Models developed for service businesses and the public sector would include topics pertinent to their specific operations.

Once a model is developed, all executive development programs should fit within the framework of the model. For example, a program in marketing to help general managers

Figure 8-3   Executive Development Strategy Model

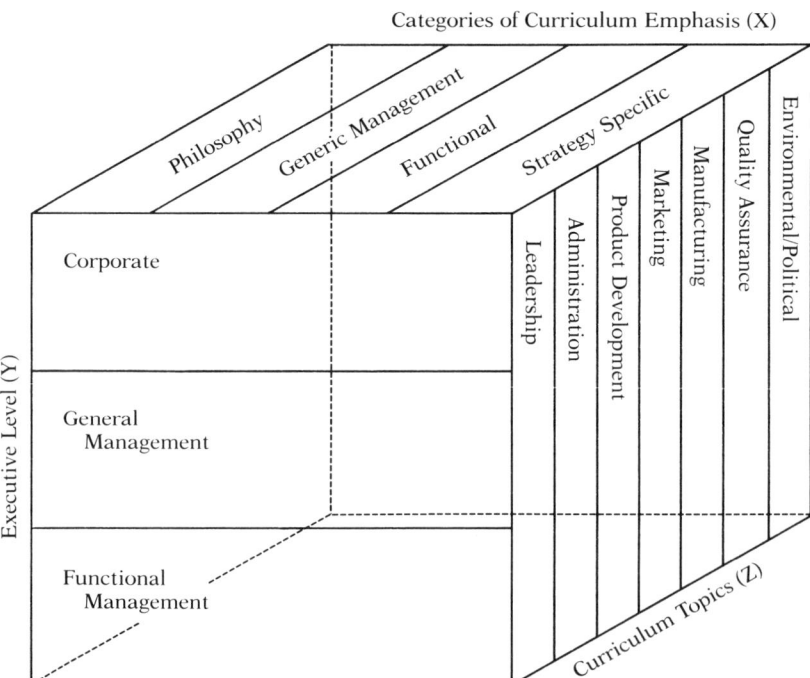

implement a companywide strategy to build marketing excellence would fit within the model as follows:

X axis — Strategy Specific

Y axis — General Management

Z axis — Marketing

Many executive development programs will consist of individual modules that may fit the model in a variety of different locations. In using a model similar to Figure 8–3, each program module should fit within the model's framework.

I used a three-dimensional model similar to Figure 8–3 to illustrate the strategy that we developed for training executives and managers at Hewlett-Packard. Any existing projects or activities that did not fit the model were discontinued. To make the point to the department staff, I asked our set designer in the television studio to build a clear plastic mockup of the model complete with wooden blocks to represent specific content topics. A proposed course in basic accounting for supervisors was represented by one of the blocks, and so on. The plastic mockup, about the size of an eighteen-inch cube, occupied a place on my conference table for several months until I concluded that everyone had received the message about what we were trying to do.[6]

Once a strategy draft and model exist, they should be tested to ensure that the strategy meets the objectives established for the executive development effort. I think that the most effective way to accomplish this verification is to review the strategy draft and model with the executives and members of the top management team who provided inputs to the strategy. The goal is to achieve consensus, and it may be necessary to go through several iterations before consensus is achieved.

At the same time that the strategy is tested for relevance, a sense of ownership for the strategy by the executive team can be built. It is natural for people to want to own what they have a role in creating, and ownership will greatly assist implementation later on. Be particularly alert for executives who can contribute their knowledge to curriculum development or their experiences for possible case studies.

GAINING STRATEGY APPROVAL

After achieving consensus, the strategy needs to be put into final form for approval by top management. The final strategy document should consist of the following parts:

1. Summary of the current executive development situation and why a new strategy is needed;
2. Summary of results of executive development needs analysis;
3. Proposed strategy that highlights how the needs are to be met, including a model of the strategy;
4. The relationship of the proposed strategy to the strategic issues that face the organization;
5. Responsibilities of the training department, executive team, and top management;
6. Implementation plan including more specific details on first priority program;
7. Summary of costs and resources needed;
8. How the strategy will be evaluated.

If possible, the training director should present the strategy at a meeting of the top management team. Ask for approval! The implementation plan should include a line item labeled "Strategy Approval by Top Management" with the actual date of the meeting shown beside it. Assume that it will be approved, but be prepared to handle any questions or objections and the possible need to modify the strategy during the meeting.

I favor a relatively short document that succinctly identifies the key points of the strategy. The effectiveness of the strategy lies in the value of the recommended actions, not in the length or detail of the document. Make sure that each member of the executive team receives a copy of the strategy, and, when approved, a copy should be sent to each executive in the organization.

ACQUIRING RESOURCES

Resources for executive development, even in the best of times, are always scarce. In economic downturns they often disappear. Training directors would do well to concentrate their resource efforts on selling the executive development strategy to top management. That is, don't be satisfied with a passive approval. Convince the top management team that the strategy deserves its enthusiastic approval and support. Requests for funds for executive training compete with numerous high-priority requests from line operations, and when members of top management view the strategy as theirs, the chances of obtaining the necessary resources are high. In addition, remember that the success of the first program is critical in getting funds for subsequent efforts. For this reason, it is important to carefully prioritize the list of executive development needs and concentrate effort on priority number one.

Resourcing the executive development effort will depend on many factors, including the extent of internal design and development activity included in the strategy, the use of outside consultants and programs, and the size of the operation. A rule of thumb for professional staff in an organization responsible for all training and development activity is one training and development specialist for every 400 to 500 employees. Staff specialization in executive development is possible only when a staff of three or four professionals is justified. Budget requests should contain estimates for each program or project in the strategy, including the number of person months of effort. The cost of the total number of person months, administration, and overhead plus the costs of any subcontracted services will yield the resource costs.

Training department costs can be reduced by the use of task forces to help develop programs, although the total cost to the organization remains the same. Significant contributions can be made by college summer interns, and salaries for these people are normally lower than for a full-time person. This is also an excellent strategy for recruiting talented young people into the organization.

INVOLVING EXECUTIVES IN THE DEVELOPMENT PROCESS

All managers have one source of strength — the knowledge, skills, and performance of their people. When a manager wants to be more successful, the best method is to work on those things that make the manager's people more successful. Training and development is the major factor in improving the performance of a team. A training program can at best be a catalyst — a way to stimulate awareness and a mechanism to learn new skills or acquire new information. Unless these skills are practiced and information is used, they are lost. Managers need to make sure that this practice and application happen, and this is part of the coaching job that managers have. Like athletic coaches who can teach and coach the fundamentals, managers are more effective when they understand the basics, can teach the basics, and know when these basics are being applied on the job. For the same reason, training programs that introduce new management methods are implemented most successfully from the top of the organization.

A very effective method for gaining support for the strategy is to find a champion for each major project. It is usually possible to identify a member of top management with a strong interest in a particular project. Try to get this individual to champion the project. This help may be useful when additional resources or support are required.

Top management will frequently assume the role of champion for an important executive development effort. Several years ago, HP's vice-president for manufacturing reminded me of the critical need for a training program in manufacturing management. At the time all of our resources were deployed in other areas, but this particular vice-president kept pushing for what he knew was an important training need. In time he succeeded in convincing me of the importance of the project and gaining top management support. His tenacity continued to help the development effort, especially when additional resources were needed.

PROGRAM OWNERSHIP AND THE "BEST PRACTICES" MODEL

The most successful programs that we developed at Hewlett-Packard were those where we involved the target population in the development effort and, through this process, gained their ownership and support. This did not mean involving everyone but enough individuals to comprise a meaningful sample. A key objective was to get ownership by those individuals whose support for the project was critical. Another goal was to obtain some "best practices" to include in the curriculum. Strategies for executive development should include efforts to gain this ownership and support.

The steps we took at HP to get target participants to think of the program under development as their program were quite straightforward, beginning with the identification of fifteen or twenty individuals who either had something to contribute to the project or whose support was necessary. The project manager would meet with each individual to explain the objectives of the program and solicit inputs on these objectives and any ideas the individual would have for content. Because essentially all programs consist of training modules, individuals would be asked to serve on module development task forces where they could contribute their ideas to the project. In addition, these task forces would review material being developed and participate in program pilot runs. On

Executive Development

completion of development, many of these individuals would act as instructors and help promote the program.

We also made use of what came to be known around HP as the "best practices" model. It simply recognizes that one of the most valuable learning resources is the experience of managers themselves. Figure 8–4 suggests that management effectiveness follows a normal distribution. The individuals to the right of point E on the curve represent the most effective managers in the organization. It makes sense to enlist their help in developing others. The objective should be to get at least half of all managers at or above this level of excellence, as suggested by the shift in the dashed curve. This can be accomplished by having the excellent managers develop others by contributing their best practices and helping with program development and instruction. I used to think that the original curve would simply skew to the right and that the excellent managers would remain stationary. I am now convinced that they get better too because teaching is an effective learning process for the instructor. Consequently, the entire distribution will shift to the right.

Figure 8-4 **Distribution of Manager Effectiveness**

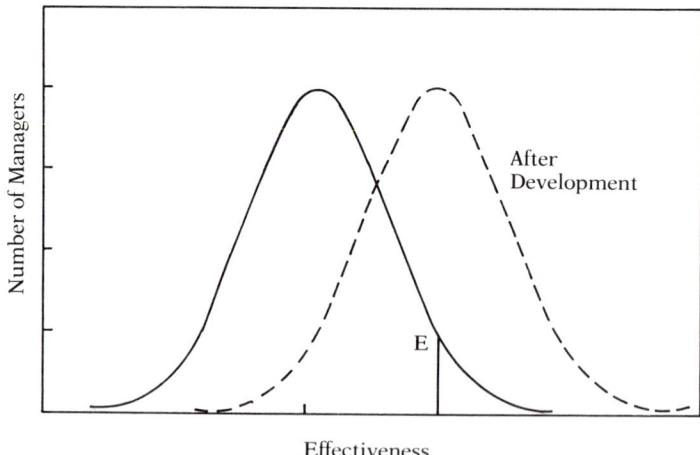

To use this model as part of your executive development strategy, enlist the help of the top management team in identifying executives within the organization who excel in their management tasks or have some exemplary practice that would strengthen the curriculum for a proposed program. Excellent managers are always trying new things and adopting new methods, and in most organizations there are bound to be managers who are well ahead of the rest in applying a new method or skill to their jobs. Once identified, these individuals are normally quite willing to contribute to an executive development effort because it provides an opportunity for their expertise to be more widely appreciated and used throughout the company. Moreover, many of these same individuals are able to bring new best practices into the company because they are not afraid to look elsewhere for new techniques and to try them in their own departments.

EXECUTIVE DEVELOPMENT AS A WORLDWIDE ACTIVITY

Strategy development should consider the needs of the entire organization and not just the needs of the executives in the headquarters country. The training director must be sensitive to worldwide needs, and this sensitivity cannot be acquired without spending some time with the overseas operations. After introducing formal executive training programs at HP in 1975, the most common critique made by HP's non-U.S. executives after attending an executive development program was that the material was too U.S. oriented. It took significant effort and expense to make sure that materials, curriculum, and instructors were worldwide in scope. We regularly included instructors from Europe and Asia in programs conducted in Palo Alto, California.

Training directors should establish contacts with some of the leading business schools outside their own country. In Europe, IMEDE in Lausanne, IMI in Geneva, INSEAD in Fontainebleau, and the London Business School have excellent executive programs and faculty. In Japan, I have visited both

Sophia and Hitosubashi Universities in Tokyo and found them to have excellent faculty. Singapore National University has excellent executive programs and faculty. It also conducts cooperative programs with some U.S. business schools.

It is important to make sure that the executive development strategy meets the needs of overseas executives and creates an international awareness in the headquarters executive staff. A major issue is cultural difference, and it is difficult to develop sensitivities to these differences through training programs. There are some excellent resources that should be included in programs oriented toward international business management.[7] A Paris-based non-U.S. executive for a U.S. company told a meeting of training directors sponsored by the Conference Board in Brussels that it takes about six years for an executive from one country to become completely oriented to a different business culture.[8] For this reason, rotational assignments of executives among countries is perhaps the best method for international executive development. Nevertheless, executives from overseas will attend executive training sessions outside their own country, and designers of programs need to be sensitive to language differences. Before finalizing the development of a program, someone should be assigned to think about how the material, particularly the words and examples used, will translate into another language.

PLANNING FOR STRATEGY IMPLEMENTATION

Chapters 9 through 12 outline in detail the processes for implementing an executive development strategy. Before addressing these processes, I would like to conclude this strategy formulation discussion with some suggestions for effective training strategy implementation.

Take some time to develop contacts with professional educators, preferably at the college and university level. I spent half of 1985 and all of 1986 as a loaned executive from Hewlett-Packard to the California State Department of Education studying the executive and management training needs of school administrators and developing specific recommendations for an overall management and executive development strategy for California public education. While engaged in this activity, I had several opportunities to work closely with faculty in university schools of education. In several instances I had the chance to learn more about the theory of formal educational processes, and many times I wished I had discovered formal educational theory and practice earlier. It appears that very few training and development people from the private sector take the effort to talk to their colleagues in schools of education. This is unfortunate because there is a highly developed knowledge and skills base that governs curriculum design, instructional strategies, and learning assessment.

Training directors must decide whether to develop a training program in house or to use an external program. Chapter 10 presents some guidelines for deciding whether to develop a program yourself or contract for its development. When the decision is to send executives to externally conducted programs, such as those run by many business schools, the training director is faced with a slightly different decision. The following points should be considered when making this decision:

- Is the program consistent with the firm's executive development strategy?
- Will the sponsor provide a complete list of past participants for evaluating program effectiveness from the perspective of executives?
- Is there a history of successful implementation?
- Are the participants attending the program at comparable levels of responsibility to your candidates?
- Are the industries, specific job responsibilities, and geographical locations of participants consistent with your business interests?
- Will the benefits provided by relating to a diverse set of participants outweigh the fact that the training will

be experienced by only one of your executives, making job transfer more difficult?

- For programs of extended duration (greater than four weeks), can the executive be away from his or her job responsibilities?

- Is the experience and research focus of the faculty congruent with your firm's interests and executive development priorities?

One final observation about executive development strategies. I am convinced of the importance of getting the basics right first as *the top priority* activity for executive and management development. The best executives at HP have a passion for simplicity. While heading HP's computer business in the 1970s, Paul Ely, now CEO of Convergent Technologies, had a sign on his office wall that succinctly suggested, "Do a Few Things Well." John Young, HP's CEO, encourages one-page strategies. General managers are typically judged on just three criteria: their product strategy, their ability to manage assets and profits, and their people leadership.

Peters and Waterman's *In Search of Excellence* characterized excellent companies with just eight common attributes.[9] Writing in *A Passion for Excellence*, Tom Peters and Nancy Austin stated, "many accused *In Search of Excellence* of oversimplifying . . . we have come to the opposite conclusion: *In Search of Excellence* didn't simplify enough!" In the later book, they offer two ways to achieve superior performance, "take exceptional care of your customers" and "constantly innovate."[10]

In a recent letter to the Editor of *Business Week*, a vice-president from another exceptional company, Disney, commented about a recent review of Buck Rodgers's book, *The IBM Way*.

> You observe, "The allocation of billions of dollars' worth of resources and people takes smarts, not just strong men and stout hearts," and "Despite Rodgers's book, IBM's secret remains secret." Like many others, you refuse to believe that the reason

for IBM's great success over the years can be as simple as it sounds: hiring the brightest and most highly motivated people it can find, training them thoroughly, rewarding them generously, and pointing all their efforts toward the singular goal of satisfying the customer. Why is it necessary that the "secret" be more complex, profound, or arcane?[11]

In thinking about the core curriculum for your executive and management development strategy, remember that there is both elegance and effectiveness in simplicity.

REFERENCES

1. Andrew S. Grove, "Why Training Is the Boss's Job," *Fortune*, January 23, 1984, pp. 93–96.
2. Due to rapid advances in technology, functional training needs to be continuous. In many functional specialities, for example, engineering and manufacturing, about half of a person's knowledge and skill base becomes obsolete in a relatively short period of time. At Hewlett-Packard the engineering education group estimated that this half-life for development engineers was somewhere between three and five years. In a forty-year career, an engineer needs to be re-educated about eight times.
3. See Peter Vaill, "The Theory of Managing in the Managerial Competency Movement," *Exchange: The Organizational Behavior Teaching Journal*, 1983, vol. 8, no. 2, pp. 50–54.
4. Peter F. Drucker, *Management: Tasks, Responsibilities, Practices*, New York, Harper & Row, 1973, p. 427.
5. See Robert Calfee, "Cognitive Psychology and Educational Practice, Review of Research in Education," Washington, D.C., American Educational Research Association, 1981.
6. See Appendix A for a description of an overall strategy for executive and management development that is similar to the strategy developed at Hewlett-Packard.
7. Copeland Griggs Productions of San Francisco, California produces an excellent film series entitled *Going International*. Also see Lennie Copeland and Lewis Griggs, *Going International*, New York, Random House, 1985.
8. "Top-Level Executive Succession and Development, A Trans-Atlantic Discussion Meeting," The Conference Board, Amigo Hotel, Brussels, Belgium, February 23, 1984.

9. Thomas J. Peters and Robert H. Waterman, Jr., *In Search of Excellence,* New York, Harper & Row, 1982.
10. Thomas J. Peters and Nancy K. Austin, *A Passion for Excellence,* New York, Random House, 1985, p. 4.
11. Erwin Okun, "IBM's Secret for Success Is Simple," a letter to the editor appearing in "Readers Report," *Business Week,* February 17, 1986, p. 8.

CHAPTER 9

EXECUTIVE DEVELOPMENT PROGRAM DESIGN

The key to the success of any executive development program is the quality of the design. In many ways an executive development program is analogous to computer software. Like software the design approach can take many forms, and the design itself leaves lots of room for creativity. The program, whether it be software or an executive seminar, must be thoroughly tested before actual use, and the designer should never lose sight of the objectives to be met. Any short cuts taken during the design phase will usually be paid for many times over during program implementation.

A basic theme of this book has been that executive development efforts need to be driven by strategic issues facing the organization. The major design consideration should be the strategic issue or issues that the program is intended to address. For this reason it is imperative that top management and the executive team play an active role in the program design, particularly in the needs analysis and project investigation phases.

Figure 9–1 shows a seven-step process for executive development program design. This chapter will explain each of the seven steps, and the design of a program for senior executives will be used to illustrate the process. Although shown as a sequential process, many of the steps in Figure 9–1 are iterative. The program designer may find it appropriate to adjust the sequence to correspond to the specific needs of the organization.

NEEDS ANALYSIS AND PROGRAM INVESTIGATION

The first step in executive development program design is to conduct a complete needs analysis for the proposed program and a thorough investigation of the objectives the program is

Figure 9-1 A Seven-Step Process for Executive Development Program Design

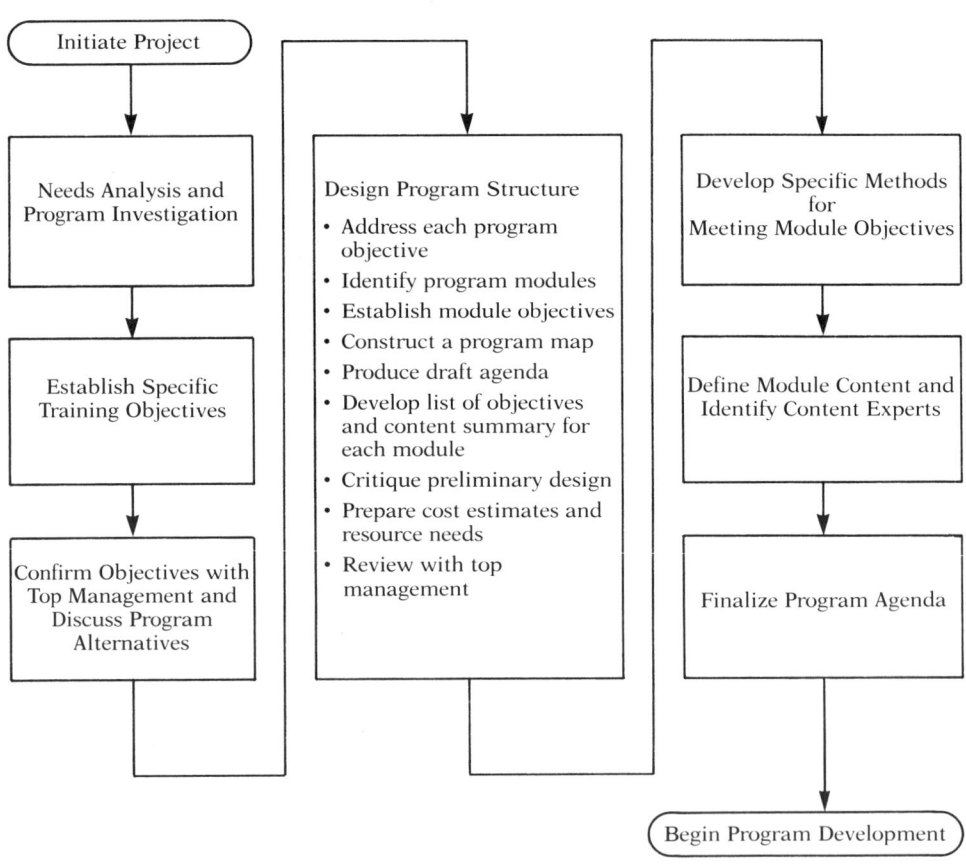

meant to address. When a decision is made to embark on the development of an executive training program, it is often made in response to a problem that top management sees within the organization. There is frequently a tendency to jump to the conclusion that training is the correct solution to the problem. It is a good idea to verify this conclusion by a thorough needs analysis. Should a training program not be needed, the needs analysis process will likely generate a more appropriate solution to the perceived problem.

Needs analyses are often done in either too much detail or as a formality to justify an existing program decision. I have seen some needs analyses occupy so much time and effort that it appeared that the needs analysis itself was the objective, not the development effort. I favor an approach to needs analysis that is based on four principles:

- Use a structured process for the analysis;
- Assess needs as perceived by target participants;
- Assess needs as perceived by top management;
- Quality of input is much more important than quantity of data.

A structured process is necessary to assure the quality of the assessment. Person-to-person interviews allow interaction and discussion that is not possible with questionnaires sent by mail, but a written set of consistent questions prepared in advance of the interview will help to assure responses that can be readily consolidated into meaningful results. This is particularly important when more than one individual is doing the analysis. A few years ago I assisted one of our course designers in doing a needs analysis for an executive development program in international business management. I had other reasons for being in the Far East and had some time available to talk to twenty or thirty HP executives in Japan and Singapore about their views on what should be included in the program. A structured questionnaire developed by the course designer made it possible to compare and combine the

Far East responses with the responses from executives in the United States and Europe.

Assessing needs as perceived by members of the target audience for the program has been the primary focus for most needs analysis efforts. This data is significant to the extent that the interviewees have taken the time to really think through what they need in order to do their jobs better. Any steps that you can take to get individuals to prepare in advance of the interview will contribute to the integrity of the data. It is extremely important to discriminate between what is perceived as necessary and what might be just desirable or fun. The interview question set can be designed for asking the same information in different ways to test both the consistency and the intensity of answers.

Needs expressed by targeted participants should be confirmed by needs expressed by the participants' bosses, particularly top management. Because these individuals have the responsibility to think about and evaluate the overall performance of the executives targeted for the development program, they should have already given considerable thought to those skills that would allow executives to improve the total results of the organization. These individuals have also had much more management experience, and their perspectives on what needs to be included in an executive's formal training are extremely valuable.

Consideration should be given to forming an executive development advisory group within your organization as a steering committee for your executive training activities. A member of the top management team should be a part of this group along with five or six executives representing a good cross-section of the firm. It is particularly important to have representation from the principal line functions, including sales. Semiannual or quarterly meetings of this group can greatly assist your needs analysis efforts as well as contribute to actual program development and implementation activities.

The most important principle of needs analysis is the value of the quality over the quantity of data produced. I would regularly tell the training and development specialists in my organization that I would much rather see needs analysis data from the right twenty or twenty-five people than from 100 to 150 people selected randomly. Selecting the right people is difficult, but it can be done if approached correctly. Top management can help in this selection, and you can expect them to suggest individuals whose judgment has attracted their attention. Personnel managers often track "comers" in their organizations, and these individuals have often thought about their own developmental needs. An important task for managers of executive development is to identify executives and managers in their organization who can provide continuous feedback on developmental needs. Continuous feedback can make formal needs analysis projects easier, as much of the data will already be at hand.

Don't miss the opportunity during the needs analysis to create interest and ownership in the project, not only with potential attendees but also with their managers. Ownership is much more likely to occur when the participants and other executives feel that they had an opportunity to help define the program. During the needs analysis take advantage of the chance to identify executives who may be able to contribute to the development of the program. Include their best practices when they fall into the subject areas to be addressed. Look also for individuals who would make effective instructors.

At the conclusion of needs analysis devote some attention to investigating various alternatives for meeting the expressed needs. This is a good time to conceptualize, diverge your thinking a bit, and be creative, before rigid objectives for the program are established. There is a time in the design cycle of any product when uncertainty should not only be tolerated but encouraged. New and innovative ways should be sought for addressing the needs uncovered during the analysis phase. Try to find out how other organizations have addressed similar needs. What would they do if confronted with the need again? What do they wish that they had done differently? What is the relevant research currently being done on topics surrounding the needs? This is the point in the life cycle of the project where very little investment has been made. Later on, uncertainty will have to decrease rapidly as investment increases during the development phase.

ESTABLISHING SPECIFIC TRAINING OBJECTIVES

A difficult challenge in program design is to take a summary of expressed needs and translate them into a few specific objectives to guide the further design effort.[1] Needs often are in conflict with each other, and, once this is sorted out, they must be prioritized. Much has been written about the development of specific training objectives, and the following is intended only to highlight some factors that were particularly important in setting objectives for executive development programs in which I was involved.[2]

The key question to answer from the needs analysis data is what you want executives to do differently after attending the training program. An equally important question is what they will likely do. How much learning will actually be transferred to the job? It is prudent to establish five or six key objectives that have an excellent chance of being met rather than a long list of wishes. You may find that writing objectives can be a highly iterative process requiring considerable verification with a few key contributors to your needs analysis. Avoid the temptation to include an objective for everyone. The only way this is possible is to settle for lowest common denominator objectives that will probably result in a lowest common denominator program.

Objectives tend to be hierarchical in nature. To achieve one objective usually requires the achievement of several subordinate objectives. For example, for an executive to better understand the impact of the economy on business performance, an understanding of the components of gross national product is necessary. The overall objectives of an executive development program are achieved by satisfactorily meeting the objectives of individual program components or modules. Don't confuse overall program objectives with the subordinate objectives of program modules.

CONFIRMING OBJECTIVES WITH TOP MANAGEMENT AND DISCUSSING PROGRAM ALTERNATIVES

Once overall program objectives are established a conference with top management should be scheduled for review and approval of the objectives. It is particularly important that top management recognize the importance of their support for the program, and this is where having a member of the top management team as a project "champion" will be extremely helpful.

In addition to objectives approval, the meeting with top management should include a discussion of the following topics:

- Ideas for program content that address the objectives;
- Ways in which the CEO and top management can contribute to program success;
- Outlines of alternative program structures including key sessions;
- Ideas for possible instructors and outside faculty;
- A tentative project schedule;
- Staffing and resource needs;
- Approval to begin program design and development.

This early meeting may worry some readers because you are going to top management with some pretty rough information. The accepted practice for such a meeting is to be prepared with more specific proposals. I favor this preliminary meeting because the top management team must play a role in the design process from the beginning if ownership of the program is to be achieved. Executive development efforts that are seen as not having the active support of top management lack impact and credibility. To achieve this necessary support, an objective of the meeting is to get top management to see themselves as co-architects of the project. Inputs received during this conference can be incorporated into the final design.

With approval to proceed with the project, the manager of executive development should begin to think about an overall schedule. It should include all principal activities from designing the program structure to program implementation. At this point in the life cycle of the project the schedule is necessarily tentative because completion dates cannot be accurately established prior to completing the design of the program. Nevertheless, the schedule should include best estimates of completion dates for the following project milestones:

- Completion of program design;
- Firm program agenda;
- Completion of leaders' outlines;
- Completion of participants' materials;
- Final selection and confirmation of instructors;
- Date for first seminar.

On completion of program design, more detailed project schedules should be established, and suggestions for these schedules are presented in Chapter 10.

DESIGNING THE PROGRAM STRUCTURE

It is most likely that during the processes of needs analysis, program investigation, establishing objectives, and the meeting with top management, some reasonably clear ideas for program structure have begun to crystallize. It is important, however, to systematically design the program by going through each of the design steps shown in the design program structure block in Figure 9–1.

Address Each Program Objective

A first step in the design of the program structure is to list several alternatives for meeting each program objective. These might include bringing in outside faculty to lecture on topics related to the objective or using a case study that is related to the objective. Each alternative should be carefully considered, and the best ones should be incorporated into the design.

Identify Program Modules

The alternatives selected for meeting the program objectives will result in ideas for specific program sessions or modules. For example, a program objective for executives to better understand cost accounting principles suggests a tutorial session on cost accounting. An objective to make more effective use of group decision-making processes may indicate the need for one of the many group decision making simulations — for example, *Lost at Sea*.[3] While identifying the major components of the program, give some preliminary thought to content and teaching methods.

Establish Module Objectives

Three or four objectives should be defined for each module in the program. Each module objective must be congruent with the primary objectives of the program. The detailed development of program content will be based on these module objectives.

Construct a Program Map

A process that I have found to be very useful is to make a preliminary map of the program by writing on a 3 x 5 card the objectives, major activities, and notes on possible content for each module. These cards can then be arranged on a table or a large piece of cardboard or plywood as illustrated in Figure 9–2. To illustrate this mapping process, Figure 9–2 shows a number of the modules for a hypothetical four-day execu-

Executive Development

tive seminar on international business management. Each program module is represented by 3 x 5 cards placed on a larger sheet of paper or board. For example, on Monday a module entitled "Marketing Outside the U.S. — Opportunities, Competitors, and Customer Needs" has been scheduled for the 1030 to 1200 time frame. If a later decision is made to

Figure 9-2   A Typical Program Map

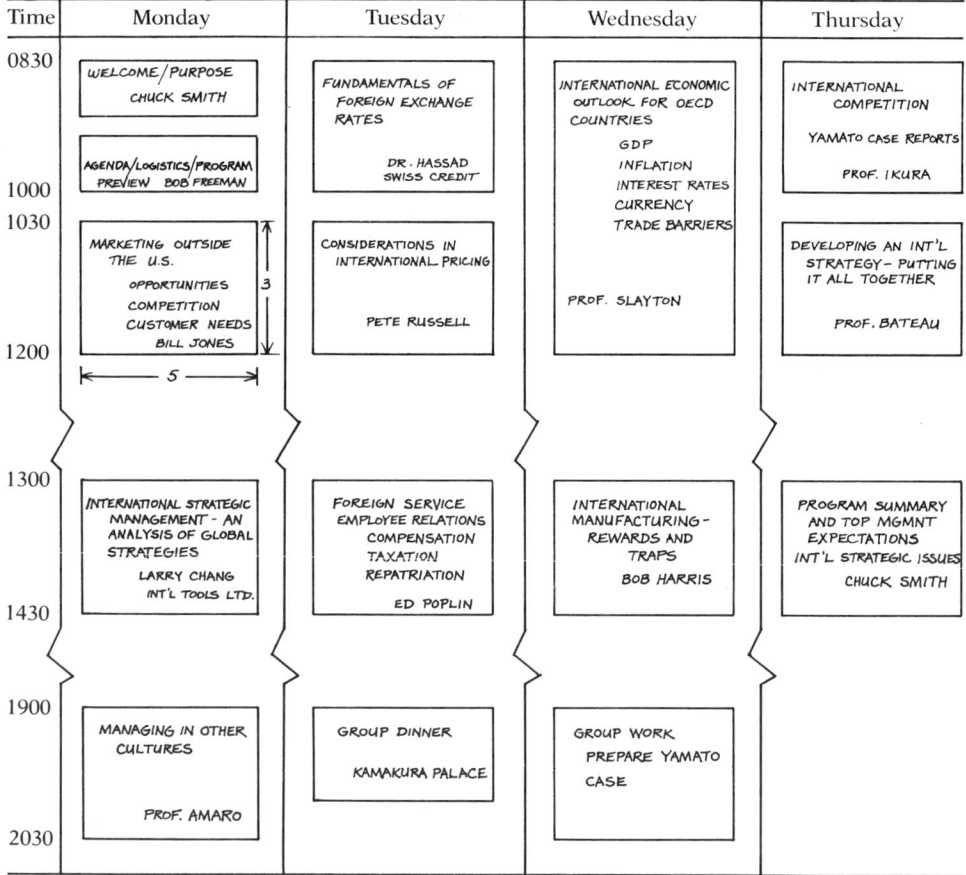

move this module to another day or time, cards can be shifted around as necessary. The program map is a way to develop a first draft of a program agenda in a manner that makes frequent adjustment easy to accomplish. Modules can be added, deleted, and moved in sequence by shifting the 3 x 5 cards. The cards can be trimmed vertically to correspond to session times, and multiple or enlarged cards can be used for sessions longer than a standard length.[4]

Produce Draft Agenda

Once you are finished moving the cards around the board and you feel that the structure is reasonably firm, a draft agenda can be typed.

Develop List of Objectives and Content Summary for Each Module

Because the design of the program structure is now at the stage where you will want it to be reviewed, a typed list of module objectives and a brief summary of the content to be included in each session should be prepared. Any other ideas for the modules — such as instructor candidates, applicable case studies, or group exercises — can be included.

Critique Preliminary Design

The draft agenda, module objectives, and content summaries should be distributed to those individuals whom you have selected to critique the design. Comments and suggestions that you decide to incorporate should be reflected in subsequent revisions.

Prepare Cost Estimates and Resource Needs

Although the design has probably not progressed sufficiently for detailed cost estimates, a tentative estimate should be prepared along with an estimate of the resources needed to finish the design and development of the program. A major decision is whether to proceed with the development of the program in-house or to contract with an outside organization.

Review With Top Management

A top management review is appropriate at this stage of the design effort. This is particularly important if resource needs turn out to be substantial. The next steps of the design will require substantial investment and commitment to instructors, and it is a good idea to make sure that top management is solidly behind your project. The project schedule should now be firm enough to establish some specific checkpoint meetings during the completion of the design phase and during actual program development. Future dates for project reviews with top management should also be established.

DEVELOPING SPECIFIC METHODS FOR MEETING MODULE OBJECTIVES

Designers of executive development programs have many teaching methods from which to choose. Methods to best meet individual session objectives should be chosen from the many alternatives available. Some consideration for program variety should also influence your decision. Figure 9–3 lists some advantages and disadvantages for common methods used in executive training programs. In addition to being aware of the advantages and disadvantages of the various teaching methods, executive development program designers need also to consider the following factors in making a choice from the methods listed in Figure 9–3.

Lecture

A lecture is often the best way to present tutorial material and can be effective when the presenter is carefully selected. In a program that includes both university faculty and line managers, the line managers will have a difficult time "compet-

Figure 9-3 Some Instructional Methods for Executive Development Programs

Method	Advantage	Disadvantage
Lecture	Simple logistics Low development cost Can use internal resources Outside lectures bring new viewpoints Dialogue is convenient Can take advantage of inexpensive visuals	Very skill dependent Can be dull Difficult to have group participation Difficult to replicate
Case Studies	Lots of group participation Simulates on-the-job conditions Brings out alternative points of view Based on actual situations Ease of integration with advance study Makes use of participants' existing base of knowledge Develops analysis and problem solving skills	Instructor dependent Some participants find internalization difficult Case selected may not be relevant Requires significant time per teaching point Case may be difficult to transfer to company's situation
Group Work	Learning from each other Active participation Develops group discussion skills Develops presentation skills	May require facilitator Requires additional rooms and equipment, e.g., flip charts Groups can get "off the track" Requires very specific instruction on expectations
Test and Examinations	Feedback to participants and instructors on participant learning When designed right can check learning success	Difficult to cover the curriculum in total Can demotivate Difficult to design
Advance Study	Increases entry-level knowledge and avoids unnecessary review of basics Previews the learning experience Advance preparation allows more effective use of class time Can contribute significantly to total learning experience	Requires time commitment from participant Creates additional materials expense Additional design time to assure relevance
Computer Methods	Can be used as auxiliary tool to facilitate learning, e.g., spreadsheets Possible to simulate actual situation "What if" scenario analysis	Hardware cost for adequate accessibility Software development investment
Video	Program consistency Professionalism Brings remote speakers to the program Very useful as role-play and replay tool	Cost of professional production Needs proper viewing equipment (size, etc.)

ing" with university professors. Inside instructors will have to work hard to make their sessions interesting and well illustrated. It is usually a good idea to avoid lectures immediately following lunch and dinner. I can't remember an occasion when an after-dinner presentation contributed much to an executive development program that I attended, designed, or conducted.

Case Studies

Most executives have already experienced case work in their university studies or in seminars conducted at universities. It is the most commonly used method in university executive training seminars and is a very popular method in company seminars using university professors as instructors. Company instructors can make excellent use of cases designed specifically for their sessions, but they need to put some extra effort into preparing the case. It is critical that the instructor know the content of the case. This is easy when the instructor has played a role in developing the case as part of the program development process, but becoming thoroughly familiar with the case when teaching it "cold" requires considerable effort. It is also important that the company instructor realize that most of the learning comes from the discussion and that most of the discussion comes from the participants not the case leader. The case leader needs to stimulate the discussion, know the right questions to ask, and guide the discussion process.

Group Work

The value of group activity in a program is based on recognizing that the participants themselves are an important learning resource. To be effective, however, group activity needs some focus and structure. The program designer needs to carefully select the objectives for proposed group activity and to design the activity to address these objectives.

Tests and Examinations

I have used exams in executive training programs with mixed results. A summary exam was a regular part of HP's first general management training seminar, and it covered what we thought were the eighteen or twenty key topics included during the week-long program. It allowed the participants to see whether they could recall these major points and the staff to see if the instruction process was getting the major content points across. Whether it contributed to the executives doing a more effective job was not measured. I doubt that it did. Results of the exam were given only to the participants, and I used it to see what points in the curriculum seemed to warrant more attention. For this reason I think that examinations in executive programs are most useful to program managers and of little use to the participants themselves. The exams were eventually discontinued.

Advance Study

A significant problem for executive development program developers is that every attendee comes to the program at different levels of knowledge and skill. Yet the program design needs to make some assumptions about where to begin. If the level is too low, attendees are bored and perhaps insulted. If too high, many of the participants will miss much of the learning presented. One way to assure that participants enter the program at a more common level of knowledge and understanding is to precede the program with a relatively thorough advance study program. This study program should include a presentation of the fundamentals that underlie the topic areas to be addressed in the seminar. At HP we regularly assigned about forty hours of advance study for a week-long seminar, and the vast majority of the attendees completed the assignments. Our executives genuinely believed that they needed to make a personal investment of their time to adequately prepare for the program.

Computer Methods

Computers can be used as both tools to facilitate learning and as learning devices themselves. In programs dealing with financial topics, computers can be used to explore "what if" scenarios. They can take some of the labor out of analyzing the financial aspects of a case study, and this leaves more time for dealing with important strategic issues. Computer simulations are excellent tools for developing skills in strategic management and business operations.

Video

Television presents an opportunity to enliven sessions with more professionally prepared materials. In-house produced videos can be used to include instruction from individuals who may not be able to personally appear at the seminar, such as an executive from overseas. It also can provide a measure of consistency in programs run frequently with different session instructors. A video segment covering the essential points for the session can be used by all instructors.[5]

DEFINING MODULE CONTENT AND IDENTIFYING CONTENT EXPERTS

A challenge for the designer of executive development programs is to ensure that up-to-date content is designed into the program. In addition, it is desirable to get the best people in their fields to participate in the program, either as instructors or consultants on program content. If these people are available within the company, you should enlist their help and support. Usually, significant research is necessary to identify appropriate content and sources.

Business and professional journals are an excellent resource for the latest thinking on management topics. *The Harvard Business Review*, the *California Management Review*, and the *Sloan Management Review* are excellent content sources and also identify individuals who are actively researching this content. Reprints from these journals make excellent prestudy material. Harvard professors have written thousands of case studies and teaching notes that are used extensively in executive development programs, and an annual index of these materials is available from the Harvard Business School.

Executive development professionals can benefit from relationships that they are able to build with faculty from business schools. Every effort should be made to expand these contacts and to build a network that will help you keep up to date with what is currently happening in executive education. Contacts with executive development professionals in other companies are a valuable method for staying up to date. Participation in the activities of the American Society for Training and Development is another good way to build an information network.

Once content has been researched the designer has the necessary background information to make decisions on content to be included in the program. It is advisable to make decisions on instructors as early as possible because they should contribute toward the design of their sessions. Once an instructor is selected, an early meeting to discuss program content should be scheduled. At this time any advance study materials and assignments for the instructor's session can be determined.

The effectiveness of the executive development programs that I designed was due in large measure to the close relationships that we were able to establish with a number of faculty from the Stanford Graduate School of Business. We valued these relationships tremendously and tried to show our appreciation by respecting their time and paying their fee on the day that they actually taught their session. Many organizations wait to pay their faculty until they receive an invoice, but we always felt that this was expecting the professor to spend time and effort preparing an invoice when we already had all the information needed to make the payment. Sometimes it requires some leaning on members of the accounting department to get them to understand why payment must be made on "delivery," but this effort pays big dividends in developing a positive relationship with valuable members of your instructor corps.

FINALIZING THE EXECUTIVE PROGRAM AGENDA

The next steps in program design are to consolidate all the inputs received in the previous steps, synthesize the final agenda, and decide where to conduct the program. Almost always there will be too much content for the time allotted for the seminar, and some materials will have to be trimmed or cut out entirely. Use the program objectives as the guide for this pruning task. In finalizing the agenda, put yourself in the shoes of a participant. Ask yourself if you will be overwhelmed by the content, and if so, allow some free time during the program for attendees to study and digest what they have already received. Look for ways that you can more effectively use evening sessions. Group exercises are a nice change of pace to end a long day. To help you establish the final agenda, it is a good idea to get some advice from some members of the executive team who are familiar with your project.

The decision where to actually run the program needs to be made well in advance of the scheduled date for the seminar. A number of factors should be considered in making the site selection, including the availability of a suitable facility at corporate headquarters and budget constraints. Figure 9-4 compares the advantages and disadvantages of on-site versus off-site seminars.

PROGRAM PACKAGING

The packaging of seminar materials should not be a last-minute decision. Careful attention should be given to overall program appearance. It is desirable for your materials to have a consistent format and design. It should appear as if the materials are part of an overall strategy rather than part of some hodge-podge collection. Use color wherever possible and incorporate illustrations. Convince your participants that you really care about the appearance of their materials. If your organization already has a standard format for management and executive training materials, it should be followed. Otherwise spend some time on a suitable design. Find someone with artistic talent to take what are often rather dull materials and jazz them up a bit.

Almost ten years ago my boss, who apparently felt that some of our materials lacked the qualities mentioned above, offered me the services of one of HP's top graphic designers on a temporary basis. This individual assembled examples of all of our existing training materials and had them photographed. He developed some alternative designs and made mock-ups that were also photographed. He asked for a meeting of the department management team where he could present his findings and recommendations. I will never forget the dramatic impression made by his 35MM slides of materials as they existed and as proposed. A new, consistent design was initiated based on his recommendations.

There are a number of significant advantages to using ring binders for program materials, particularly for leaders'

Figure 9-4   Program Location — On Site Versus Off Site

	Advantages	*Disadvantages*
On Site	More likely to have top management involvement (less travel) Less expensive Close proximity to training center staff and development specialists Have control of your own facility	Easy for attendees to be interrupted Local attendees may not participate in informal gatherings
Off Site	Away from telephones and interruptions More opportunity for informal interaction Local people don't go home Availability of recreational facilities	Some facilities have marginal rooms, limited break out rooms, and poor visual aid equipment Difficult to duplicate services of a well-trained in-house training center staff Usually more costly

guides and participants' manuals. Binders allow easy integration of article reprints, class notes, and handouts. They lay flat and are easy to use during sessions. Binders inventoried for later sessions of the same seminar are easily updated when changes need to be made. They come in all shapes, colors, and sizes and can be readily customized with your company's logo and the program title.

It is important to give some thought to the actual layout of the leaders' and participants' binders. The first consideration should be ease of use. Binders should be divided into logical sections with distinctive tabs. Session leaders must be able to rapidly find any materials used during their sessions, and participants must also be able to find relevant exhibits, group assignments, and other references needed during class. A good layout will make the participants' binder more valuable as a reference for use on the job. Tabs can be printed and coated with plastic for an added professional appearance. A printed title page can be designed for adding participants' names using a graphics plotter and personal computer.

There are an infinite number of ways to lay out the binder sections. The program agenda, table of contents, and logistical information are usually put at the front of the binder. The remaining sections might follow by topic area, for example, marketing, economics, leadership, finance, and so forth. Alternatively it might be helpful to have the layout according to the order of individual sessions. An example layout for a typical executive development program is shown in Figure 9–5.

There are few things more irritating to an attendee than an overstuffed binder with half of the material falling out because the rings won't close properly. Avoid this frustration by providing binders that will hold all of the materials used during the seminar. With a little advance planning the right size binders can be provided. There is nothing wrong with having more than one volume, but you will need to plan ahead early in the design and development process. The only sure way to plan for the correct size is to have an accurate page count for *all* items that will eventually be put in the binder. Don't forget handouts, previously distributed advance study materials, and notes taken during the sessions. To be on the safe side, specify one size larger than you think you will need.

Leaders' materials should be designed to maximize the success of the instructor and therefore the overall effectiveness of the session for the participants. I favor making maximum use of line managers as instructors in executive development programs, and these individuals need your assistance in conducting an effective session. Leaders' guides should be designed for ease of use while in front of the class. Every effort should go into making the experience a rewarding one for the instructor, especially if you want the executive to teach in one of your seminars on a regular basis. The format of leaders'

Figure 9-5 **Binder Layout for Typical Executive Development Program in International Business Management**

Section	Contents
Agenda	Program Agenda List of Participants Program Objectives
Logistics	Group and Evening Assignments Messages and Obtaining Assistance Instructor Biographical Summaries
International Marketing Strategic Management International Cultures International Finance Human Resource Management Economics International Manufacturing Global R&D	Module Objectives for Each Session Exercises Session Handouts Session Notes
Miscellaneous	Notes and Other Materials Collected during the Seminar

guides should be consistent, so that instructors do not have to relearn the layout with each new course.

A STRATEGY EXAMPLE: A MANAGEMENT SEMINAR FOR SENIOR EXECUTIVES

Many of the steps in designing an executive development program can be illustrated by a program designed for senior executives at Hewlett-Packard. The original need for this program arose from the fact that many senior executives had not been to any formal executive training since they had attended the basic general management program some three or four years earlier. These individuals expressed a desire for a refresher course. The company had also grown very rapidly in the latter half of the 1970s, and a number of new divisions had been added. Several members of the top management team expressed a concern that many of the division managers were focusing so heavily on their divisions that they had lost some perspective for issues facing the company as a whole. These two basic needs stimulated a project to develop an advanced training program for senior executives.

I decided to manage this project and asked Bob LeDuc, at the time our manager of management development and previously on the faculty of the Harvard Business School, to co-develop this program with me. To participate in the needs analysis and preliminary design, we created a short duration task force made up of an executive vice-president and group and division general managers. This task force met on several occasions over a three-month period to advise us on program needs and comment on some early design ideas. During this period, program needs were discussed with a representative cross-section of general management. Program objectives were established and approved by top management.

The need to design and develop a refresher program was relatively easy to address, as curriculum needs could be met by a general updating on business economics, the environment in which we were managing, and new strategic issues that had surfaced during the past few years. The need to get

Executive Development Program Design

division-level managers to look beyond their particular division was more challenging. We needed to figure out a way to get the division general managers to participate in strategy development at the corporate level.

Two summers earlier I had the chance to sit through several sessions of an executive management program run by the University of Hawaii. One of the visiting professors in this seminar was Dr. Howard Perlmutter of the Wharton School, University of Pennsylvania. Professor Perlmutter conducted a session on the importance of scenario design to executive actions. At the time I had thought that scenario design might be a topic to include in a future executive development program. This was perhaps a way to address the program objective for getting general managers thinking beyond their own business unit. One approach would be to have program participants construct a scenario for the future and a corresponding strategy for optimizing total corporate performance in the environment created by the scenario. A subsequent meeting with Professor Perlmutter resulted in his participation in the seminar.

The design approach decided on was to bring in some outside speakers who could address what were some likely scenarios for international economics, social forces, political forces, customer expectations, trends in technology, competitive trends, and so forth. Based on these presentations, seminar groups were asked to develop scenarios for the next ten years. On completion of scenario design, each group was asked to put themselves in the shoes of the chief executive officer and develop a strategy for the entire corporation. The objective for the strategy was to optimize corporate performance in the scenario they chose as being most likely. In doing this we hoped to get the participants to think beyond their own individual business entity. The design was approved, the program was developed, the instructors were chosen, and the first seminar was conducted.

Early in the design the decision was made to run the program in house. We wanted to make it convenient for the numerous instructors who were senior managers at corporate headquarters. We also wanted to encourage maximum interaction between seminar participants and top management in the social events surrounding the instruction. Adequate facilities were available in the corporate training center, and logistics could be managed by a very competent staff.

Although judged to be quite effective by the participants, an analysis of the outcome of the first seminar indicated that executives required more knowledge and skill in strategy formulation. To meet this need, Dan Thomas, at the time a Stanford Business School professor specializing in strategic management, was invited to participate in the program to conduct sessions on the fundamentals of strategic management. This was the last major change to the program, which continued to run for several years.

The major lesson learned from this experience was that often the final design of a program cannot evolve until a session or two has been conducted. It is difficult for executives to identify every real need before the program is developed and run for the first time. The task force that helped to guide our efforts consisted of some of the top managers in the company, but the need for tutorial sessions on strategy was a need that was only identified after the program was actually run. This tends to support my assertion at the beginning of the chapter that executive development program design is an iterative process, and one should not be afraid to try what appears at first to be needed and then be willing to modify the design from the experience. The next chapter outlines the principal steps required to take a program design into the development and production phases.

REFERENCES

1. The term *objective* is used synonymously with the term *goals*, following the convention established in the discussion of strategy in Chapter 2.
2. For a detailed treatment of training objectives, see Robert F. Mager, *Preparing Instructional Objectives*, Belmont, Calif., Fearon Publishers, 1972.

3. *Lost at Sea* is a group decision-making exercise available from University Associates, Inc., San Diego, California.
4. At Hewlett-Packard we tried to standardize on a session length of ninety minutes. A typical morning could contain two of these sessions from 8:30 A.M. to 12:00 with a thirty-minute break between sessions. Sessions requiring additional time could either start at 8:00 A.M. or standard sessions could be linked together.
5. For a more detailed description of the use of computer methods and video in executive training programs, see Appendix C.

CHAPTER **10**

PROGRAM DEVELOPMENT AND PRODUCTION

The starting point for translating an executive development program design into a finished program is the formulation of an overall plan and schedule for developing, testing, and packaging the content. This chapter will outline the steps necessary for effective management of an executive development project, offer some suggestions for successful program development, and review the key considerations for producing a deliverable program.

Figure 10–1 is a checklist of things that the manager of executive development must consider from the outset of the development activity.

OVERALL PROJECT MANAGEMENT

Project management responsibility must be clearly assigned. One individual needs to manage the many diverse activities of the project and be accountable for the results. For a large program, a project team consisting of the project manager and several training and development specialists must be formed.

If the project manager did the needs analysis and designed the program, the transition to program development will be a logical extension of the design. If not, the needs analysis and design rationale should be discussed with whoever was responsible for that activity. It is essential to have complete session objectives, a tentative agenda, a list of potential instructors, preliminary session content, and the proposed project schedule prior to beginning detailed program development.

Give first priority to the project schedule and staffing needs. The schedule obviously is affected by the number of staff members to be deployed on the project, and it is important to clear up any questions on staff availability as quickly as possible. The staff assigned to the project is also dependent on how much of the program is to be developed in house and how much by outside contractors and consultants. In arriving at this decision, consider the points summarized in Figure 10–2.

The decision does not have to be for either in-house *or* outside development. To the extent that the program deals with company strategy and other proprietary information, in-house development may be essential. For those sessions that do not require stringent security, it may be possible to subcontract the development. Some companies establish long-term relationships with outside consultants to assist in the design and development of executive training programs. The relationship is based on mutual trust, and work done by the consultant is treated as thoroughly confidential and private. During the relationship the consultant is able to become socialized into the company environment and culture. The consultant can gain an understanding of the strategic issues

Figure 10-1   Checklist for Executive Development Program Development and Production

- ☐ Project Management Responsibility
- ☐ The Make or Buy Decision
- ☐ Staffing Assignments
- ☐ The Project Schedule
- ☐ Project Checkpoints
- ☐ Project Reviews
- ☐ The Project Budget
- ☐ Module Development Task Forces
- ☐ Material Selection
- ☐ Media Selection
- ☐ Organization of Content Materials and Files
- ☐ Writing and Editing
- ☐ Integration of Outside Materials
- ☐ Development of Leaders' Materials
- ☐ Relationships with Support Services
- ☐ Material Publication and Reproduction
- ☐ Media Production
- ☐ Content Testing and Pilot Runs
- ☐ Materials Distribution

Program Development And Production

facing an organization and yet maintain an outside perspective that is often extremely helpful to the top management team.

STAFFING ASSIGNMENTS

What kind of experience is best for project team members? Is training experience, content knowledge, or operational experience more valuable? Ideally some mixture of the three should be sought. At HP I assembled our training and development staff from people with experience in personnel administration, training, and line management. Finding any one individual with a strong background in all these areas is rare. I first looked for people with experience in management training, particularly the processes that result in effective learning. I also wanted to include on our staff people with line management experience within the company, as it is difficult to build credibility with a group of managers when you have never managed a team.

A significant amount of content knowledge was provided by many of the people whom we brought into our department. The people from training or personnel administration brought expertise in the areas of group processes, motivation, and organizational behavior. Individuals who

---

Figure 10-2 **The Make or Buy Decision**

A. Some Advantages of In-House Development
  1. Consistency with Organization's Culture
  2. Security
  3. Ownership of the Program by the Organization
  4. Taking Advantage of In-House Best Practices

B. Some Advantages for Development by Consultants or Outside Training and Development Firms
  1. Does Not Require Ongoing Staff and Support Expense
  2. Avoids "Reinventing the Wheel"
  3. Likely to Conserve Time
  4. Exposure to Outside Ideas and Practices

came from the line brought experience in effective leadership and the functional skills of marketing, engineering, manufacturing, and finance. This content knowledge was supplemented as necessary by directly involving line managers in program development as members of module development task forces.

In selecting training and development specialists to work on executive development program projects, remember that these individuals will frequently work closely with top management and the executive team. They will represent you and your department. Pay careful attention to the following criteria for staffing decisions.

- Ability to work effectively with all levels of management in a consultative mode, both individually and in a group;
- Demonstrated skills in effective oral and written communication;
- Possession of superior classroom training skills;
- Educational background or experience that provides a solid foundation in basic business management principles;
- Experience in applying adult learning theory to management and executive development;
- Evidence of motivation toward high levels of achievement.

THE PROJECT SCHEDULE, CHECKPOINTS, AND PROJECT REVIEWS

The project schedule is a critical tool for effective management of an executive development project. In basic form it is a simple time line of all major activities to be accomplished during the development phase. The schedule should be updated as necessary and distributed to all development team members as well as top management. Figure 10–3 is an abbreviated project schedule for the executive development program in international management used as an illustration in the last chapter.

The project should be divided into logical chunks or modules. The completion of a module or, alternatively, a logical grouping of modules can mark a significant checkpoint in the development process. Checkpoints may include final selection of media to be used, completion of leaders' materials, release of materials for publication and duplication, and pilot run. Whatever checkpoints are chosen, they should be clearly identified on the project schedule with specific target dates.

Development projects should be reviewed on a regular basis. I favor a comprehensive review at least four times during the project life and, for a project lasting longer than about nine months, a review every eight weeks. Avoid scheduling reviews to coincide with checkpoints, as a delay in completing the activity defining the checkpoint would also delay the review. Project reviews should be scheduled for specific dates regardless of project status.

The project manager should conduct the project review and invite participation from the individuals responsible for program modules. I recommend that everyone participating in the development effort be present at the review, including the support people who will later play a major role in producing the final materials for distribution. The review should begin with an overall status report from the project manager, followed by status reviews of each module. Key topics to present are the general approach to the development of the module, examples of specific content and methods for presenting the content, estimated completion date, and any issues that may affect the quality of the module or the actual completion date. The climate of the meeting must encourage idea and information interchange rather than excessive critique. The review process should provide everyone with a status report and an opportunity for constructive discussion on maximum program effectiveness. Attention must be focused on the right issues.

Figure 10-3 Format for Executive Development Project Schedule

Module Number and Title / Checkpoint	1 Welcome and Purpose	2 Agenda	3 Marketing Outside the United States	4 International Strategic Management	5 Managing in Other Cultures	6 Fundamentals of Foreign Exchange	7 International Pricing	8 Foreign Service Employee Relations	N Additional Modules
Objectives	Complete	Complete	Mar 3	Apr 4	Mar 10	Etc.			
Outline	Aug 1	Aug 1	Apr 11	Apr 18	Mar 24				
Research Complete	NA	NA	May 2	May 9	Apr 11		Etc.		
Design Complete	NA	NA	May 2	Jun 6	May 2				
Final Content	Aug 1	Aug 1	Jun 6	Jun 20	Jun 6			Etc.	
Advance Study Assignments	NA	NA	May 2	Jun 20	Jun 6				Etc.
Media Complete	NA	Aug 1	Jun 6	Jul 11	NA				
Leader's Outline	Aug 15	Aug 22	Jul 18	Jul 11	Jul 18				
Pilot Run/Test	NA	NA	Jul 25	Jul 25	Jul 25				
Final Materials	NA	Aug 1	Aug 1	Aug 8	Aug 1				
Leader's Guide	Aug 15	Aug 22	Aug 8	Aug 8	Aug 1				
Materials Reproduction	NA	Aug 15	Aug 15	Aug 15	Aug 15				

Program Development And Production

The executive development program checklist, shown in Figure 10–4, is another useful tool for managing an executive development project, particularly the activities critical to program production and implementation. The checklist was designed for the international management program example of Chapter 9 and covers major activities from program development to implementation with an emphasis on specific tasks that are critical to the successful running of a seminar. The checklist includes columns for completion dates, a description of the activity, and the person responsible for activity completion. The date column shows actual date as well as the number of weeks before the start of the seminar. A similar checklist is very useful for managing programs that are to run more than once. Individual checklists can be prepared for each seminar with appropriate activity dates.

THE PROJECT BUDGET

If your accounting system has provisions for accumulating and reporting actual expenses associated with the development project, a formal project budget will usually be required. The largest expense category is usually salaries and benefits for the training and development staff unless most of the work is contracted out. In that case it is necessary to budget for consulting services. Other major expenses are textbooks and materials used in the seminar and as advance study. For textbooks, deal directly with the publisher. Most publishers offer institutional discounts to companies buying even small quantities of textbooks for executive training programs. Outside faculty fees are another substantial expense. The costs of meals, refreshments, facilities, and living accommodations are also significant expense items. Travel and lodging expenses are frequently billed back to the location of the attendee, but be sure that you understand the practice in your organization.

Many companies do not formally account for program development expenses against a particular project. All expenses are lumped together under the training director's lo-

Figure 10-4 Executive Development Program Checklist

Week	Ending	Activity	Responsibility
−20	Apr 11	Confirm dates with session instructors	Program Manager
−18	Apr 25	Purchase textbooks, cases, and other materials Typeset preliminary agenda	Program Manager Support Person
−17	May 2	Select participants/obtain approval Prepare participant invitation letter Schedule classrooms Confirm hotel accommodations for attendees	Program Manager Program Manager Program Manager Support Person
−14	May 23	Invite participants Confirming letters to instructors	Program Manager Support Person
−12	Jun 6	Send advance study materials and logistics information to participants	Support Person
−8	Jul 4	Finalize all curriculum materials Send second mailing to participants including instructor biographies and any additional assignments	Program Manager Support Person
−6	Jul 18	Send second mailing to instructors	Support Person
−4	Aug 1	Produce master participant binder Reproduce all participants' materials Select menus Final mailing to participants with final agenda and last minute information Final mailing to instructors	Program Manager Support Person Support Person Support Person Support Person
−2	Aug 15	Invite appropriate executives to social events Request stipend checks for outside faculty Develop logistical notes	Program Manager Support Person Program Manager
−1	Aug 22	Assemble participants' binders Assemble session handouts Produce name cards Write faculty introduction cards	Support Person Support Person Support Person Program Manager
Day Before Seminar Week		Arrange seminar room/breakout rooms	Program Manager

cation. Even when the accounting department provides no formal report, it is still a good idea to keep track of actual costs for developing the program. This can be done by keeping track of the major expenses outlined above. An estimate accurate to within 10 percent is usually adequate. This information is useful in preparing future budgets and is a way to remind everyone working on the project that cost control is important.

USE OF MODULE TASK FORCES

Successful executive development efforts are always "owned" by the executive team. To build ownership, get executives directly involved in the development of the program. One method for doing this is by asking executives to participate in module development task forces. These task force members are able to contribute their knowledge, experience, and best practices to the curriculum and provide overall guidance on content matters.

The success of the task force approach is based on getting the right executives to participate. Top management can be of assistance on this. It is particularly helpful to have a member of top management championing the development of the program. For example, the logical champion for an executive development program on manufacturing strategy and methods is the vice-president of manufacturing. Champions will be aware of executives within the company who have developed best practices that should be included in the seminar. They can help you enlist these people for service on module task forces.

Should you decide to follow the module task force approach on your project, start by designating the training and development specialist responsible for the module as the task force chairperson. Include on this task force training and development specialists working on other modules because this will ensure program cohesiveness. Task force members should include executives who will contribute program content and any consultants or outside faculty involved in the module. The executives on the task force may have suggestions for others who could make significant contributions.

The task force chairperson must employ assertive leadership. It is common for executives to like to share their ideas but not want to be saddled with committing their thoughts to writing. Task force work by busy managers is often eclipsed by other pressing demands, and the chairperson must be willing to occasionally crack the whip to refocus attention. The chairperson is responsible for keeping task force activity moving forward. Members must occasionally be reminded of their responsibilities and commitments to the development of the module.

SELECTION OF MATERIALS AND MEDIA

During the design phase of the project, a number of ideas for program content are generated, and development of some of the content may even have started. Some materials may have been tentatively selected. During the development phase, final selections must be made.

The primary sources for program content are

- College and university faculty and the curriculum base for courses in general and functional management;
- The existing experience and expertise of the executives and functional specialists within your organization;
- Current research studies and reports on management and functional skills;
- Professional and trade organizations;
- Executives in other organizations.

The problem in program development is usually not insufficient content. The trick is selecting the most relevant content for your program objectives. Contacts in other companies and in universities can be of help in the sorting process. They are also an excellent source for content and materials ideas. For example, when I was interested in investigating a program in international business management, a colleague in another company and two professors at the Stanford Graduate School of Business were very helpful to me in establishing some contacts with faculty at Japanese universities.

Selecting materials requires several iterations of searching, evaluating, testing, and adapting. This usually proves to be the most time-consuming process in the program development task. It is important to maintain a balance between theory that is applicable to your program and proven practice. This is another reason why executives in your own company should be involved in the program development process. Test your ideas for content and materials on a sample of your executives.

Media selection, especially video and film productions, requires care. Much commercially available media will not exactly meet your specific needs, and a decision must be made whether a seminar module can be adjusted to use the media. Producing your own video media is expensive but may be worth the cost if the production is to be used in numerous seminar sessions. If you decide to produce your own video, acquire the services of a professional television producer with experience in industrial and educational television.[1]

More common media — such as overhead transparencies, 35MM slides, and illustrations for participants' manuals — need attention too. These items should be prepared professionally because they directly bear on the learning experience and testify to the overall quality of your program. Think of the seminar participants as your customers, and select media and materials that will benefit them.

CONTENT DEVELOPMENT

Most of the activities discussed up to now are the fun part of the development job. Sitting down to actually write the content is the tough part. Content generation proceeds more smoothly when you organize yourself for the task. The following ideas have been of help to me in generating executive development program content.

Organization

When the agenda is firm and objectives are established for each module, set up a file for each module and a set of ring binders for participants' materials, instructors' materials, materials to be sent out as advance study, and items to be handed out during the sessions. The module file folders are a convenient place to keep content ideas, articles dealing with content, outlines of the session, correspondence, and miscellaneous notes. Figure 10–5 shows a method for organizing files for a typical executive development project.

As draft material is generated for each module, it should be placed in the appropriate ring binder depending on whether it is material for prestudy, for the participants' binder, for handouts, or for a leader's guide. Each binder should be tab indexed with the name of the module. As the materials are refined and put into final form, each binder becomes a prototype for the final set of program documentation.

Most writers today use personal computers for word processing. It is a good idea to set up a file for your discs by seminar module. I prefer using a separate disc for each module, but this is a personal choice. My backup copies, however, contain several modules per disc.

Writing and Editing

Although a discussion of writing is beyond the scope of this book, there are some points that should be considered by developers of training and development programs. Materials need to be organized in a logical, step-by-step fashion with the needs of the learner foremost in mind. Simplicity, clarity, and relevance should be paramount. Choice of words and style should be consistent with the group that will read the

Figure 10-5 Executive Development Program Project File Organization

	File Folders	Participants' Materials Binder	Advance Study Binder	Session Handout Binder	Leaders' Materials Binder
Format	Manila file for each program module	Ring binder(s) with index tab for each module plus program objectives, agenda, logistical information, group and evening assignments.	Ring binder tabbed for assignment list, books and articles, and other materials	Ring binder(s) tabbed for each module	Ring binder(s) (1 for each module) tabbed by module sections, overhead slide copies, handouts, and advance study
Typical Content	Module outline Module content references and articles Content ideas Module task force meeting notes Correspondence relating to module	Draft of materials for final participants' binders Final participants' materials when complete	All materials used for advance study	Copies of all handouts	Draft of leaders' materials Copies of handouts and advance study materials Final leaders' materials when complete
To be Used For	General reference file on the project	Prototype participants' binder	Reference	Reference	Prototype leaders' guide

material. The materials advertise the professionalism of the program developers.

Major considerations should be *transferability* and *translatability*. The materials should be written with sufficient examples and illustrations to make it relatively easy for the reader to transfer the points being made back to his or her job situation. It is extremely important to consider executive participants whose native language is different from yours. Slang and uncommon idiom should be avoided.

I was always surprised by the fact that so many training and development specialists with excellent educational backgrounds wanted to rely heavily on editors. Perhaps writing skills are not stressed enough in universities. It is important to staff your organization with individuals who can express their thoughts clearly in writing. By writing your materials correctly the first time, many editing delays and expenses can be avoided. The services of an editor can be helpful in providing consistency and uniformity from module to module, but they should not be used as a crutch by developers unwilling to put sufficient effort into their writing.

Integration of Outside Materials

The use of outside materials can add significantly to the effectiveness of executive training programs. Thought must be given to integrating these materials into the program. Materials used for advance study need to be explained in the study assignment, particularly how they relate to the situation in your company. The relevance of outside materials handed out during the session should be discussed by the instructor. Quotes included in the body of curriculum materials need to be properly footnoted, and copyrights need to be stringently observed. Questions concerning the use of copyrighted material should be either directed at the copyright holder or discussed with your legal department. It is a relatively simple process to obtain permission to reprint sections of copyrighted material that pertain to your project. Copyright law is complex and should not be interpreted by training and development specialists. All staff members need to be aware of the importance of respecting the work of others.

Preparing Final Drafts

Take every opportunity to solicit comments from other session developers and content experts on early drafts of session materials. As soon as your materials meet your session objectives, are well written, and integrate into the program as a whole, it is time to quit the editing process and prepare the final draft for production. A decision must be made to either print the materials or duplicate copies from a final manuscript. There are many formats for printing, and the services of an experienced layout person should be employed. Laser printing is becoming very popular and has the advantage that the materials can be printed directly from your central computer or from a personal computer. If you will be using a laser printer, it is necessary to follow the proper formatting procedures while the final draft copy is being input to the terminal or personal computer.

Participants' Materials

In addition to content materials needed during program sessions and seminar logistical data, participants' binders should include brief biographical sketches of the program instructors, especially outside faculty. Even if this information was distributed with the advance study, it should be included in the binder. When I first began to manage executive programs at HP, I found that I was spending considerable time reminding attendees about what they were supposed to be doing in group discussion sessions. I developed a simple checklist entitled "Group and Evening Assignments" and put a copy in the participants' binders. Each group session, scheduled as part of the regular agenda, and evening study period or event was listed chronologically by day, date, and time, and specific instructions were included beside each listing.

DEVELOPMENT OF LEADERS' MATERIALS

In addition to the basic design and development of the seminar, a major determinant of seminar success is instructor effectiveness. Every effort should be made to maximize their chances for success. When university faculty members are used, seminar managers are often reluctant to properly prepare the faculty for their sessions. It is easy to assume that they automatically know what to do to make their sessions successful. Being expert faculty gives them a significant advantage over line manager instructors, but they still need to be adequately prepared.

Detailed leaders' outlines should be prepared as soon as session content is firm. These outlines should include the following information:

- Overall objectives for the seminar;
- Session objectives;
- Relationship of the session to other sessions;
- References and prestudy assignments;
- Methods to be used during the session;
- Visual aids required;
- Detailed outline of the session content.

In developing the leaders' materials it is important to remember that emphasis should be placed on making the experience successful for the leader. If the materials don't help the instructor conduct a successful session, it is doubtful that you will be able to convince the leader to participate again. Pay particular attention to format. The materials should be typed in large, easy-to-read characters using a typeface like Orator. The outline should be clearly marked at points where overhead slides or other visuals are to be used. An innovative training and development specialist at HP came up with an idea for using a standard set of symbols to mark the leader's guide when it was time for an overhead slide, class discussion, questioning the participants, a videotape, and so forth. Some very effective leaders' outlines are typed on pages divided vertically into three columns — one for the method to be used for a particular section, the second column for the outline, and the final column for notes made by the leader during preparation.

CONTENT TESTING AND PILOT RUNS

Before finishing the development of the program, the content should be tested to see how well session objectives are met. If the program is scheduled to be conducted on a regular basis to a large target audience, it is worthwhile to schedule a pilot run with a representative sample of the target population. The objective of such a test is to simulate an actual class. Every effort should be made to conduct the pilot session in as real an environment as possible.

An alternative to a complete pilot run of the seminar is to test each seminar module individually with a smaller group of representative attendees. These tests should include members of module development task forces.

Things to look for in either a program pilot run or the testing of individual modules include the following:

- Are objectives achieved?
- Are materials effective?
- Are leaders' materials appropriate and effective?
- Is the media effective?
- What is the level of enthusiasm displayed by test participants?

In a one-shot seminar, it may not be practical to conduct a simulated test of the program or individual sessions. It is still possible to get a feeling for the effectiveness of the materials by asking managers from the target population to participate in an in-depth review of session content. The module development team can walk several managers through the content and observe their reactions. Although not as reliable a test method as an actual simulated run, much can be learned from this effort. At the conclusion of the test a thorough evaluation should be made and any necessary changes to the content, media, methods, or leaders' materials should be incorporated into the program.

PROGRAM PRODUCTION CONSIDERATIONS

On completion of program development, emphasis must shift to the critical phase of actual program production. So far, the prospective program exists only in the form of sheets of content, leaders' outlines, an assortment of handout material and article reprints, advance study assignments, and various logistical supplies. Now all of these materials must be turned into a deliverable program.

Liaison with Support Services

During the development phase of the project, regular meetings should be held with the individuals who will be responsible for printing and publishing the seminar materials. If your organization has an individual responsible for this effort, he or she needs to be included in the project review meetings. A number of decisions affecting materials production are made during program development, including size and number of participants' and leaders' binders, the color of materials, whether printed index tabs are to be included, labeling of binders, order quantities, and storage of purchased materials. These decisions need to be made in accordance with your project schedule, and many purchased items carry relatively long lead times.

Format, Typesetting, and Reproduction

For ease in reading, participants' materials are often commercially printed. This is particularly justified for programs with a large target audience. Program modules are typed in rough draft form and delivered to a professional reprotypist who typesets the module copy. A page layout designer works beside the module developer and the reprotypist to design the proper format for the module. I frequently used an outside graphics design consultant who was able to interface directly with content developers, illustrators, typesetters, and printers. Trying to do a major project without the help of a professional would be like trying to build a house without a general contractor.

Computer-based word processing systems have simplified the publishing task. Today it is common for program developers to input their materials directly into a computer. Subsequent editing and page formatting can be done on-line. Master copies of materials can be stored easily and retrieved for any necessary updating. Computer-prepared text stored on magnetic tape or floppy discs can be delivered to a commercial printer or printed on a laser printer. The results are professional-looking seminar materials. A number of computer manufacturers and software suppliers offer desk-top publishing systems that offer executive development program designers a new level of flexibility in program production.

Before you go out and purchase a word processing system, it is important to find out what systems are already available in your company for publication work. Effort spent on ensuring hardware and software compatibility can result in significant savings and increase the probability that someone in your company can provide help when needed. Developers that write and produce customer instruction manuals are frequently well equipped with computer-based publishing systems and staffed with knowledgeable people. Talk to them and benefit from their expertise.

Program materials often incorporate graphics within the text. Common examples are organization charts, graphs of financial performance, charts of market and competitor information, and so forth. Computer graphics programs should be used to create this data for reasons of both graphics quality and ease of storage, editing, and reproduction. Many word processing programs can integrate computer-prepared graphics into the text, and the integrated materials can be easily printed on a laser printer. Overhead slides for use in the seminar sessions can often be produced from the same graphics software by using an X-Y plotter.

Graphics and Media Production

Most executive development seminars make extensive use of overhead transparencies. It is possible to develop excellent overhead transparencies using software packages designed for personal computers and graphics plotters. A complete system is relatively inexpensive when compared to outside production of overhead slides, and this investment can be recovered rather quickly. It is easy for existing staff to learn to use these systems, and self-teaching programs are available.

There is considerable argument on the relative merits of overhead transparencies and 35MM slides. I can't add much to the debate except to describe how each was used in executive development seminars at Hewlett-Packard. Formal presentations incorporating photographs of manufacturing processes, new products, customer applications, and so forth were always more effective with 35MM slides, but a darkened room was required. We tried to minimize the use of 35MM when overhead slides would serve equally well. More effective learning takes place when there is a high level of participant interaction with the session leader. This interaction is more difficult to achieve in a darkened room. Most sessions in HP programs were conducted with overhead slides prepared on graphics plotters. The seminar room could remain at the ambient light level, slides could be annotated during the discussions, and a more informal discussion environment was preserved.

During the development phase it is also necessary to maintain close contact with the individuals responsible for developing television segments for your project. Television production people work extremely well from a set of detailed objectives for the segment. Let them do the creative work. Most television productions today are developed by electronically editing videotape footage that is shot on location or in a studio setting. The person responsible for the session incorporating video should try to be present during the videotaping to become familiar with the process being used to produce the television segment. During the editing phase, close cooperation between the seminar segment developer and television staff is essential.

Materials Management

Coordinating the specification, procurement, receiving, and consolidation of all materials going into an executive development program is not an easy job; the overall success of the project depends on no glitches in the process. Materials need to be purchased well in advance of their need, paying close attention to lead time on custom-designed items — such as silkscreened binders and printed divider tabs. Purchasing departments should be alert to discounts on books and other printed materials. Because books are frequently shipped at the cheapest rate, allowances need to be made for either early purchase or air delivery at higher cost.

The receiving departments in large organizations can sometimes create bottlenecks. Most receiving problems are related to improper paperwork. Purchase orders should be clearly marked with the name of the individual in the training department to whom the materials should be delivered. The program manager should maintain a file of all purchase orders and related correspondence, along with a tickler file to initiate expediting. Getting to know the people who work in purchasing and receiving can often lead to better service for the training department. Your success is tied to the services that these people provide.

I was surprised at the quantity of materials required to support just one executive training seminar. At HP we set aside a storeroom to hold these materials, and the room was sectioned into spaces for advance study materials, uncollated participants' and leaders' materials by session title, handouts for each session, and completed participants' and leaders' binders. Extra copies of all materials were inventoried because an extra copy or two were frequently needed during the course of a seminar. We kept the shipping boxes that the binders came in and put the collated binders back into them for storage.

Training departments can easily become loaded with outdated materials, old files that are no longer relevant, unnecessary references, and lots of miscellaneous clutter. At Hewlett-Packard I instituted an annual departmentwide clean-up day on the last day of the company's fiscal year, October 31. Department employees dressed in their old clothes, and a dozen or so trash barrels were situated strategically throughout the building. The day ended with a beer bust where prizes were awarded to the person disposing of the most trash, for the biggest improvement in a work area, and for other achievements that the clean-up day committee chose to recognize. Once each year we were able to clean out what was not needed and free up valuable space. Not only did this make the department a more attractive and efficient workplace, but it also saved the company money. At an occupancy charge approaching $3.00 per square foot per month, we did not want to have to invest in unneeded storage space.

Materials were collated into their binders well in advance of the seminar. An unscheduled classroom was turned into an assembly and collating room, popularly referred to as the bindery. Temporary help was used for much of this work, but a department employee was responsible for supervision and the quality of the finished binders. The program manager was responsible for assembling a sample binder to be used as a model for producing the others. This same manager was also responsible for checking the materials against the program design.

It is important to remember to punch materials that will be handed out during the sessions, otherwise it is difficult to insert them into the participants' binders. This represents a problem when session leaders bring their own handouts to the seminar. In addition to reminding session leaders to punch their handouts, we always kept a punch in each seminar room just in case.

A strategy for distributing program materials is an important component of your production plan. For centralized programs, the task is relatively simple because the only shipments to be made are normally advance study assignments to participants. In the United States, the use of UPS represents an excellent compromise between cost and delivery time for advance study materials. Leaders' guides for out-of-town instructors will need to be sent far enough in advance to allow time for instructor preparation. The other distribution challenge is to get everything to the seminar site when it is needed.

Programs implemented by entities in the field require more attention to materials distribution. Both instructors' and participants' materials are usually ordered from the corporate training department, and an order processing system should be set up. Procedures need to be established for billing decentralized sites when materials are shipped. An effective materials usage and inventory management system is required to make sure that orders can be expeditiously filled.

A balance needs to be reached between economies of central procurement versus the costs of shipping from a central site. It is usually less costly to procure books and articles locally, especially if a purchase contract is negotiated that allows multiple order and shipping points. The transmittal of materials via computer networks to laser printers at remote sites should also be considered. In any event top priority should be given to getting the materials to the decentralized sites in a complete and timely fashion. Economies that jeopardize material availability are false economies.

QUALITY ASSURANCE

To be a credible institution for teaching excellence in management, the training department should set an example by its own management excellence. Executive development managers and their organizations are on constant display to the senior management of the organization. The quality of the materials used in a training seminar, the quality of overall instruction, and the quality of program management will play a major role in how the training organization is evaluated by the executive team.

Program quality is a function of each step in the project beginning with program design. The principles of total quality control outlined in Chapter 6 can be quite easily applied to the process of designing, developing, producing, market-

Figure 10-6   Key Steps in Executive Development Programs

Design	Development	Production	Marketing	Implementation
Needs Analysis	Selection of Instructors	Purchase of Outside Materials	Program Launch	Invitations
Site Selection	Participants' Materials	Printing Quality	Program Literature	Confirm Accommodations
Room Scheduling	Instructors' Materials	Duplication Quality		Advance Study
	Audiovisual Quality	Accuracy of Material Collation		
	Accuracy of Visuals			

ing, and implementing an executive development program. By paying attention to each step in the project, superior quality can be achieved. The trick is to identify those critical factors throughout the project that will determine program success. Figure 10-6 is a simple checklist showing the key steps in each phase of the project. It can be used to develop specific performance measures.

The major contributors to program quality are the people involved in the project. It is impossible to overstress the importance of a close working relationship among all members of the project team. When the program is viewed by all as "our program," a significant step toward program excellence has been achieved.

The final two chapters outline processes for marketing your executive development efforts, running a specific program, and evaluating program effectiveness.

REFERENCES

1. See Appendix C for a detailed discussion of the use of television in executive development programs.

CHAPTER 11

MARKETING EXECUTIVE DEVELOPMENT

Earlier chapters have asserted that achieving success in executive development requires a high level of commitment from the top management team and the executives in your organization. There may have been an implied assumption that your CEO and the firm's executives will readily "buy in" to the strategy and programs that you propose. Suppose they don't. How do you go about obtaining the level of commitment that will assure success? What specific techniques will help you achieve that commitment?

This chapter argues for the importance of marketing to executive development efforts. The discussion will include an approach for defining specific marketing objectives, a review of some basic concepts and principles of marketing, how these principles can be applied to the marketing of executive development programs, and the necessary steps for developing a marketing plan.

APPRAISING WHERE YOU STAND AND SETTING MARKETING OBJECTIVES

The first step in gaining a strong commitment to your executive development activities is to assess where the concept of executive development is positioned relative to all the other activities going on in your organization. How much attention is being paid to executive development? What obstacles must you overcome? There are four measures to include in your assessment:

- The general level of *awareness;*
- The degree of *interest;*
- The extent to which the *benefits* are appreciated;
- The degree of actual *commitment.*

Awareness

If you have followed an approach to executive development strategy formulation similar to that outlined in Chapter 8, your top management team should be aware of your plans and the executive development tools available to the organization. If this approach was not followed, schedule a meeting with the CEO to assess awareness. Meet with other members of the top management team as well as several executives at lower levels. Your function is to help them be more successful and to make sure that they understand that. Remember that the level of awareness will fade with time, and your marketing plan must include the necessary activities that will reinforce it.

Level of Interest

When you approach executives with what you think is a really great program, don't be too surprised if they fail to share your excitement. Executives are paid to focus their attention on the many pressing issues of strategy implementation. Your executive development programs are usually not on their lists of the ten most critical things to worry about. Even when they show you the courtesy of listening to what you have to say, typical responses are:

- We already know this stuff.
- I can learn it better on the job.

- After we resolve our current problems, perhaps we will have time for some formal training next year.
- I had all this in business school.

Failing to Recognize the Benefits

Some executives may have a difficult time seeing how executive development can benefit their immediate job needs. Most people look at learning as an activity with longer-term payoff. Ideally, executives should have faith that the knowledge and skills acquired from an executive development program will help address critical operational issues in the near term. No one but the training director is going to take the time to convince executives that their development efforts can result in an immediate return.

Commitment

In marketing a product or service, the objective is the order. In marketing executive development efforts, the objective is commitment. It is important to identify the specific objections or reasons that are making it difficult to gain either top management or executive team commitment. Once these are identified, you can deal with them.

Marketing people have to face lack of commitment as a constant component of their jobs. They must operate with the philosophy that lack of commitment is only a temporary phenomena, and the majority of their time and effort is spent finding ways to overcome the many objections that customers raise. Sales presentations, promotional brochures, and advertising messages are designed to overcome customer objections. Many marketing techniques can be applied to building strong commitment for executive development, and training and development directors should learn how to use them. The following section will review some of these basic marketing principles and techniques.

ESSENTIAL ELEMENTS OF MARKETING FOR TRAINING AND DEVELOPMENT DIRECTORS

Marketing Begins with the Customer

Effective marketing is based on customers and their needs. A fundamental marketing concept is that customers do things for *their reasons, not yours.* A corollary to this concept is that customers purchase products or services based on *perceived benefits to them.* You may think that you have the greatest product or service in the world, but your opinion really doesn't count. It's no wonder that Tom Peters's and Nancy Austin's best seller, *A Passion for Excellence,* has five full chapters on customers.[1] The customer's opinion is everything.

It is important to recognize that the users of your product or service are not your only customers. Many people are typically involved in either approving the purchase decision or in some manner exerting strong influence. In developing a marketing strategy, it is necessary to consider all parties to the buying decision.

Years ago, when I first went into the field as a sales engineer for Hewlett-Packard, I stopped by a customer's facility one afternoon to pick up an order that was supposed to have been approved. Much to my surprise, I found that the decision had been made to purchase the equipment from a competitor. I had failed to cover the people who had ultimate approval authority for the purchase. It was an expensive lesson.

Sell Benefits, Not Features

An important marketing principle is to recognize the difference between a product or service *feature* and the *benefit* provided to the user. A feature — for example, the fact that your television set has remote control — is meaningful only to the extent that this feature provides a real benefit to the user. The benefit from remote control is the ability to change channels and sound level without having to get up and walk across the room. Easily identifiable user benefits should be the focus of a marketing effort.

Characteristics about the Product or Service that Must Be Addressed in a Marketing Plan

In marketing a product or service, there are a number of variables that need to be considered. Marketing textbooks usually refer to these variables as the marketing mix, and they include such things as product characteristics, price, distribution methods, promotion, and after-sales support.[2] Some marketing variables are controllable, such as price and product packaging, and the marketing strategy can precisely specify the variable. Strategies are developed to define these variables in a way that will maximize profitable sales of products and services to customers. For example, products are usually developed to provide the characteristics that market research data show are important to customers. The resulting products are described in a way that makes them appear superior to similar products marketed by competitors. Strategies for distribution are designed to make it easy for customers to purchase and receive products.

Three of the most important marketing variables are promotion, selling, and after-sales support. Promotion of the product is designed to convince prospective customers that the product or service will deliver the expected benefit better than competing brands or services. Advertising is used to position the product in a more attractive light than the product of the competitor. Because most products involve person-to-person discussion, firms support their overall marketing program with a concerted sales effort by well-trained people. Because the long-term viability of any business is based on creating repeat business, most companies give significant attention to helping the customer get maximum utilization from the product or service through training, application support, and fast and convenient repair service.

Some variables are uncontrollable, such as customer needs, competitors' actions, and the environment. These variables actually control the marketing strategy, and firms that ignore them seldom succeed. This concludes the general discussion about marketing. Now let's see how these principles can be applied to the marketing of executive development.

APPLYING MARKETING TECHNIQUES TO EXECUTIVE DEVELOPMENT

There are three critical questions to consider when formulating a marketing strategy for your executive development activities.

- Who are your customers or clients?
- What do you want them to do?
- What are the benefits provided?

Figure 11–1 shows the interrelationships between these factors and some suggested answers for a typical executive development effort.

Customers

For formulating a marketing strategy, it is useful to define two categories, or segments, of customers. The first is obviously the chief executive officer and the executives who report directly to the CEO. This group is responsible for setting the overall policies and operating agenda for the firm. Executive development will not be on their agenda unless the management team places it there. The other customer segment consists of the remaining executives in the organization. They are your consumers as well as important resources for developing and implementing programs.

What You Want Your Customers to Do

The first column of Figure 11–1 lists several key objectives for your marketing efforts for both the CEO and top management team and the executive team. These are the things for which you need to gain their commitment. They should be prioritized according to your earlier assessment of awareness, degree of interest, and sense of general commitment to executive development activity. For example, if your top management team generally provides the necessary resources

Marketing Executive Development

Figure 11-1 Executive Development Marketing — Customers, Objectives, and Benefits

	Objectives — What You Want Your Customers to Do	*Benefits Provided*
CEO and Top Management Team	1. Active Involvement 　Teach in programs 　Set expectations 　Set an example 2. Provide resources necessary for strategy implementation 　Facilities 　Operating expense 3. Provide Other Support 　Encourage developmental efforts 　Reward and reinforce development results	More knowledgeable and skilled team More success in strategy implementation Ability to more effectively cope with change Improved goal congruency Provides a framework for subsequent coaching Develops a tradition of continuous improvement Clarifies and communicates expectations Pride in a well-prepared executive team
Executive Team	1. Involvement in Program Development 2. Act as Instructors 3. Attend Programs 4. Promote Programs 5. Commit to Transfer of Learning to the Job	More knowledge and improved skills lead to organization and individual success An effective means for sharing best practices Teaching is an effective way to learn More effective interfunctional relationships Builds strong networks with other executives in the organization Establishes a framework for continual development Contribution to the development of others

and encouragement for executive development but seldom finds the time to actively participate in the programs, gaining this participation should head your list of marketing objectives.

Benefits Provided

Training and development departments provide two of the most sought-after products in existence — knowledge and skills. They are fundamental to achieving both individual and team success. Many years ago the founder of a large cosmetics company suggested that his company's product was beauty, not just cosmetics. In commenting about beauty he warned that it is a product so much in demand we have to be careful not to misrepresent it. The achievement of knowledge and skills commands a similar demand.

The righthand column of Figure 11–1 lists some of the major benefits for each of the objectives in the first column. These benefits answer the question, "Why should I do this?" For example, benefits that come from active involvement from top management include more succcessful strategy implementation, clearer communication of expectations, and a framework for continuous performance improvement.

Before attempting to persuade top management or executives to buy in to your proposals, spend some time thinking about the benefits from their perspective. Expand the list to include benefits that tie specifically to the strategic issues facing your organization. Use the benefits as the central theme of your personal selling efforts. The best strategy for overcoming an objection is to outweigh it with a substantial benefit.

MARKETING AN EXECUTIVE DEVELOPMENT PROGRAM

In addition to the need to market the overall executive development strategy, it is also necessary to develop marketing plans for specific programs. Figure 11–2 is a convenient

Figure 11-2 Program Marketing Checklist

Marketing Variables	Marketing Activity
Uncontrollable	
Customers	Identification of target audience Identification of managers who will make and influence executive development decisions
Competitors	Identification of actual competition Uncovering apathy
Environment	Understanding impact of business climate on program implementation
Controllable	
Program Characteristics	Program objectives Program prerequisites Program content Program design features — learning methods Program description — agenda Faculty Program materials Program packaging Logistics
Positioning	Translating program objectives into participant benefits Relationship to other programs
Price/Cost	Participant cost
Distribution	Advance study materials Centralized vs decentralized implementation
Promotion	Program introduction Program data sheet Article in company magazine/newsletter Personal contact with top management Attention to implementation
Selling	Identifying decision factors Articulating benefits Overcoming objections
Support	Program followup Contact with prior participants Distributing updated materials to past participants

checklist of the most common marketing variables and the associated marketing activities that should be addressed in a marketing plan.

In the earlier section that described the essential elements of marketing, the characteristics about a product or service that need to be addressed in a marketing plan were labeled as controllable and uncontrollable variables. The major controllable and uncontrollable marketing variables for an executive development program are shown in the first column of Figure 11–2. The three uncontrollable variables — customers, competitors, and the environment — will be discussed first.

Customers

For a specific program, the customers are the executives in the target audience *and* the managers who will make the decision to send an executive to the program or in some manner influence that decision. Marketing activities should focus on benefits and be congruent with the needs that were uncovered during the program needs analysis and design phases.

Competitors

Outside seminars that claim to offer the same benefits as your program may represent competition. The most effective way to counteract this competion is to make your program better. I think the most formidable competitor is executive apathy, and if this is present, it must be overcome.

Environment

The economic environment will substantially affect most executive development strategies. Programs are often classified as postponable investments during economic downturns, and aggressive marketing efforts may be counterproductive. However, some executive development activity may abate the effects of an economic slowdown. Programs on marketing and sales management will likely produce more orders. Programs on manufacturing productivity and quality can help reduce production costs. When executive development efforts are closely linked to the strategic issues facing the firm, programs are less likely to be cancelled or postponed.

Program and Activity Characteristics

The first of the controllable variables is the set of characteristics that defines your program. Decisions on these characteristics are usually made during program design and development, and a data sheet or other description of the program should be produced as one of the first steps in a marketing program. Data sheet content is outlined below under promotion.

The importance of program packaging is easy to forget, and marketing strategies should specify ways to enhance overall appearance and ease of use of the materials. Also, pay attention to decisions on program logistics, particularly those that affect the learning environment.

Positioning

Positioning has to do with perception — the way your customers perceive your product with respect to others and with respect to their needs. An executive development program should be positioned squarely on top of your executives' expressed needs. To do this, you must translate the program objectives into realistic participant benefits and communicate these benefits to participants and their bosses.

When your organization has a family of executive training programs, executives frequently get confused on where a particular program fits into the family. Make this clear in your marketing efforts, particularly in program descriptions.

Price/Cost

Most companies do not price their programs in the usual marketing sense but bill actual costs back to the participants' home locations. These costs should be included on program data sheets.

Distribution

Executive development programs can either be distributed as a centralized seminar in one location or put on the road for decentralized implementation in each of the firm's major entities. Both methods offer tradeoffs to the participants, and the benefits of these tradeoffs should be made clear. Decentralized implementation avoids participant travel and permits customization to local needs. This may be quite important for entities outside of the firm's headquarters country. It is also easier for a complete management team of an entity to experience the program when it is implemented in their entity. A centralized program provides for more interaction with executives from other parts of the world and offers an opportunity for more participation from the top management team. It is also easier to assemble the very best faculty for a centralized seminar.

Marketing strategies must also address the distribution of program materials. Especially important is the sending of advance study materials to seminar participants. Late distribution of these materials, or missing items, can seriously undermine the reputation of your executive development department.

Promotion

Promoting executive development involves the promotion of both the general concept of continuous executive training as well as specific programs. I think promoting the concept is the critical challenge. The best-designed and best-run program in the world will have little long-term impact if the executives' bosses back home fail to reinforce the knowledge and skills acquired during the seminar. It does no harm to continually remind the members of the top management team of this fact and of the need for their personal commitment and involvement in executive development activity. Often, the best way to promote this concept is through personal one on one contact with top level executives. The best way to promote executive development activity is through earning an excellent reputation with past programs. A marginal reputation is a sure source of apathy. Provide some general promotional information on the executive development programs regularly offered by your company. At Hewlett-Packard we published an annual training and development resource guide that included descriptions of executive development programs and resources. Individual data sheets for major programs included the following items:

- An abstract of the program;
- The target audience of the program;
- Program prerequisites;
- Program objectives;
- Program format including a typical daily schedule;
- Program cost;
- A description of program materials;
- How to order materials (for decentralized programs);
- How to obtain additional information.

The formal promotion of a specific program begins with program introduction. The chief executive officer should play the major role in the official launch of the program. The CEO is in a unique position to explain why the program was developed, describe the objectives for the program, and set top management's expectations of the participants. Prepare a letter or memo to the executive team for the CEO's signature. If possible, write a draft of an article for the CEO to publish in the company's newsletter or magazine. It is important to establish management and executive training as a high-priority activity in your firm, and any publicity you receive benefits your department's efforts. In the article draft be sure to recognize the contributions made by the many people who worked on design, development, and implementation.

Selling

Selling the executive development strategy and activities is a key role for the executive development director and substantial time should be allocated to it. Selling is always necessary to obtain sufficient resources, but it is also necessary at the participant level. Frequently, an executive selected to attend a program has a "good" excuse why he or she will be unable to attend. Often, a cancellation is attempted at the last minute. Both executive development directors and specific program managers need to be well briefed on the benefits provided by a program and possess the skills necessary to avert most of these cancellation and postponement efforts. In my experience, most executives can be convinced that staying in the program is possible and preferable to postponement.

Support

When the program is over, it is a good idea to maintain contact with participants to see how they feel about the program after a few months have passed. What have they been able to use on their job? What did they wish had been included in the seminar they attended? This information is extremely valuable for updating the program as well as for the design of follow-up training activity. Your marketing strategy should include this follow-up support activity.

Programs run on a regular basis have a tendency to evolve, and new materials are often incorporated into the design. Past participants can benefit from individually reviewing the new materials, and a strategy for updating them should be formulated.

The most important marketing tool that you have is the reputation you build by designing, developing, and implementing outstanding seminars. During implementation you have the opportunity for continuous contact with executive participants as well as top management. What happens during implementation will normally be remembered the longest.

REFERENCES

1. Thomas J. Peters and Nancy K. Austin, *A Passion for Excellence,* New York, Random House, 1985, chs. 4, 5, 6, 7, and 8.
2. For a detailed treatment of marketing, see Philip Kotler, *Marketing Management,* 5th ed., Englewood Cliffs, N.J., Prentice-Hall, 1984. For a discussion of marketing in public sector or nonprofit institutions, see Kotler's, *Marketing for Non-Profit Organizations,* 2d ed., Englewood Cliffs, N.J., Prentice-Hall, 1982.

CHAPTER **12**

PROGRAM IMPLEMENTATION AND EVALUATION

The success of your executive development strategy, the effectiveness of individual program design and development, and all your efforts in production and marketing are ultimately judged in the running of an actual program. All effort so far assumes that the program will be implemented successfully. Many implementation decisions have been made as part of the design and development phases. Some need to be made in the weeks just prior to the first session. Other decisions will have to be made on a real-time basis during the seminar. This chapter will outline the steps that are necessary for a well-run program and provide some suggestions for evaluating overall effectiveness.

PROGRAM MANAGEMENT

In the early 1970s I had the opportunity to attend an executive program on federal government operations designed and run by the Brookings Institution in Washington, D.C. I remember being impressed with how well the program was managed. Beginning with our arrival in Washington on the Sunday before the program, every detail was arranged. A welcoming session previewed the week and gave all of the attendees a chance to become acquainted with each other. The Brookings staff member who acted as the program leader made us feel at home. During the week of the seminar he was always with us. He provided continuity with the program agenda and helped the participants take maximum advantage of this learning experience. When I was later asked to establish and manage Hewlett-Packard's executive development operation, I used the Brookings Program as a model to emulate.

About ten years later I had the opportunity to attend an executive development program in organizational management conducted by the Stanford Graduate School of Business. Like the Brookings experience, I was again impressed with how important program management is to the overall success of the executive development experience. The staff at Stanford did a superb job. Even though I had been managing HP's programs for several years by then, I learned a number of new methods that I was able to incorporate into our own processes. In addition to acquiring new knowledge and insights into organizational management, sitting in the program as a customer provided me with the opportunity to experience the impact of program management on the success of the seminar.

Like the Brookings leader, the director of the Stanford program was with us constantly during the two-week seminar and provided a much-needed sense of program continuity. The staff addressed all of our logistical needs so that we could concentrate on the seminar curriculum. You have to be an attendee to really appreciate how helpful it is to have seminar faculty join you for lunch, cocktails, and dinner. Many of the informal sessions that resulted from this interaction during meals and in the evening were highlights of the seminar. I left the program with a new reassurance that we were not wasting our time worrying about program management matters back at HP. I strongly recommend that anyone responsible for running a management or executive development program spend at least a week each year attending a program run by another organization. It is good to occasionally look at things through the eyes of a customer.

A number of factors affect the success of executive seminar implementation. Figure 12–1 lists some of the items that executive development directors need to consider before and during the running of a seminar. The essential factor in good program management is to have one individual in charge of running the program who is personally dedicated to making it successful. This individual needs to be free of other responsibilities to focus 100 percent attention on the program. This includes attending the seminar sessions, hosting meals and social functions, directing the activities of support personnel involved in program implementation, working closely with session instructors, and generally anticipating the needs of program participants during the seminar. The importance of the program may dictate that management of the seminar be undertaken by the executive development director. Even if this responsibility is delegated to another professional on the staff, the director should make every attempt to be present at as many seminar sessions and activities as possible.

The program manager needs to be intimately familiar with the program design and content in order to provide continuity from session to session. For this reason, it is a good idea to select as program manager one of the training and development specialists who was heavily involved in program design and development.

A primary tool for effective seminar management is the executive development project checklist of Figure 10–4. The program manager may find it helpful to prepare an expanded version of this checklist to cover more details on activities particularly important to program implementation. For example, the checklist suggests reminding both instructors and attendees about their participation on several occasions during the months before the seminar. This is easily done by sending out reminder letters that also transmit additional in-

---

Figure 12-1   Factors for Effective Program Management

    Specific Assignment of Management Responsibility
    Use of Program Checklist to Achieve Quality
    Avoiding Last-Minute Preparation
    Establishing Good Relationships with Participants
    Effective Management of Faculty
    Paying Attention to Details of Program Logistics
    Session Punctuality
    Program Manager Presence in Classroom
    Clear Instructions for Group and Individual Assignments
    Providing Assistance during Group and Individual Work
    Check of Facility and Equipment Each Morning

formation — a revised agenda or an article to add to the pre-study readings. These activities could be scheduled in more detail on an expanded version of the checklist that focuses on implementation.

There seems to be a tendency for last-minute time crunches with all executive development programs. Often materials are not ready until the last minute, and this creates additional expense in reproduction and collation. The highest price, however, is on the people who are asked to work long hours of overtime during the several days preceding the program. I think this can be avoided by effective program management. Effective planning, coupled with active management, is the primary responsibility of the program manager.

PARTICIPANT SELECTION

Many variables influence the optimal class size for an executive development seminar, the most common being cost, desire for interaction, and whether all executives must go through the program immediately. At Hewlett-Packard we tried to hold functional management programs to twenty-one participants and general management programs to no more than sixteen. Some follow-on programs for senior executives were designed for twelve participants. The number of seminar participants is also influenced by the number of small groups that can be effectively managed. Our experience suggested that small groups of four to six executives worked best for us, although a functional management program that made use of a computer-based simulation had groups of seven. In this program we assigned a group member to each of six functional management positions and to the position of general manager. Three such groups made up the twenty-one seminar participants. These are relatively small numbers of participants, but we greatly valued the chance for our executives to have frequent interaction with seminar faculty. Programs with larger numbers of participants can be very effective, if this tradeoff can be made.

A data base of eligible participants should be made for each executive program being actively used. Organizations having formal systems for executive tracking and succession planning may find it possible to combine data on prospective participants for executive development programs with the data in succession planning data bases. Regardless of what system is used, the data base should include priority of attendance, geographical area, functional background, and current management assignment. Class lists can be made up from the data base, and proposed classes can be balanced for geography, functional background, and current assignment. I always tried to assemble a diverse group for each class. We were convinced that some of the enduring benefits from seminar attendance were the knowledge and ideas that the attendees acquired from each other.

In many organizations the top management team may want to review the attendee list before invitations for specific programs are issued. If possible, get the CEO to sign the letter inviting the executive to the program. This procedure more closely associates top management with the program and results in fewer postponements and last-minute cancellations. I always had top management approve a few alternate candidates for each seminar because we usually had several invited participants unable to attend for various reasons. Immediately issuing an invitation to an alternate saves time and gives the alternate sufficient time to prepare any prestudy assignments.

We also could usually predict the number of cancellations that we might get just prior to the seminar when it would be very difficult to obtain a replacement. We borrowed a procedure that is used by some airlines and hotels — overbooking — and always invited one or two extra people to each seminar. This would occasionally unbalance a small group, but we were able to work around this without inconveniencing the other participants.

INSTRUCTOR TRAINING, COACHING, AND EVALUATION

Although a little talent helps, the major determinant of success in leading an executive development session is adequate preparation. The program manager has the responsibility to make sure that each session instructor has complete materials and is adequately briefed well before the seminar. The briefing should include specific objectives for the session, how that session integrates into the program as a whole, and what the instructor might expect from the participants. I found it helpful to provide each instructor, especially outside faculty, with an attendee roster listing each participant's current assignment and educational background.

Each instructor has the responsibility to prepare his or her session. This is not a problem for professional faculty, but session leaders from inside your company may need some help in how to adequately prepare. A common rule of thumb for advance preparation is about two hours for each hour of class time, assuming a thorough knowledge of the content, a complete leader's outline, and already prepared visual aids. For executive development program leaders doing a session for the first time, it is safer to double this figure. Session leaders who are not professional instructors should be encouraged to rehearse their presentations before a video recorder. Your department may want to make a system available for this purpose. Should the instructor want to fine tune the presentation, an audiotape cassette recorder can be used at home.

The training and development staff can offer much assistance to session leaders before the program. I was often asked to sit through and critique a leader's rehearsal, particularly when they had had a problem in a previous seminar. The staff should not hesitate to coach senior management instructors. They are standing before their peers and bosses and will appreciate your help in preparation. Your contribution to their success will win support for the future.

It is important to adequately brief university faculty. Although they seldom lack effective teaching skills, they may not have had experience in teaching executives. This is a problem with some new assistant professors whose sole experience is teaching young MBA students. In selecting university faculty, verify that they have had experience in executive education. Try to sit through one or more of their classes. Outside instructors need to be thoroughly briefed on your company's business, recent performance results, and strategic goals and issues. They need to understand any cultural norms that might influence their session. Be wary of individuals who show lack of interest in this briefing.

PROGRAM LOGISTICS

Running an executive training seminar has many of the characteristics of managing a stage production. There is the audience. There are performers. Everything is happening at once, and it is exciting. The proper handling of program logistics can help assure a successful seminar. The executive development project checklist (see Figure 10–4) lists the major logistical items that need to be managed. Some suggestions and the rationale behind these items follows.

The arrangement of the main seminar room should reflect an environment conducive to learning and discussion. A U-shaped seating arrangement with the leader at the open end of the U worked best for me. Seats should be comfortable and spaced away from each other to allow room for shifting around and stretching. At HP we built the U from tables that were two-feet wide and of lengths varying from three to six feet. We allowed a minimum of two feet of table for each participant. This gave sufficient room for participants' binders, books, and note pads. A similar table was put at the head of the room for the use of the instructor. As some instructors liked a podium, small table-top units were constructed to fit the tables. The open end permitted instructors to "wander around" the inside of the U as desired. Figure 12–2 shows a typical seminar room layout.

The program manager had the responsibility to decide how to place participants around the table. We tried to avoid seating together people who knew each other. We mixed people according to geography and nationality, and in this manner we hoped to build new associations. Place cards were made in advance using a graphics plotter. Cards were also made for each instructor. Each position around the table was equipped with a pad and pencil. Participants' binders were carefully laid out, unless they had been distributed at a welcoming dinner the night before. Ice water was available

Executive Development

Figure 12-2 Typical Room Layout for Executive Seminars

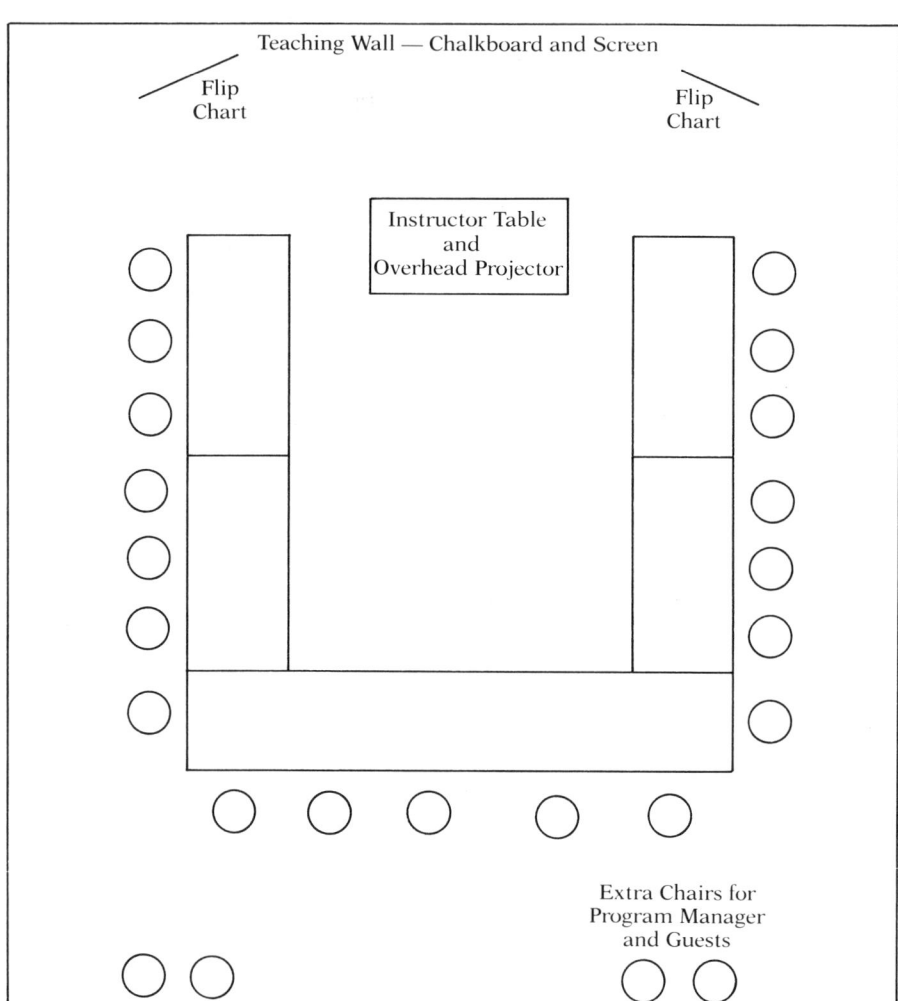

Program Implementation And Evaluation

on the tables, and coffee, tea, and decaffeinated coffee were available on a table at the rear of the seminar room. The training center staff looked on each attendee as a guest, and every effort was made to make the attendees welcome and comfortable.

Immediately outside the seminar room was a lounge area for breaks. A message board was posted outside the room entrance. A copy of the program agenda, a list of participants, and a list of group assignments and breakout rooms were also posted on this board. The logistical information sheet sent to the participants in advance named an individual who could be called to take messages. For outgoing calls, a number of phones for participants were located in the lounge area.

Breaks were programmed into the agenda to allow sufficient time for answering important messages and to talk informally with instructors and other participants. The morning break was always thirty minutes. Afternoon breaks were nominally fifteen minutes, but instructors were given latitude on the actual timing and frequency.

Because a significant amount of executive development programs consists of group work and case preparation, a sufficient number of breakout rooms should be provided. Although we frequently used the main room as a breakout room, we had better experience assigning a separate room to each group. This is particularly important when the program design includes a lengthy series of group work sessions where the groups may want to develop analyses and conclusions on flip-chart paper posted around the breakout room. The rooms were equipped with flip-chart easels, pads, marking pens, and masking tape.

The most common visual aids used in executive programs are overhead transparencies, 35MM slides, videotape, flip charts, and writing boards. The overhead slide projector should be bright enough to be useful without darkening the room. A remote control 35MM projector should be available for instructors who wish to use it. Spare bulbs should be available *in the room* for all projectors used. The video cassette player should be accessible from the front of the room, and a sufficient number of television monitors should be available for easy viewing. Instructors should be encouraged to pre-cue their videotapes. Although large-screen projection televisions can be used, at HP we preferred individual monitors suspended from the ceiling. Should a problem occur in one monitor, the others can still be used.

Two flip-chart easels should be available with a sufficient quantity and color selection of pens. Pens always seem to run dry, so plenty of extras should be on hand. Although chalkless writing surfaces are becoming more popular, I found that chalkboards were preferred by most of our outside faculty. Make sure that plenty of chalk of various colors is available. Should you prefer chalkless boards, have an ample supply of the special pens that are required. Some conventional pens used for flip charts will damage a chalkless writing surface, so have a method to keep the pens separate.

I think it is a good idea to develop a seminar room checklist for the training center staff. Each morning check the cleanliness of projector surfaces and lenses, sufficiency of participant note pads and flip-chart paper, chalk and writing pen supply, operation of all audio-visual equipment, and general orderliness of the room. Never underestimate the value of a top-notch training center staff. If you are running your program off site, the program manager will most likely have to do this daily check. Few commercial conference centers take the time and effort to check these things.

A word about food and beverage. Regardless of whether the program is run on site or off, prepare a menu in advance. A simple continental breakfast is a good way to greet the attendees each morning. Have plenty of coffee available for the participants in the seminar room. This is often difficult when conducting a program at a hotel, because many restaurant people want to bring coffee at specific times rather than having it available all day. Select something light for lunch. A make-your-own sandwich buffet allows participants to choose their own fare and conserves time. A cocktail hour prior to dinner provides an excellent opportunity for other executives to join the group for informal discussions. The critical thing is to close the bar at an appropriate time and go in to dinner. If your facilities permit, a barbecue dinner during the week provides variety. Program managers need to remember their priorities when managing the food and beverage part of the program. The main objective is learning.

It is often a good idea to precede a seminar with a welcoming dinner. This allows people to meet one another and renew past acquaintances before the seminar starts. The program manager can provide an overview of the seminar, and even distribute an assignment for the next day if needed. Participants' materials can be distributed. Expectations for punctuality and interruptions can be established. If the program is held off site, a dinner and program the night before the first day assures that all attendees can find the facility and their accommodations.

CLASSROOM OPERATIONS

It is important to get the program off to a good start, and this requires the active involvement of the program manager. Attendees will have some expectations for the program. They will certainly expect that the program will be fast paced, cover their needs, and capture their interest. Their first impressions last throughout the program.

The program manager should be at the seminar site for a last-minute check of logistics well before any attendee is likely to arrive. Attendees should be enthusiastically greeted and told where they can find the continental breakfast and the seminar room. The program manager is the host; the attendees are guests.

At the time appointed to begin the seminar, the manager should guide attendees to their places and the seminar should begin — on time. The first agenda item is normally a welcome from the CEO or another representative from top management, and this individual should be introduced briefly. Logistical and agenda comments from the program manager should wait until after the welcoming session.

During the discussion of program logistics and a preview of the agenda, it is important to stress beginning and ending the sessions on time. The participants should be told that each session will start exactly on time and that they are expected to be in their seats ready to proceed. The alternative is getting so hopelessly behind that chaos sets in. I have never had a problem getting the support of the attendees on punctuality. Most executives demand it.

Each instructor should be introduced personally by the program manager, even though a biography may have been included in the participants' binder. A good way to remember the salient facts about an instructor is to list them on a 3 x 5 card. A course leader for a sales training program at HP would do such a good job of introducing his speakers and making them feel welcome that he never had a problem in getting them as speakers again. They probably worked harder to prepare for their sessions as a result of the superb introductions.

As stated earlier, I feel that it is critical that the program manager remain in the room during all presentations. I was regularly told by university faculty that it was a great help to the instructor. It also helps attendees. Frequently an attendee forgets to bring some materials to class, or the instructor needs some logistical help. These things are the responsibility of the program manager.

It is impossible to do a proper job of evaluating a session without experiencing the session and observing the instructor and the participants. This is a primary duty for the program manager. There is another benefit, however. The more that training and development professionals know about the management of their company, the better their position to help executives develop their knowledge levels and skills. Sitting in an executive development program provides content knowledge as well as knowledge on the behavior of the company's executives. It is an excellent opportunity for developing training and development professionals.

Without the attention of the course leader or program manager, a well-designed, well-integrated executive seminar can easily become a disconnected series of individual sessions. Program continuity is needed, and the program manager is the logical person to meet this need. I think it is important to start out each morning with a preview of the day's sessions and how they relate to one another. Key points from previous sessions can be reiterated in one or two minutes prior to introducing the next speaker. During the course of the session, a question may arise about how the current session content relates to a previous session. The program manager can answer these questions or concerns. In programs that I ran, I told the attendees that I would be going through the program with them. By being present and actively involved in the seminar, I could provide any assistance necessary throughout the seminar.

Inevitably we all encounter instructors who go over their time allotment. Although I try to be courteous, I am rather ruthless in signaling to the instructor when time is about to expire and I sense that the session will not end on schedule. If this doesn't work, I stand up in the back of the room at the scheduled ending time, and again make a signal. After another two minutes, I politely announce to the instructor that we must end this session because we are scheduled to go into the next session. In an attempt to lessen the times that I have to use these measures, I point out to each instructor during the preseminar briefings that it is *essential* that all sessions end on time because we have a very tightly packed agenda. This should always be done.

PROGRAM EVALUATION AND FOLLOWUP

It is important to get immediate feedback from participants on their feelings about the program. I designed a written questionnaire and asked each participant to evaluate each session on a scale of 0 to 10 for program content, relevance to their job, and overall instructional quality. Additional questions were asked as to which sessions were the most helpful, which were superfluous, what should be added to the curriculum, the relevance of advance study, and comments on logistics. The questionnaires were analyzed, and a composite report was forwarded to each instructor and attendee. The main purpose of the evaluation was to get ideas on how we could improve the program. Instructors had no problem with our publishing their scores, and I think it contributed to their motivation to properly prepare.

The critical question is whether executives perform better as a result of training. It is difficult for training departments to make this measurement because job performance is not easily measured by a person's manager, let alone by a training professional. I think the best approach to this evaluation of whether seminar learning is transferred back to the job is to gain program ownership by all executives in the company. For instance, a program designed to provide executives with additional knowledge and skills in marketing should be evaluated as follows. All executives beginning with the CEO should agree on the overall objectives of the executive development program expressed in terms of specific job behaviors. If one objective is to do a better job of market research, executives attending the program who are responsible for marketing research need to have specific goals established by their managers. Then their managers need to measure whether more effective market research is being done. It is arguable whether the better job is being done as a direct result of the training, but I think this argument is academic. It wasn't being done before the training. Now it is being done. Whatever the cause, the objective has been met.

To transfer learning back to the job, the returning manager needs to find an environment that supports the transfer. The key factor is the expectation of the manager's boss. This is why top-down executive training is so critical. The ideal case would be for every executive sending an executive to a seminar to sit down with the participant prior to the course and outline several items that he or she expects the participant to bring back from the program. On return, specific job-related objectives should be established and measured. This is actually applying total quality control to the evaluation of executive training. It is the classic *Plan, Do, Check, Act* cycle discussed earlier in this book. Figure 12–3 illustrates how TQC can be applied to the evaluation of executive development program effectiveness.

PROGRAM SUPPORT

Executive development programs that are conducted numerous times have a tendency to evolve over time. Each seminar results in experiences that influence both program content and instructional methods. New materials become available, and different instructors bring fresh approaches. This is a desirable process, but the program manager needs to make sure that changes are documented and materials are revised as

Figure 12-3   TQC and Executive Development Program Evaluation

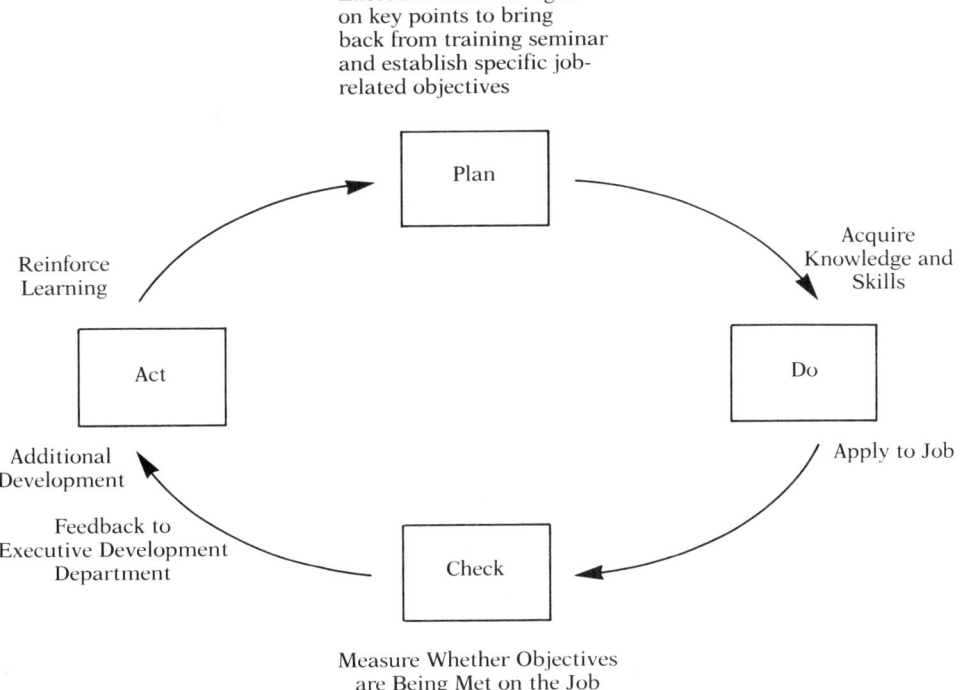

needed. This is especially important when staff turnover results in the assignment of a new program manager.

It is also important to provide past attendees with any materials that would help them apply the seminar to their jobs. It is helpful to send new articles and books to past attendees, but as a minimum they should be informed of their availability. At Hewlett-Packard we experimented with sending videotapes of speakers new to the program to prior attendees. An effective strategy for executive development should address the need for continual executive education.

STRATEGY FOR PROGRAM UPDATING AND ULTIMATE OBSOLESCENCE

The evolution of an executive seminar is a helpful process, but occasionally a program needs thorough revision and updating. This is especially true for a program that has been run for the entire original target population and is now sitting dormant on the shelf. Frequently the program manager has transferred to another position, and there may be no one left in the department with program familiarity. Is there anyone who could successfully resurrect it?

A generic executive program in general management or functional management should be formally updated every few years. A strategy for redoing the needs analysis, program design, program development, and production should be formulated and the project assigned to a new program manager. Care should be taken to not reinvent everything, but a new perspective is valuable. The obsolescence of the existing program should be a part of the strategy.

Programs that have lain dormant are another problem. Is it worthwhile to salvage an old program, or is it better to scrap it and start anew? The question cannot be addressed until a preliminary needs analysis is done to see if there is still a requirement for the program. Assuming that the old program is well documented, it should be matched against preliminary needs, and a decision made for renewal or a new program. Perhaps the need for the program no longer exists.

In that case a formal obsolescence should be initiated. Other than archival documentation, there is little sense in continuing to store obsolete materials. They are excellent candidates for donation.

SUMMARY OF PART III

This final section of the book began with a discussion of executive development strategy. The formulation of this strategy, although the specific responsibility of the executive development director, must involve top management and the executives of the firm. An approach was outlined for focusing development efforts first on getting the basics right and then on addressing those issues that will help executives do a better job of business strategy implementation. A model for strategy development was shown. Chapter 8 concluded with some planning ideas for training strategy implementation.

Chapters 9 and 10 described methods for designing and developing executive training programs, from the needs analysis phase to program production. The CEO can play an important role in the design of a program to ensure a close tie to strategic issues and top management expectations. Program content should be balanced between new ideas and methods from outside the firm and best practices developed internally. The organization's executives are an important source of content ideas, and they can contribute to program development by serving on module development task forces. As executives should also be assigned as instructors, an important part of program development is the leaders' guides that facilitate the instructional role. Chapter 10 included a discussion on key steps to consider in producing program materials. In all phases of program design, development, and production, effective project management is essential.

Executive development directors must plan and implement a marketing strategy for their executive development activities. A review of basic marketing principles and how they can be applied to executive development was discussed in Chapter 11. Guidelines for developing a marketing plan for a specific program were also provided.

The final test of an executive development strategy comes through program implementation and the evaluation of actual results. The basics of program implementation were reviewed in Chapter 12, and particular attention was paid to the importance of program management. The program manager is responsible for managing the logistics to optimize the learning environment. This can be done best by being in the program with the participants. Recognizing that development does not stop at the conclusion of a seminar, strategies for making executive development a continuous activity were discussed.

Finally, executive development will not be effective without the active involvement of the boss. No one else can evaluate whether the knowledge and skills acquired are being applied to better execution of strategy on the job. Executive development programs that are continuously reinforced on the job greatly increase the chances of achieving strategic goals.

APPENDIX A

A MODEL FOR MANAGEMENT DEVELOPMENT

Management and executive development strategies are more easily understood when a simple model illustrates the strategy's salient points. Such a model is also useful in selling the strategy to top management. This appendix describes a model similar to the one that I developed at Hewlett-Packard to guide executive and management development activity.

After assuming responsibility for HP's corporate training department, I found a potpourri of programs that had been developed, were being used, and were planned for future development by various entities within the company. Yet no overall strategy for management development existed. Formulating a strategy was the first order of business for my new department, which had been formed through a merging of a corporate personnel development group, a marketing training and television department, and a new project to develop an executive training program.

The approach taken for the strategy was to define those points in a manager's career where he or she might need a formal development program. Specific programs could then be designed to match these transition points. Figure A-1 is an abbreviated organization chart for a typical business entity and shows four major management transitions. The bottom and top transitions are somewhat obvious, when one becomes a manager in the first place, and when a senior manager assumes the responsibility for the general management of the entity. The two intermediate transitions were identified as promotional steps that involved significant change in responsibilities and management focus.

Achieving Strategic Goals Through Executive Development

The transition to manager of managers is a subtle yet crucial step. Most management development occurs on the job, by doing it, rather than in the classroom. Formal management development programs, particularly at the lower levels of management, are at best a catalyst for development. Although much cognitive knowledge and some skill development can result from formal programs, lasting development comes from the job experience itself. The most successful managers develop their skills on the job working under the

Figure A-1 **Basic Management Transitions**

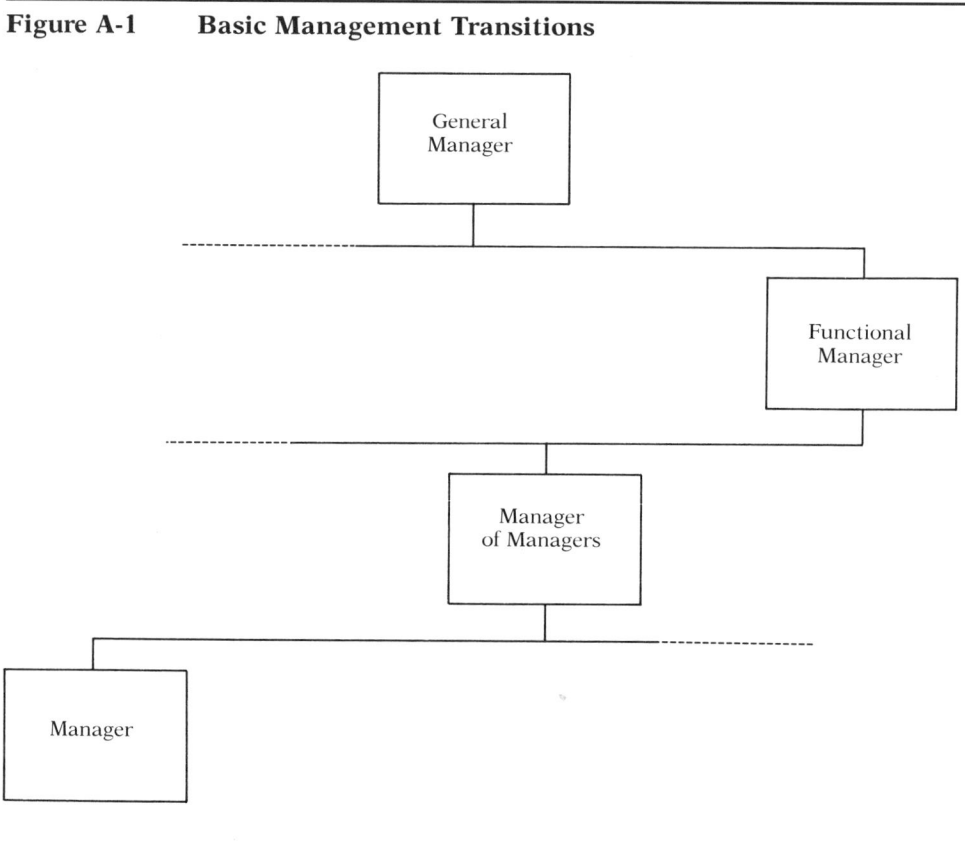

direction of a manager with excellent coaching skills. A new manager's own manager, then, plays an extremely important role in this experiential learning process. Managers who are new to managing other managers require some formal training in basic coaching and teambuilding skills.

The transition to functional manager is often a difficult transition because many managers reach the functional level without experience in functions other than their own. This is commonplace in high technology companies where promotion can be rapid and little time is available for job rotation. When I became a marketing manager at Hewlett-Packard, my entire career had been spent in marketing and field sales. Although an engineer by training, I had only passing familiarity with the issues that confronted my counterparts who were managing the product development and manufacturing functions. Production master schedules and the importance of sales forecasts to the manufacturing manager were not things that I had spent much time worrying about. Yet as a functional manager, I had joined the management team of a major business unit, and my new responsibilities were inextricably tied to the management of other functions. I had to learn the hard way, and I was determined to spare other newly promoted managers from many of the frustrations that I had experienced.

One may argue about whether four transitions are the correct number. It worked for us at HP, and the actual number is somewhat irrelevant. The important thing is to define the *critical* transitions for your organization, and then design your management and executive development strategy around them. These transitions represent one dimension of a management and executive development strategy model.

The second dimension in the model is the category of curriculum emphasis. For example, new general managers will usually need some additional training in accounting and finance, and this topic would represent an area of curriculum emphasis. First-level managers need a thorough understanding of the management philosophy of the firm, so management philosophy is another area of curriculum emphasis. Leadership is another important curriculum area.

The third dimension of the model is specific content within the area of curriculum emphasis. For example, capital asset management is a topic within the accounting and finance area. Coaching skills is a topic within the leadership curriculum area.

Figure A-2 is a three-dimensional model that shows the relationships between management transitions on the Y axis of a cube, categories of curriculum emphasis on the X axis, and specific program content on the Z axis.

At HP we initiated the development of what we called basic core programs for each of our management transitions. The important categories of curriculum emphasis were identified for each transition, and training programs were de-

Figure A-2   A Model for Management Development

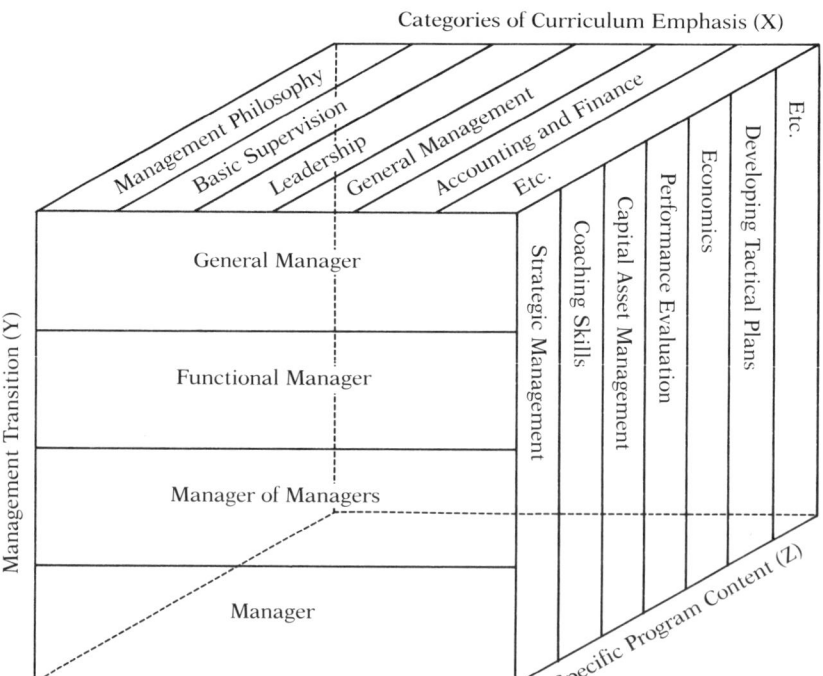

signed to cover the essential content in each curriculum area. Some general examples of curriculum categories and program content are outlined below:

> Categories of curriculum emphasis (X axis)
> Management philosophy
> Basic supervision
> Leadership
> General management
> Accounting and finance
> International business management
> Marketing
> Product development
> Manufacturing
> Quality assurance
> Human resource management

> Specific program content (Z axis)
> Strategic management
> Coaching skills
> Capital asset management
> Performance evaluation
> Economics
> Developing tactical plans
> Government relations
> Market research
> Financial analysis
> Management by objectives
> Interpersonal communications
> Meeting management
> Managing foreign exchange rate fluctuations

A model such as the one described above is a useful device to illustrate a training strategy. Like all models it represents the ideal and will most likely evolve as the organization gains more experience with its management and executive development activities.

APPENDIX B
TEN STRATEGIC ISSUES FOR TRAINING AND DEVELOPMENT

In February 1986 I was invited by the Conference Board to give a presentation on critical training and development issues that affect competitiveness at their Conference on Management Training and Development in New York. Because these issues have a direct influence on the ability of a business organization to achieve its strategic goals, the presentation is repeated here.

The basic strategic goal for a free enterprise business is to achieve a competitive advantage over others in the industry. Firms that skillfully compete not only survive but flourish. Improving competitiveness, therefore, should be a fundamental goal for training and development professionals. Ten strategic issues that affect competitiveness are outlined below. The list is based on my experiences while directing Hewlett-Packard's management and executive development operation. Before describing these issues, I would like to review some reasons that competitiveness should be the number one concern in the United States today and what human resource professionals can do about it.

WHY COMPETITIVENESS SHOULD BE EVERYONE'S NUMBER ONE CONCERN

Unless we start worrying about our ability to compete in an increasingly complex world marketplace, we had better get used to a declining standard of living vis-à-vis other developed countries. This was the bottom line of *The Report of the*

President's Commission on Industrial Competitiveness released in January 1985. This blue-ribbon commission, consisting of leaders from business, government, and education, cited five factors that directly affect our ability as a nation to compete. First is a series of trade deficits. The alarming thing to those of us at Hewlett-Packard is that last year there was a trade deficit of $15 billion with Japan in electronics alone, and that was *larger* than the trade deficit in automobiles! Next is the fact that we've lost market share in high technology industries since 1965. Out of ten sectors that were measured, we have lost market share in seven. Third, U.S. productivity growth has been outstripped by all of our major competitors around the world. Using a measure of real gross domestic product per employed person, the numbers for the average annual productivity increase during the period 1960 through 1983 are Japan, 5.9 percent; Korea, 5.3 percent; France, 3.7 percent; Germany, 3.4 percent; United Kingdom, 2.3 percent; and the United States, 1.2 percent. The Japanese increased productivity about five times as fast as the United States. Next, the report cited a declining rate of return on assets in the manufacturing sector. Finally, stagnant real wages in the United States are causing a decline in the standard of living compared to other industrialized countries. Take some time to read the actual report; it is a sobering document.

THE CHALLENGE AND OPPORTUNITY FOR HUMAN RESOURCE DEVELOPMENT

I wish that we were not faced with these tough competitive problems, but I also see a tremendous opportunity. Human resource development efforts can play a significant role in helping organizations regain competitiveness. This contribution can be made by recognizing that training and development activities must be driven by the strategy of the organization. All developmental activities must be focused on helping the organization compete in a complex and changing environment. We must spend more time on those things that will help management do a better job today, tomorrow, next week, next month — not just several years down the line when the battle might not be possible to win.

I believe there are two legitimate functions of training and development. The first is to get the basics right. By *basics* I mean the perpetuation of the organization's philosophy and shared values and the basic generic and functional knowledge and skills required by all employees to do their jobs. The second legitimate role is contributing to the implementation of business strategy. This includes acquiring new knowledge and skills for implementing specific strategic actions, using development as a tool for facilitating change, and helping the CEO set overall expectations and share the vision of where the organization is to go.

TEN STRATEGIC ISSUES FOR TRAINING AND DEVELOPMENT

1. *Impact of modern manufacturing methodologies.* The word *automation* doesn't begin to describe the revolution that is going on in the way we make things. Computer technology, particularly the use of computers to aid the design and manufacture of products, is changing the way that factories look. The manufacturing function is a key strategic element in most companies today, and proprietary processes and methods, like just-in-time inventory management, can provide substantial competitive advantage. To achieve this competitive advantage, managers and employees in manufacturing, as well as managers and employees in other functions, need to keep up to date with these technologies and methods. Consequently, training and development efforts must be focused on providing process and methods skills to help these people position their company favorably. In addition, new manufacturing methods are causing significant changes in the workplace, particularly the skills that are needed for continued employment. Several of the following issues result from these changes in manufacturing.

2. *Quality as a competitive element.* Customers today expect much higher quality in the products they purchase, and firms must provide this quality or face declining sales. The Japanese have set the quality standard for many industries and have challenged competitors around the world to match their quality accomplishments. In the final analysis, quality comes from people doing the job right the first time, whether the job be in the mailroom, the office, or the factory floor. We must pay attention to how well we are training these people; better training results in better quality.

People used to think that higher quality meant higher manufacturing costs. Quite the contrary is true. At HP we found that about 25 percent of our production space was necessary to fix products that were not produced right the first time. A lot of really unnecessary facilities were needed to inventory parts and materials for reworking defective products, for people to do the rework, and for space to do it in. The costs that were necessary because the work was not done right the first time were being added to overall production costs. If we could eliminate the rework, this unnecessary cost would disappear. Consequently, attention paid to quality makes your product or service more competitive because it better matches customer quality expectations at a lower cost. Focused training and development efforts can directly produce this highly desirable effect, and the results flow right to the bottom line.

3. *Productivity improvements.* To compete successfully it is necessary to lower costs even further than is possible through paying attention to quality alone. An interesting exercise for human resources people is to plot a measure of productivity — such as revenue or profit dollars per employee for your company and for your major competitors. The important thing is not the absolute value but trends. Are your competitors increasing their productivity faster than you are? If so, why? Look beyond manufacturing productivity. What are you doing to improve productivity in design, marketing, sales, and administration?

4. *Need for understanding the "guts" of the business.* It should go without saying that people managing employee

and management development activities must have a thorough understanding of the firm's businesses, the processes used in producing your products and services, customers' major applications, and the strategies that are being followed to grow these businesses. How else can one devise a training strategy to help managers and employees compete more effectively? Yet I don't think that most training professionals take the time to sufficiently develop this understanding. To understand a business, you have to spend some time doing what the other employees do, wandering around their work areas, asking lots of questions, finding out what customers do with your products, and trying to understand some things about the firms with whom you compete. Several years ago at HP we assigned newly hired training and development specialists to one of our divisions for several weeks of hands-on experience, including working in the manufacturing areas. It was helpful to the new employee and also demonstrated that the training operation stayed in touch.

5. *Mismatch between jobs and available people.* This is an outgrowth of issue 1, the impact of new manufacturing technologies, and is a significant problem for HP as well as most other firms. At one time HP required hundreds of sheet metal workers, but enclosures for new products are now produced primarily through an automated plastic injection molding process. Employees with skills no longer in high demand cannot fill the new jobs that are being created without a dedicated effort to retraining. Most companies are committed to retraining strategies, for it is not right to simply discard employees when their skills are no longer needed. Reshaping their workforces are key strategic issues for most organizations.

6. *Need to define future skill/aptitude requirements three to five years out.* You can't do a proper job of retraining unless you can accurately predict the kinds of job skills that you will need in the future. This is the dilemma that faces many of us. I think that most companies are just beginning to learn how to do this, and I doubt whether any organization is yet doing it as well as will be necessary in the future. The challenge for training departments is to be ready to provide effective train-

ing as new job skills are defined. To do this, training managers need to stay close to the action in engineering and manufacturing.

7. *Cost of improper training.* The cost of an improperly trained employee is a tragic waste. Quality and productivity suffer, and often customer relationships are damaged. Improper training results in several costs. Salary and benefits costs already invested in the employee yield little return to the company. Add to this the cost of doing the training job that you should have done in the first place. The unfortunate thing is that in most organizations these costs are buried somewhere and are not easily measured or managed. When the improperly trained employee is a manager, the cost is extremely high, for managers set the example for the people they lead. They also should be providing much of the on-the-job training.

8. *Commitment to continuous training.* Technological change provides many benefits, but it also precipitates knowledge and skill obsolescence. Those firms that recognize the need for commitment to continuous training and retraining of their employees will most likely win out over their competitors. At HP we estimated that about half of an engineer's education becomes obsolete in five years. For software designers this figure is about two and one-half years. To keep these people current, HP delivers engineering and computer science courses via a company-owned satellite television network. To compete effectively in the future, I anticipate that many companies will expand training via television networks to cover most job categories.

9. *Process versus task orientation.* Today's manufacturing processes require workers who can think *and* do, not just do. Whether in an administrative office, the laboratory, or in production, employees must have an understanding of their particular process, not just the task that the process is designed to accomplish. The Japanese have taken the lead in recognizing the value of a thinking worker, and much of their success is attributable to initiatives taken by their employees.

10. *Commitment to continuous process improvement.* Like many other organizations, Hewlett-Packard has ambitiously pursued a program of total quality control. TQC is a

management philosophy that originated in Japan to ensure product quality. Gone are the quality control inspectors who look for products to reject. The employees themselves are responsible for ensuring quality. Rather than just focus on the product, the employees focus on all the processes used to make the product. Each process has performance measures that are continuously monitored. Feedback from these measurements results in actions taken to improve the process. The only acceptable goal is perfection. Because the key to TQC is the involvement of people in understanding and improving their processes, continual training is a key element in implementing a total quality control program. I think that this is another major opportunity for human resources development managers to impact the bottom line.

SUMMARY

The common denominator in these ten training and development issues is that competitive advantage comes from all members of the organization doing their jobs just a little bit better than their competitors. Companies with training strategies that continuously improve the knowledge levels and skills of their employees will be able to capture and hold competitive advantage. Training and development managers have never had such a wonderful opportunity to help shape their organization's future.

APPENDIX C

TELEVISION, COMPUTERS, AND SIMULATIONS AS EXECUTIVE DEVELOPMENT RESOURCES

INTRODUCTION

This appendix describes some applications of television, computers, and simulations to the executive development process. It is based largely on my experiences at Hewlett-Packard, and I would like to acknowledge my indebtedness to the many people at HP's Corporate Training Department who taught me much of what I know about this topic and for their willingness to explore how these devices could be applied to executive and management training.[1] I hope that the following discussion will convey some ideas and stimulate your imagination for applying innovative methods to enliven your executive development activities.

Two fortunate events gave me a head start in applying television and computers to management training. One was the fact that my previous assignment at HP was in computer marketing. The second was that I inherited HP's television studio as part of my responsibilities for setting up a new management and executive training operation.

TELEVISION

The Hewlett-Packard television studio had been built primarily to provide training programs on new products and applications for field sales and support people. The person who was originally responsible for its development was an outstanding pioneer and champion and, like many pioneers, developed a capacity before many people knew how to use it. I was able to direct this extra capacity to management training applications.

Early productions from the HP studio included some short video vignettes for training programs in performance evaluation and the metric system. The first application for executive training was to videotape a speech that Dave Packard delivered at HP's executive seminar for general managers. The tape was made originally as a backup because Dave was not always able to appear personally. Once it existed, it was used in other executive training sessions. The second major application was to videotape a talk delivered by Tom Peters at a new executive program for senior managers. We had asked Tom to address the subject of maintaining innovation, and his message was most enthusiastically received. We decided that this message should be heard by a broader cross-section of HP managers, and a videotape was produced. It didn't take long for the training and development staff to realize what a powerful tool television could be. Before long, all excess capacity was gone, and management training applications had to compete with the television needs from the product marketing groups.

A major attraction of television as a management training medium is that you can personalize a given production to the specific needs of your firm. Videotape is more convenient to use than film, is easily transportable, can take advantage of the fact that almost every home has a VCR, and is inexpensive to copy and distribute. The following are some of the major applications for television as an executive or management training resource.

Use as a Basic Audio-Visual Device

In this application, videotape replaces 16MM film to deliver segments of a management training session. Program and message consistency is a common objective, particularly when a program is implemented throughout a large organization on a decentralized basis. Television is an excellent medium for assuring this consistency. It is also effective for documenting "best practices" that need to be communicated to all managers in the organization.

For a program that will be conducted many times, it is frequently difficult to schedule a faculty member for each program. A videotape of the session can capture the essence of the instructor's message. This has been a common practice in many HP programs, particularly those that are implemented in the divisions and sales entities.

Setting Top Management Expectations

Central to the design of many training programs is a central theme or message from top management. The most effective way to communicate this message is for the CEO to participate directly in articulating clear expectations, but it is usually impossible to schedule the CEO in all subsequent programs. A videotape can provide this message. Often the message is appropriate for a wider audience than the seminar was designed to address. Here again a videotape can be used.

Members of the top management team are usually not comfortable before a television camera, and coaching is usually necessary for effective television communication. At HP we were fortunate in having, as our television network manager, an excellent coach with major network experience. When planning to use top management in television segments, plan also for their coaching.

Setting the Scene for Case Discussion

An early HP application of television for management training was a series of video vignettes for a performance evaluation workshop. The vignettes described typical situations that occur in a performance evaluation interview. During the workshop, the tape would be stopped at appropriate moments for group discussion. The production of your own vignettes tailors the training to your own management philosophy and methods.

A video production can also supplement or substitute for a written case study. A number of professionally produced cases are available. The Harvard Business School has a substantial library of video cases.[2]

Tutored Videotape Instruction and Satellite Delivery

Although used primarily for continuing education in the sciences, the delivery of graduate-level continuing education via videotape or satellite transmission shows promise for executive development. Tutored videotape instruction, originally developed by Stanford's engineering school dean, Jim Gibbons, has been used for the past decade for delivering graduate courses in engineering and computer science to engineers in HP divisions away from the San Francisco Bay area.[3] The process involves sending videotapes of actual classes to divisions that have Stanford certified tutors. Students do homework and take the same examinations that are administered on campus.

Hewlett-Packard has also delivered graduate courses in computer science from California State University in Chico via the HP Television Network to all HP sites in the United States. In the future, these courses will be delivered directly from the university on an uplink being provided by HP's Roseville Division. Similar courses in engineering and computer science are delivered by the National Technological University via videotape and satellite to participating organizations throughout the United States.

The HP satellite television network is frequently used to deliver live presentations to customers. Major new products have been introduced at televised press conferences conducted at sites throughout North America and Europe. Live two-way audio hookups allow customers and the press to direct questions to HP executives.

Role Play and Behavior Modeling

One of the earliest uses of television at HP was for videotaping role-play exercises in sales training. The sales representative can witness how he or she comes across to the customer in a simulated sales situation.

Television is frequently used to illustrate processes for effective communication between managers and employees. Desired behaviors can be modeled, and by customizing the videotape, a firm can model behaviors that are congruent with the organization's style and management philosophy.

Presentation Rehearsal and Public Relations Training

Instructors in Hewlett-Packard training programs include faculty from major universities as well as HP line executives. Because they are not full-time instructors, the HP people usually need to rehearse their sessions, particularly those sessions broadcast live over the satellite network or videotaped for later use. Formal coaching is provided by the television staff. Instructors and other seminar speakers often find videotape replay an excellent tool for fine tuning these presentations. Training departments should have the necessary equipment available for these practice sessions and make it easy for instructors to use the equipment and receive any coaching that they may desire.

Senior executives frequently make presentations to customers, speak before trade and professional associations, meet with the press, and appear before other public gatherings. Often, press conferences or public meetings can turn into unfriendly and stressful experiences, and executives need to develop skills to counteract hostile or aggressive questioning tactics or disruptive behavior. A number of firms offer coaching for executives to better cope with these situations, and video is a medium where instant feedback is possible. Some of these coaching sessions directly address the use of television as the communication medium and help executives overcome any apprehensions they may have about appearing before the camera.

SOME FACTORS TO CONSIDER BEFORE JUMPING INTO A VIDEO PRODUCTION

The major decision to be made about video is whether to go outside for production services or to produce the program in-house. If you have a television production facility in your firm, the question narrows down to one of capability. If you are considering investing in an in-house television production capability, you should be aware of the fact that the easiest thing is buying the equipment. The difficult part is developing the staff. Professional television people are artists. They excel in taking your ideas and figuring out ways to make them come alive in video. Don't underestimate the effort that it will take to develop a professional television staff.

Assuming that your organization already has a television production operation, your first objective should be to go to the person who manages it and learn about its capabilities. Develop a good relationship with the manager and the staff. You will need to work closely with them when you begin to produce a program. Executive development specialists need to understand the basics of television, so spend some time learning about your firm's facility. Try to schedule some time observing an actual production and program editing processes.

If you must go outside for television production services, you should be aware of the fact that there are many categories of production services. You can get anything along a continuum starting with the equivalent of a home movie, advancing to industrial quality, and at the extreme, broadcast-quality television. For programs for marketing or satellite transmission, the closer you get to broadcast quality the better. You have the choice of contracting with an independent producer who will in turn arrange for actual production, editing, and duplication services, or you can deal with one firm that will provide all services needed. Before selecting a contractor, be sure to check the satisfaction of prior clients.

From my experience, the most common problem with producing a program for management and executive development is the training and development manager who is unprepared to proceed with the project. It is essential to define the precise objectives for what you want the television production to accomplish, and this is not the responsibility of the television people. The second most common problem, and one that costs a lot of money, is changing the objectives during the production and editing processes. Thorough advance preparation from the training staff can significantly reduce the costs of television programs.

COMPUTERS

Computers, particularly personal computers, are very useful tools for executive and management development. Although the discussion below will emphasize the application of computers to management training simulations, computers find much application as training delivery systems and for training administration. Extensive curriculum software is available, and many of the traditional textbook publishing companies have expanding catalogs of computer courseware. Numerous scheduling programs are available for administration. In addition, project management software can help you keep track of program development projects. Word processing programs and desk-top publishing software have revolutionized the writing and production of course materials.

To help your staff maximize the benefits that computers can offer to the executive and management development processes, recruit someone with functional management experience and an understanding of computers and computer programming. Although you can get assistance from your firm's EDP and office automation people, having someone on your staff who is dedicated to the application of computers to train managers will be a worthwhile investment. This is particularly important if you plan to make extensive use of computers during executive development seminars, or if you will be using a computer simulation as part of a program.

The primary educational uses for computers are reviewed briefly below. For an in-depth treatment of the topic, refer to the extensive literature on computer-based training.[4]

The Computer as an Analytical Tool

One of the most common applications of personal computers during an executive program session is its use as an analytical tool. Financial data, from the firm itself or from a company being studied via a case, can be analyzed very efficiently using computer spreadsheets. "What if" scenarios studied by computer provide immediate answers to the effect of alternative actions. Trend analysis is made easy by graphics software extensions to spreadsheet programs.

The first use of computers for executive training at Hewlett-Packard was in the original general management seminar. Alex Robichek, a Stanford finance professor who was one of the architects of the seminar, had developed a financial analysis program that ran on a computer timesharing system. Terminals and telephones were placed in the seminar room, and groups of executives could access the program during a session. From this early beginning, our needs for both classroom use and training administration increased enough to justify a dedicated computer system for the training department.

Computer-Based Training

Almost as soon as computers became commonplace tools for science and business, they were applied to education, and computer-based training (CBT) was born. More recently, the widespread availability of personal computers has created significant interest in CBT for management and executive training. Some of the more common benefits provided by computer-based instruction include the following:

- Instruction can be individualized and geared to the pace of the learner.

- Learning is available at the time and place desired.
- The learner is actively involved in the process.
- Curriculum implementation is consistent.
- Curriculum can be easily updated.
- Record keeping is an integral part of the system.

Computer/Videodisc Personal Learning Stations

Some critics of computer-based training point to the boredom that can result after watching a computer screen for any length of time. It's hardly exciting for most people. The addition of color displays with graphics capability has helped overcome this difficulty, but the combination of videodisc technology with personal computers may make individualized computer-based learning both effective and exciting.

Videodiscs can store over 50,000 pages of text or pictures on a relatively inexpensive plastic disc. Any page can be randomly accessed in milliseconds. Where conventional CBT had to rely on text and graphics, a computer and videodisc system can add full motion video to the lesson. Learner boredom and disenchantment can be significantly reduced.

A number of interactive video disc/computer learning projects were initiated at HP, and this technology looks particularly attractive for many training applications. A number of companies are using videodisc learning systems, and interested readers will find numerous descriptions in the training and educational technology literature.

The Distributed University

I think that one of the more exciting potential technologies for executive education is the use of interactive computer networks and video technology for distributed learning. The development of asynchronous computer conferencing, where a group of individuals carry on a meeting or seminar via their personal computers connected to telephone lines, makes it possible to remotely participate in a class where case discussion is a required part of the learning process. Homework and examinations can be administered via the computer network. The addition of satellite delivery of live lectures makes it quite possible to have a truly distributed university.

One of the pioneers in the use of computer networks for executive education is the Western Behavioral Sciences Institute in La Jolla, California. In January 1982, WBSI convened the first class in The School of Management and Strategic Studies, and the vast majority of the classwork and student interaction takes place via a network of personal computers linking the students and faculty.[5]

SIMULATIONS

Effective executive development has increasingly involved the use of training experiences designed to simulate real-life situations. A popular way to simulate an actual business experience is the case study method used by the majority of business schools. Students study the background information provided in the case, and the instructor leads a class discussion. The significant issues in the case are addressed and alternative decisions are debated and analyzed.

The availability of low-cost computing power has spurred the development of computer-based management simulations for graduate level and executive education. These simulations are particularly effective for developing skills in strategic management. Examples of these simulations include "Strategic Perspectives," a competitive business simulation by Executive Perspectives, Inc., Charlestown, Mass., and "Markstrat," a marketing strategy game developed by INSEAD/CEDEP, Fontainebleau, France. A number of companies, including Hewlett-Packard, have developed computer-based simulations to meet their own specific needs.

Executive development managers have found that training situations that simulate a typical day in the life of a manager are excellent tools for building team effectiveness skills. Early examples of these simulations were the popular in-basket exercises designed to see how manager trainees react to hypothetical reports, letters, memos, requests for action, telephone messages, and other stimuli. Recently, sophisticated large-scale behavioral simulations of a typical day in a manager's life have been developed, and these simulations are excellent tools for executive team development. Two examples of these behavioral simulations are Looking Glass, Inc. (LGI), developed by the Center for Creative Leadership, and Financial Services Industry (FSI), created at New York University Graduate School of Business Administration.[6]

Simulations are extremely effective teaching tools for middle- and upper-level executives, as they can be tailored to address many specific management development objectives. Common applications for simulations include the following:

- Improving executive skills by delineating the critical competencies required for successful performance on the job and highlighting the relationships between executive behavior and organizational performance;

- Building executive skills in strategic management, both the processes and techniques for strategy development and the implementation of strategies in an increasingly competitive and complex business environment;

- Developing teamwork and enhancing interpersonal skills;

- Helping executives understand the critical management challenges for executives in other functions, and how to more effectively interrelate with these functions.

Computer-Based Simulations

My first experience with a computer simulation for executive training was in 1976 when we developed an executive training program for Hewlett-Packard functional managers. A key objective for the program was an exercise that would allow managers to experience the activities of their counterparts in other functions. An HP division had already developed a simple management game for a management retreat, and we decided to try this game in the new functional management seminar.

The game consisted of an in-basket containing correspondence and reports covering the development of a hypothetical new product. Participants were asked to make R&D, manufacturing, marketing, and general management decisions. A computer was used to simulate the operating results of the decisions in a typical HP division, and a computer printout of the results and the score was provided to each team. Teams competed for the highest score. After the game, a senior manager conducted a debriefing and explained the reasons for each team's score.

This basic game, which went through several iterations over a five-year period, was the first computer-based simulation used in an HP management or executive training seminar. This initial success encouraged further application of simulations to executive training.

During a period of recession in the late 1970s, HP's CEO, John Young, asked me to investigate the availability of a management game that might help managers sharpen their skills for managing a division in a down economy. If we could find a game with the right variables, we could teach the application of these variables to managing in uncertain times.

I was unable to find a suitable game, primarily because we wanted to customize the simulation to the operation of a typical HP division. It began to look as if we would have to develop a simulation ourselves. In the summer of 1977, I was in Geneva to participate in a functional management seminar that our training group in Europe ran on a regular basis. In a seminar session on economics, Professor Keith Lumsden of Heriot-Watt University in Edinburgh used a simulation of the U.K. economy. Keith had done extensive work on teaching economics by using simulations in which the students could manipulate various economic parameters and observe the effects on inflation, interest rates, and gross domestic product. I was impressed with how closely his basic model approached the simulation that I was trying to find. That evening Keith agreed to develop a simulation for HP, and work began that fall. The original simulation developed by Lumsden's team went through several versions and is still in use as a central element in HP's functional management seminar.[7]

Computer-based management simulations allow participants to learn by making operating decisions over a period of time, usually quarterly for several years. Results of the decisions are provided almost immediately, and participants have to make future decisions based on these results. Executives are assigned to teams and assume a specific management role. For maximum learning, executives should assume an unfamiliar role during the simulation. Simulations designed for competition between teams add additional motivation to the learning process. During a typical one-week seminar, the simulation may occupy one-third of the time and tutorial sessions the remainder. In seminars on strategic management, lectures on competitive strategy would precede the simulation, and principles studied in the lectures would subsequently be applied in the simulation.

When using simulations, the program manager needs to have the necessary knowledge and skills in the subject matter that the simulation is designed to address. Learning takes place through the experience of the simulation, and the program manager needs to be an effective tutor to the executive teams.

Behavioral Simulations

Behavioral simulations focus on the processes of executive management and provide participants with feedback on how well they have mastered these processes. These simulations depict the working of a typical business organization. Each participating manager is assigned an executive role in the organization and faces multiple strategic and tactical challenges and opportunities. Executives are provided with extensive information detailing the demands, constraints, and choices affecting their positions and the firm as a whole. The information comes from a variety of sources, including memos, meetings, and annual reports. Participants identify and deal with issues, establish priorities, and solve problems in a simulated, but realistic, management environment.

A typical simulation begins with an introduction to the simulated organization and an opportunity to become familiar with its products, services, organizational structure, and financial status. Past decisions are reviewed, and present issues and opportunities are described. The executive team is charged with running the company for a day, and they may run it as they choose. Objectives are established and actions are taken based on the group's interactions as well as on individual initiative. Participants are observed by executive training professionals, as well as by other participants. At the completion of the simulation, participating managers receive data on the results of the decisions that were made, the financial impact of these decisions, and their individual and team effectiveness. The feedback and discussion focus on the relationships between management process, individual performance, and organizational effectiveness.

Simulations offer many advantages over traditional management games, role plays, and in-basket exercises. Major advantages include the following:

Duration. Simulations, typically lasting from six hours to several days, are longer than traditional exercises. During the course of the simulation, executives become immersed in their roles, and they soon begin to behave as they would back on the job. Early in the simulation, managers stop asking, "What would someone in this position do?" and begin to ask, "What would I do in this situation?"

Realism. Simulations can offer a high degree of realism, and this facilitates learning transfer back to the job. Unlike a conventional case study, managers must do more than just talk about what they would do in a given situation. They must act and live with the consequences of their actions.

Scope. Simulations can address a broader range of management issues than other types of executive development activity.

Teamwork. Simulations are excellent methods for developing executive teamwork. A well-run simulation can dramatically demonstrate the value of team decision making and strategy implementation.

Flexibility. Because of the many different learning experiences possible from a simulation, the experience can be structured to emphasize particular knowledge and skills needed by the participants.

REFERENCES

1. Marika Ruumet, manager of the Hewlett-Packard Television Network, played a major role in shaping HP's innovations in the application of television to executive and management development. Terry Gildea, HP's manager of Educational Technology, developed the later versions of the management simulation originally developed in Edinburgh. They were both major contributors to our management team at Corporate Training and outstanding tutors for all of us. The material on behavioral simulations was contributed largely by Steve Wall and Rich Lepsinger of Manus Associates in New York. Steve introduced me to the concept of behavioral simulations when we were co-chairmen of the Conference Board's Council on Education, Training, and Development.
2. See the most recent issue of *Directory of Harvard Business School Cases and Related Course Materials*, Harvard Business School, Soldiers Field, Boston, Mass., 02163.
3. See J. F. Gibbons, W. R. Kincheloe, and K. S. Down, "Tutored Videotape Instruction: A New Use of Electronics Media in Education," *Science*, March 18, 1977, vol. 195, pp. 1139–1146, and James F. Gibbons, "Tutored Videotape Instruction — An Approach to Educational Productivity," *The Stanford Engineer*, Spring/Summer 1984.
4. For an excellent discussion of the selection and implementation of computer-based training systems, see Greg Kearsley, *Computer-Based Training*, Reading, Mass., Addison-Wesley, 1983.
5. See Roy Rowan, "Executive Ed. at Computer U.," *Fortune*, March 7, 1983, and "California Institute Uses 'Teleconferences' to Teach Business Strategy, Computer Use," *Wall Street Journal*, February 10, 1983.

6. For a survey of simulations used in management and executive training, see Jack Gordon, "Games Managers Play," *Training*, July 1985, p. 30.
7. The major work on the last several versions of the HP management simulation, DIVSIM, was done by Terry Gildea of Hewlett-Packard.

BIBLIOGRAPHY

Barnard, Chester I., *The Functions of the Executive*, Cambridge, Mass., Harvard University Press, 1938.

Bennis, Warren, and Burt Nanus, *Leaders*, New York, Harper & Row, 1985.

Besterfield, Dale H., *Quality Control*, 2d ed., Englewood Cliffs, N.J., Prentice-Hall, 1986.

Cleveland, Harlan, *The Knowledge Executive*, New York, E. P. Dutton, 1985.

Copeland, Lennie, and Lewis Griggs, *Going International*, New York, Random House, 1985.

Cornish, Edward, *The Study of the Future*, Washington, D.C., World Future Society, 1977.

Drucker, Peter F., *Management: Tasks, Responsibilities, Practices*, New York, Harper & Row, 1973.

Eurich, Nell P., *Corporate Classrooms — The Learning Business*, Princeton, N.J., The Carnegie Foundation for the Advancement of Learning, 1985.

Feigenbaum, Armand V., *Total Quality Control*, 3d ed., New York, McGraw-Hill, 1983 (originally published in 1951).

Germane, Gayton E., ed., *The Executive Course — What Every Manager Needs to Know About the Essentials of Business*, Reading, Mass., Addison-Wesley, 1986.

Hayes, Robert H., and Steven C. Wheelwright, *Restoring Our Competitive Edge — Competing Through Manufacturing*, New York, John Wiley & Sons, 1984.

Helfert, Erich A., *Techniques of Financial Analysis*, 6th ed., Homewood, Ill., Dow-Jones Irwin, 1987.

Horngren, Charles T., *Introduction to Management Accounting*, 6th ed., Englewood Cliffs, N.J., Prentice-Hall, 1984.

Iacocca, Lee, *Iacocca*, New York, Bantam, 1984.

Imai, Masaaki, *Kaizen — The Key to Japan's Competitive Success*, New York, Random House, 1986.

Ishikawa, Kaouru, *Guide to Quality Control*, 2d rev. ed., Tokyo, Asian Productivity Organization, 1982.

———, *What Is Total Quality Control*, Englewood Cliffs, N.J., Prentice-Hall, 1985 (translated by David J. Lu).

Kanter, Rosabeth Moss, *The Change Masters*, New York, Simon and Schuster, 1983.

Kearsley, *Computer-Based Training*, Reading, Mass., Addison-Wesley, 1983.

Kepner, Charles H., and Benjamin B. Tregoe, *The New Rational Manager*, Princeton, N.J., Princeton Research Press, 1981.

Kotler, Philip, *Marketing Management*, Englewood Cliffs, N.J., Prentice-Hall, 1984.

———, *Marketing for Non-Profit Organizations*, 2d ed., Englewood Cliffs, N.J., Prentice-Hall, 1982.

Kotter, John P., *The General Managers*, New York, The Free Press, 1982.

Leavitt, Harold J., *Corporate Pathfinders*, Homewood, Ill., Dow-Jones Irwin, 1986.

Levitt, Theodore, *The Marketing Imagination*, New York, The Free Press, 1983.

Mager, Robert F., *Preparing Instructional Objectives*, Belmont, Calif., Fearon Publishers, 1972.

Ohmae, Kenichi, *The Mind of the Strategist*, New York, McGraw-Hill, 1982.

Ouchi, William, *The M-Form Society*, Reading, Mass., Addison-Wesley, 1984.

———, *Theory Z*, Reading, Mass., Addison-Wesley, 1981.

Pascale, Richard Tanner, and Anthony G. Athos, *The Art of Japanese Management*, New York, Simon and Schuster, 1981.

Peters, Thomas J., and Nancy K. Austin, *A Passion for Excellence*, New York, Random House, 1985.

Peters, Thomas J., and Robert H. Waterman, Jr., *In Search of Excellence*, New York, Harper & Row, 1982.

Porter, Michael E., *Competitive Advantage*, New York, The Free Press, 1985.

———, *Competitive Strategy*, New York, The Free Press, 1980.

Ries, Al, and Jack Trout, *Positioning — The Battle for Your Mind*, New York, Warner Books, 1981.

Schonberger, Richard J., *Japanese Manufacturing Techniques*, New York, The Free Press, 1982.

INDEX

Administrative support, linkages with, 67, *68*, 70, *71*, 72–73
Advanced study, as executive development program method, *155*, 157
Advisory board, for executive/staff development, 120, 146
Agenda setting function of management, 102, 104
Airline flight selection, process of, 88, *89*
American Telephone & Telegraph, 6
Austin, Nancy, 140, 196
Automation, 235
Awareness of executive development programs, 194

Backlund, Bob, 6
Basics of management, *124*, 140, 235, 236–37
  functional knowledge and skills, 126, 141 n.2
  generic business management, 126
  philosophy, 125–26, 229
Behavior modeling, 245
  simulations, 253–55
  on video, 245
Bell Advanced Management Program, 6
Benefits of executive development programs, *199*, 200
  failure to recognize, 195
  selling benefits over features, 196
Bennis, Warren, 33
Best practices model of managerial effectiveness, *136–37*, 243
Binder layout, 162, *163*
Black & Decker Co., strategic repositioning, 28–29
Breaks during seminar programs, 217
Brookings Institution, 209
Budgeting for executive development, 133–34, 153–54, 175, 177. *See also* Price/cost of executive development programs

Business environment. *See also* Economic conditions
  increased competition in, 1–3, 38, 234
  new technologies in, 38
  and strategy development, 27
  and strategy issues, 38–40
Business journals, 121, 158
Business strategy. *See* Strategy, business
Business Week, 140

California State Department of Education, 138
Capital assets, ability to manage, 104, *105*
Case studies. *See also* Simulations
  as executive development program method, *155*, 156, 250
  on video, 243–44
Cause and effect analysis,
  of management processes, 110, *111*
  of production processes, 92–95
CEO. *See* Chief executive officer (CEO)
Champions, for executive development programs, 134–35, 177–78
Chief executive officer (CEO), 13 n.5
  business strategy responsibilities of, 7, 10
  as customer for executive development, 198, *199*, 200
  responsibilities for executive development, 122–23
  strategic management by, 20–21
Chrysler Corp., 24
Classroom operations, 219–21
Cleveland, Harlan, 92
Commitment, as the marketing program objective, 195
Competency-based management training, 127
Competition,
  gaining advantage over, 27–28
  increased international, 1–3, 38, 234
  as number one concern, 233–34

Competitive Advantage, 17, 28, 67
Competitive Strategy, 17
Competitors, to your executive development program, 202
Computer(s), 235
  as executive development program method, *155,* 158, 247–50, 251–53
Computer-based training (CBT), 248–49
Content of executive development programs, 178, 179–83, 230. *See also* Curriculum emphasis, executive development
  file organization, 180, *181*
  integrating outside materials, 182–83
  materials, 183, 184–85. *See also* Materials in executive development programs
  preparing final drafts, 183
  testing and pilot runs, 185–86
  writing and editing, 180, 182
Corporate Pathfinders, 35
Curriculum emphasis, executive development, 123–28, 229–31. *See also* Content of executive development programs
  categories of, *124*
  getting the basics right, 125–26, 140
  strategy specific training, 127–28
Customer(s),
  executives as, 198, *199,* 200, 202
  needs of, and marketing, 196–97
Customer satisfaction,
  process performance and, 91
  quality control and, 81
  and strategy implementation, 37

Data, quality of needs assessment, 146–47
Deming, W. Edwards, 82
Deming cycle, 82–85
  Act step, 83–84, 95–96
  applied to management processes, 99–105
  Check step, 83, 90, 99–100
  as closed-loop feedback control system, *84*
  corrective action, 95–96
  Do step, 83, 86, 90
  Plan step, 82, 90
  as a process, *87*
  process analysis with, 85–90
Deming Prize, 82, 91
Distributed learning, 249–50

Distribution of executive development programs, 204
Documentation, executive development strategy, 132–33
Doyle, John, 74–75
Driving forces, in strategy implementation, 34, *35*
Drucker, Peter, 65, 127

Economic conditions, 34. *See also* Business environment
  and competitiveness, 233–34
  effect on marketing executive development programs, 202–3
Educators as a resource, 137, 138–39, 159
Effectiveness in management, 65, 74–75
Efficiency in management, 65
Ely, Paul, 140
Evaluation. *See also* Total quality control (TQC)
  of executive development programs, 221–22, *223*
  of management processes, 102, 104, *105,* 106–10
  and measures of performance, 77–78
  of tactical plans, 58–59
Executive(s),
  defined, 13 n.5
  involving in executive development programming, 134–35
Executive development,
  and business strategy formulation, 31
  in the Deming cycle, *101*
  for developing linkages and teamwork, 73, 77
  increased competition and need for, 1–3
  international, 137–38
  limitations on current practices, 3–4
  link between strategy, operations and, 7–9
  link to tactical planning, 59–60
  marketing. *See* Marketing of executive development
  model of, 10, 129, *130,* 227–31
  need for business strategy to drive, 4–7
  overview, 11–13
  priorities, 128–29, 140
  programming for. *See* Program design for executive development; Program implementation/evaluation for executive development; Program production for executive development

strategy for. *See* Strategy formulation for executive development
  synchronizing with strategic issues, 45–47
  unconventional approach to, 9–11
Executive team,
  as customer for executive development, 198, *199*, 200
  defined, 13 n.5
  responsibilities of executive development, 123
Expenses, ability to manage, 104, *105*
External factors. *See* Business environment

Feedback control system, Deming cycle as, *84*
Feigenbaum, Armand V., 79
Financial analysis with computers, 248
Fishbone diagram of cause and effect analysis, 92, *93*, 94–95, 110, *111*
Flowchart,
  of airflight selection, *89*
  of management processes, 102, *103* with specific goals, *105*
  of process analysis, 85–90
  symbols, *86*
Food and beverages during seminars, 218
Ford Motor Co., 24–25
Functional management, 101–5, 126
  goals/performance measures for, 108, *109*
  transition to, *228*, 229
Function(s) of an organization,
  linked processes of, 66–73
  model of linkages among, *68*, *71*
  strategies for each, as business strategy component, 29–31
  teamwork among, 74–75 processes for developing, 75–76
Future skills, need to define, 237–38

Genentech Co., 18
General Electric Co., 18, 31 n.3
  report on competition, 1–2
General management, 101–5, 126
  agenda setting/networking functions of, 102, 104
  evaluating, 102, 104, *105*, 106–10
  goals/performance measures, *107*
  linkages with, 67, *68*, 70, *71*, 72–73
  transition to, 227, *228*

General Motors, 24
German auto industry, 24
Gibbons, Jim, 244
Goals and objectives of business, 18, *20*. *See also* Strategy, business
  congruency of, 49 in tactical plans, 50, 56
  definition, in tactical plans, 56
  executive development and, 4–7, 10
  for general management, *107*
Goals and objectives of executive development programs, 148
  addressing each, 151
  confirming with top management, 149–50
  developing methods for meeting, 154–58
Governmental policy, 34
Group work, as executive development program method, *155*, 156
Grove, Andy, 121

Harvard Business School, 244
Hewlett, Bill, 5, 122–23
Hewlett-Packard Company, 11
  changing executive behavior at, 5–6
  executive development program design, 164–66, 167 n.4
  functional linkages model, 67, *68*
  model for executive development, 227–31
  quality control at, 80
  strategic issues at, 40–41
  teamwork at, 74, 75–76
  television production at, 241, 255 n.1
High Output Management, 121
Human resource development, 234–35. *See also* Executive development

IBM, 140–41
The IBM Way, 140
Implementation. *See* Program implementation/evaluation for executive development; Strategy implementation and execution
In Search of Excellence, 140
Instruction, methods of, 154–58, 241–56
Instructors for executive development programs, 159. *See also* Training director in executive development programs
  materials for, 184–85
  training, coaching, evaluation of, 213–15

Interest levels, for executive development program, 194–95
International business,
  competing in, 1–3, 233–34
  executive development for, 137–38
Interviews, needs assessment, 145–46
Ishikawa, Kaoru, 92

Japanese auto industry, 24, 29
Japanese business schools, 137–38
Japanese management practices, 2
  total quality control, 79, 80–82, 91
Job and people mismatch, 237
Job rotation, 113
Juran, J., 82

The Knowledge Executive, 92
Kotter, John, 33, 102

Leadership, 229
  characteristics of effective, 74–75
  and strategy implementation, 37
  and tactical plans, 57
  vision of, 33, 49
Leavitt, Hal, 33, 35–36
Lecture, as executive development program method, 154, *155*, 156
LeDuc, Bob, 164
Linkages among functional model elements, 66–73
Location of executive development programs, 160, *161*
Lumsden, Keith, 252

McKinsey & Company, 21
McKinsey 7S Framework, 21
Makita Electric Works, Ltd., 28
Management, 65
Management. *See also* Chief executive officer (CEO); Executive(s); Executive team; Strategic business unit (SBU), managers; Top managment
  basics. *See* Basics of management
  effectiveness, 65, 74–75 best practices model of, *136*, 137
  efficiency in, 65
  evaluation of, 102, 104, *105*, 106–10
  of executive development programs, 169–71 factors for effective, *211*
  functional. *See* Functional management
  general. *See* General management
  participative, and tactical planning, 57
  processes. *See* Processes, management
  strategic. *See* Strategic management
  strategic issues as tools for, 40–42
  training of. *See* Executive development
  transitions, 227, *228*, 229–31
Management by Objectives (MBO), and tactical planning, 56–57
Manager of managers, transition to, 228–29
Manufacturing. *See also* Processes, production
  linkages with, 67, *68*, 69, 70, *71*, 72
  teamwork and, 75–76
  new technology in, 235
Marketing,
  approach of, to executive development, 9–11
  goals/performance measures for function of, 108, *109*
  linkages with, 67, *68*, 69, 70, *71*, 72
  tactical plan for XYZ Products, *54*
  teamwork and, 75–76
Marketing of executive development, 193–207
  applying marketing techniques, 198–200
  assessment of position/setting objectives for, 193–95
  checklist for, *201*
  elements of, for training directors, 196–97
  marketing implementation, 200–6
Materials in executive development programs,
  format, typesetting, reproduction of, 186–88
  graphics and media production, 188–89
  for leaders, 184–85
  management of, 189–91
  organizing, 179–83
  packaging of, 160–64
  selection of, 178–79
  transferability and translatability of, 182
Measures of performance, 77–78. *See also* Evaluation; Total quality control (TQC)
Media in executive development programs, 158, 179, 217. *See also* Appendix C
  graphics and media production, 188–89
The Mind of the Strategist, 17, 49
Mission, business, 18, *20*
Models,
  best practices, *136*-137

executive development, 10, 129, *130*, 227–31
fishbone diagram of cause and effect analysis, 93
multibusiness organization, *51*
strategic issues, *35*
strategic positions, *23*
Modules, executive development program, 173
　content summary, 153
　defining content/identifying experts, 158–59
　establishing objectives for, 151
　identifying, 151
　methods for meeting objectives of, 154–58
　task forces for, 177–78
Motorola Company, organizational factors, 21–22, 32 n.7
Musashi Institute of Technology, Tokyo, 92

Nanus, Burt, 33
Needs analysis, 9
　for executive development program design, 144–48
Networking function of management, 102

Objectives. *See* Goals and objectives of business
Ohmae, Kenichi, 17, 24, 49
Operations. *See also* Strategic management; Strategy implementation and execution; Total quality control (TQC)
　linked to business strategy and executive development, 7–9
　tactical plans as tool for, 57–58
Organization, typical multibusiness, *51*
Organizational competencies, 120
Organizational factors,
　and effective strategy, 21–22
　internal, and strategy issues, 36–38
Overhead transparencies, 188
Ownership of programs, 10, 57
　executive development, 135–37, 147, 177–78
　tactical plans, 58

Packard, Dave, 5–6, 123
Participant selection, in executive development programs, 212–13
A Passion for Excellence, 140, 196
Pathfinding, 33. *See also* Leadership

People management, effectiveness at, 104, *105*
Performance appraisal, vs. process performance measurement, 111–12
Perlmutter, Howard, 165
Personnel,
　mismatch of jobs with, 237
　XYZ Products tactical plan for, *55*
Peters, Thomas J., 140, 196
Philosphy of management, 125–26
Porter, Michael, 17, 27–28, 67
Price/cost of executive development programs, 203. *See also* Budgeting for executive development
Processes, management, 99–114
　alternatives for improvement of, 112–13
　cause and effect analysis of, 110, *111*
　for developing teamwork, 75–76
　evaluating effectiveness of, 102, 104, *104*, 106–10
　general and functional, 101–5
　linked, 66–73
　performance measurement vs. performance appraisal, 111–12
　real-time, 19–21
　total quality control applied to, 96–97
Processes, production, 81
　committment to continuous improvement of, 238–39
　Deming cycle analysis of, 85–90
　measuring performance of, 90–92
　process vs. task orientation, 238
Process performance measurement, vs. performance appraisal, 111–12
Product development,
　linkages with, 67, *68*, 69, 70, *71*, 72
　teamwork and, 75–76
Productivity, 37, 236
Profit targets, ability to manage, 104, *105*
Program design for executive development, 143–67
　confirming objectives/discussing alternatives, 149–50
　designing program structure, 150–54
　establishing specific training objectives, 148
　finalizing program agenda, 160
　methods of instruction to meet objectives, 154–58, 241–56
　module content and content experts, 158–59
　needs analysis and program investigation, 144–48

program packaging, 160–64, 203
seven step process, *144*
strategy example of, 164–66
Program implementation/evaluation for executive development, 209–26
 classroom operations, 219–21
 evaluation and followup, 221
 instructor training, coaching, evaluation, 213–15
 logistics of, 215–19
 longterm support, 223–24
 participant selection, 212–13
 program management, 209–12
 program updating and revising, 224–25
Program map, 151, *152*, 153
Program production for executive development, 169–92
 budget for, 175, 177. *See also* Resources for executive development
 checklists, *170*, *176*
 content development, 179–83
 content testing and pilot runs, 185–86
 in-house vs. external, 139–40, *171*
 key steps in, *192*
 leaders' materials, 184–85
 materials and media selection, 178–79
 module task forces, 177–78
 overall project management, 169–71
 production considerations, 186–91
 quality assurance in, 191–92
 schedule, checkpoints, and reviews, 172–75
 staffing assignments, 171–72
Promotion of executive development programs, 204–5
Public relations training on video, 245–46

Quality assurance,
 as a competitive element, 236
 of executive development program production, 191–92
 of products/services. *See also* Total quality control (TQC)
 and strategy implementation, 37
Quality circles, 81, 82, 97 n.4

The Report of the President's Commission on Industrial Competitiveness, 234
Resources for executive development, 133–34, 153–54, 175, 177
Restraining forces, in strategy implementation, 34, 35, 36

Review of executive development programs, 173
Robichek, Alex, 248
Rodgers, Buck, 140
Role playing on video, 245

Sasaoka, Kenzo, 91
Satellite delivered video education, 244
Schedule, executive development program, 150, 170, 172–73, *174*, *176*
School of Management and Strategic Studies, 250
Selling the executive development program, 196, 206
Seminar rooms, arrangement of, 215, *216*
Shared values of an organization, 21
Simplicity, in tactical plans, 56
Simulations, 250–55. *See also* Case studies
 behavioral, 253–55
 computer-based, 251–53
Slides, 35mm, 188
Staffing of executive development programs, 170, 171–72
Stanford Graduate School of Business, 210
Statistical tools for process performance analysis, 92
Strategic business unit (SBU), 50, *51*
 managers, 20–21
Strategic issues, 7–8, 11, 33–47
 identifying, 35–40 external environment, 38–40 internal factors and implementation effectiveness, 36–38 strategy effectiveness, 36
 impediments to strategy implementation, 34–35
 synchronizing to executive development, 45–47 for training and development, 233–39
 using, as a management tool, 40–42
 XYZ Products example, 42–45
Strategic management. *See also* Processes, management
 as linked processes, 66–73
 of production. *See* Processes, production
 as real-time process, 19–21
 total quality control applied to, 96–97
Strategic position, 22–24
 of executive development programs, 193–95, 203
 strategy as repositioning, 24–25, *26*, 27–29
Strategy, business, 17–32

basic considerations in formulating, 25–29
basic definitions, 17–19, *20*
in the Deming cycle, *101*
executive development driven by, 4–7
executive development's importance to, 31
functional strategies as components of, 29–31
vs. goals and objectives, 18
issues. *See* Strategic issues
manager's ability to formulate/execute, 104, *105*
operations/executive development linked to, 7–9
organizational factors related to, 21–22
positioning. *See* Strategic position
as real-time management process, 19–21
vs. tactics, 50
Strategy effectiveness, 36
Strategy formulation for executive development, 117–42, 227
acquiring resources, 133–34
basic responsibilities of, 117–23
determining overall needs, 123–28
gaining strategy approval, 132–33
involving executives in, 134–35
planning for strategy implementation, 138–41
program ownership/best practices model, 135–37
strategy development, 128–32
ten strategic issues for, 233–39
worldwide nature of, 137–38
Strategy implementation and execution, 19, 65–78. *See also* Tactics and tactical planning
in the the Deming cycle, *101*
executive development and, 77
functional model of, *68*
interfunctional teamwork in, 74–75
processes for developing, 75–76
less margin for error, 2
as linked processes, 66–73
measures of performance, 77–78
strategic issues as impediments to, 34–35 identifying, 35–40
through tactical planning, 49–61
Strategy specific training, 127–28
Support for executive development programs,
followup for participants, 206, 223–24

from production staff, 186, 218
Tactics and tactical planning, 7–8
defined, 19, *20*
evaluating, 58–59
interlocking plans, *52*
linking executive development to, 59–60
planning guidelines, 55–58
planning process, 50–55
XYZ Products example, *53–55*
Task force process, 76
Teamwork,
among organizational functions, 74–75
processes for developing, 75–76
and strategy implementation, 37–38
Techologies, new, 38
Television. *See* Video and television
Tests and examinations, as executive development program method, *155*, 157
Thomas, Dan, 19, 166
3M Company, 6
Top management. *See also* Chief executive officer (CEO)
approval of executive development strategy, 132–33
business strategy responsibilities of, 7, 10
confirming program objectives with, 149–50, 154
as customer for executive development, 198, *199*, 200
defined, 13 n.5
expectations of, and video productions, 243
responsibilities for executive development, *118*, 121–23
Total quality control (TQC), 98, 238–39
applied to executive development program, 222, *223*
applied to management processes, 96–97
basics of, 80–82
cause and effect analysis, 92–95
corrective action, 95–96
Deming cycle, 82–85
measuring process performance, 90–92
process analysis, 85–90
Training and development, 233–29. *See also* Executive development
challenge of human resource development, 234–35
commitment to continuous, 238

265

competitiveness as first concern, 233–34
cost of improper, 238
ten strategic issues for, 235–39
Training director in executive
  development programs,
  essential marketing elements for, 196–97
  management by, 169–71, 210, *211*
  responsibilities of, *118*, 119–21
Triad process, 76
Tunstall, Brooke, 6
Tutoring, videotaped, 244

U.S. auto industry, 24–25, 29
Updating and revising executive
  development programs, 224–25

Value chain, 67
Video and television, as executive
  development program method, *155*,
  158, 179, 188–89, 241–47
  as a basic audio-visual device, 242–43
  case discussion scene setting, 243–44
  factors to consider before initiating, 246–47
  presentation rehearsal and public
    relations training, 245–46
  role playing and behavior modeling, 245
  top management expectations for, 243
  tutoring and satellite delivery, 244
Videodiscs, 249
Vision for the organization, 33, 49

Waterman, Robert H., Jr., 140
Western Behavioral Sciences Institute, 250

XYZ Products, Inc. example,
  strategic issues for, 42–45
  tactical plans for, *53–55*

Yokogawa Hewlett-Packard Ltd., 91
Young, John, 28, 140
  on organizational vision, 49
  strategic issues list, 40–41